Waste Land, this book examines anew the literary and philosophical backgrounds of the work and shows in detail how these bear specifically on a complete understanding of it. Rather than speak in safe generalities, the author cites lines and episodes that reflect the principles described. The book centers on a detailed exegesis arranged first by section and then by line. The reader can instantly find explicit commentary on any episode, image, line, or even word in Eliot's dense and rich poem.

Schwarz's presentation deliberately strays far from the aridity of standard academic prose. In this work of reverent scholarship, the author directs the full resources of his language, not excluding an occasional poetic turn of phrase, to the exposition of his subject. Whether long a student of *The Waste Land* or coming to it for the first time, the reader will unquestionably find in these pages much that is new, much that appears in no other source. The first-time reader of Eliot's masterpiece will find Mr. Schwarz's study a Virgilian guide to the labyrinth of the poet's creative process. The reader who knows the poem well—even intimately—will experience the pleasurable shock of knowing the work anew, freshly illuminated by the author's discoveries and insights.

BROKEN IMAGES

BROKEN IMAGES

A Study of *The Waste Land*

Robert L. Schwarz

Lewisburg
Bucknell University Press
London and Toronto: Associated University Presses

Associated University Presses
440 Forsgate Drive
Cranbury, NJ 08512

Associated University Presses
25 Sicilian Avenue
London WC1A 2QH, England

Associated University Presses
P.O. Box 488, Port Credit
Mississauga, Ontario
Canada L5G 4M2

The paper used in this publication meets the requirements
of the American National Standard for Permanence of Paper
for Printed Library Materials Z39.48-1984.

Library of Congress Cataloging-in-Publication Data

Schwarz, Robert L., 1937–
   Broken images.

   Bibliography: p.
   Includes index.
   1. Eliot, T. S. (Thomas Stearns), 1888–1965.
Waste land.   I. Title.
PS3509.L43W3813   1988   821′.912   87-40502
ISBN 0-8387-5137-7 (alk. paper)

PRINTED IN THE UNITED STATES OF AMERICA

Contents

Acknowledgments

As Eliot pointed out, in our beginnings are our ends, a truth found much less elegantly stated in many textbooks of child psychology. In my beginnings I was fortunate enough to have had parents who unflaggingly supported my natural inclination to study; and all the tools for that enterprise were placed at my disposal. For that understanding, I publicly extend my undying appreciation to my parents: my late father, Harry C. Schwarz, and my mother, Leona M. Schwarz.

Along the way, I was taught the wonderful art of book collecting by F. Purl Johnson, who showed me how a modest income could suffice to build a scholar's library. The vicissitudes of life have kept us apart of late, but some of my finest recollections remain those of "making the rounds," as he called it, with Mr. Johnson, who conducted me, a mere boy, into the secret sources of the avid bibliophile.

The manuscript for this book passed through the hands of many disinterested publishers before coming to rest as so much excess baggage in my basement, where it probably would have remained, had it not been for the vigilance of a former student and now long-time friend, Mitchell J. Stephenson, whose gentle but persistent prompting finally moved me to submit it to the present publisher.

For preparing the multiple copies of the manuscript required for submission to Bucknell University Press, I would like to thank my good friend, Jeff Forker, and his daughter, Shannon. Subsequently, Dr. Alan Wolf assisted in the mechanical preparation of the finished draft; and Robert Hamilton extended me many patient hours, helping to collate the footnotes.

My thanks goes to Louis Salvator for his advice in making the final revision of this book. Lou has that rare editorial ability to think in terms of another's writing style. His suggestions have unquestionably lent additional coherence to this book.

Finally, I would consider it remiss not to acknowledge the efforts of my copy editor, Megan Benton, and Beth Gianfagna, managing editor at Associated University Presses, both of whom have dispatched their services with exemplary acumen and professionalism.

BROKEN IMAGES

Introduction

INTELLECTUAL history evolves in endless cycles between the poles of uncertainty and certainty, as the inchoate shadow of existence is illuminated by the paradigms of human conception, disorder giving way to order. Knowledge involves the imposition of form. It begins with perception, in which the world apart from man—so-called objective reality—is informed with the structure of the human sensory and nervous systems. And it ends when the intellectual forms that perception engenders have completely replaced the initial perceptions, leaving behind the bare skeleton of thought, shadow into shadow, having the substance of a reflection only.

In this larger framework of intellectual history, the reputations of literary works, painting, and sculpture rise and fall in this cycle between ambiguity and perfect explicitness. To maintain a favorable reputation, a work must retain possibilities for meaning and implication not yet resolved to final and absolute clarity. As soon as a work is drained of possible meaning and implication, it becomes a cliché, no longer worthy of attention, absorbed into common knowledge and forgotten as a separate entity. We return to Shakespeare, the Bible, Keats, and Shelley because we cannot exhaust their resources of expression, while we read the latest bestseller novel and usually forget it, never prompted to return to it because it presents no more than a story, and we apprehend that on the first reading.

"Certainty," said Sir Edward Coke, "is the mother of Quietness and Repose; and Incertainty the cause of variance and contentions." So long as a literary work provides a core meaning from which refinements of detail can gradually be deduced, we are comfortable with it. It is not so difficult to appreciate that it baffles the critical senses. But if that core is not readily visible, we are troubled. And if concerted and prolonged effort fails to uncover any such core, the reputation of the work is bound to be in dispute.

The matter is simple, of course, if research and sympathetic reading discover no reason to believe that a particular work has a coherent import. The work can then conscionably be rejected as an aberration or a bland failure. Quite the contrary applies if there is good reason to believe that the work has a coherent thrust but the thrust cannot be

11

established with any consensus. Uncertainty reigns, then, and gives way to variance and contentions.

Such is the case with *The Waste Land* and many other of the poems of T. S. Eliot. "In the past quarter-century," observed Horace Gregory in *A History of American Poetry 1900–1940*, "no poet of Eliot's generation has been so fortunately reviled, denounced, defamed, buried so often, revived so often, been so enthusiastically defended, and so passionately denied (by his adverse critics) the merits of human contact and of sincerity."[1] He goes on to single out *The Waste Land* as the chief cause of the critical equivocation. Certainly *Ash Wednesday* and *Four Quartets* present similar difficulties in interpretation, but they are religious poems in the mystical tradition; and in the tradition of mysticism, obscurity is expected and accepted. *The Waste Land* belongs in this tradition, too, but falls rather more to the metaphysical side than to the purely religious and so cannot be readily exculpated for its expressive transgressions.

The whole question of meaning in *The Waste Land* is complicated by the established position of the poem as a preeminent influence in twentieth-century Anglo-American poetry. "He articulated the mind of an epoch in words that seemed its most natural expression," Kenneth Rexroth writes in his recent *American Poetry in the Twentieth Century*. "He is the most difficult author in the twentieth century to avoid. Two generations of poets learned to write largely by carefully, year by year, shedding his influence, his metrics, his reading matter."[2] And of his body of poetic works, Rexroth singles out *The Waste Land* as "the epic of l'entre deux guerres."[3] These statements are of peculiar significance in that they come not simply from a literary scholar but from a poet who was in the mainstream of poetry during the period in question. They are echoed by other poets both within and without the tradition to which Pound and Eliot belonged. Hart Crane, for example, within the tradition but disappointed with *The Waste Land*, nevertheless declared to Waldo Frank:

> I am certain that a number of us at last have some kind of community of interest. And with this communion will come something better than a mere clique. It is a consciousness of something more vital than stylistic questions and "taste"; it is vision, and a vision alone that not only America needs, but the whole world. We are not sure where this will lead, but after the complete renunciation symbolised in "The Waste Land" and though less, in "Ulysses" we have sensed some new vitality.[4]

Even a poet as divorced from the sensibilities of Eliot as W. B. Yeats, in his introduction to the 1936 edition of *The Oxford Book of Modern Verse*, attested to the primary influence of Eliot on poetry to that time.

The situation may be resolved to the simple fact that *The Waste Land* has had an indisputable impact on the literature, especially the poetry, of this century; yet it stands as a monument whose inscriptions remain largely undeciphered. It is surely a paradox—a maddening one to the aristarchs and decriers—that a work largely incomprehensible should shape the sensibilities of two generations. It is a paradox worth closer examination.

It is relatively easy to explain why the poem is difficult to understand: it does not proceed logically, it contains only partially disclosed references personal to the poet, and it depends upon allusions many of which have not been identified. But if it cannot be understood clearly, why does it fascinate so many readers? The answer is manifold.

First, it exemplifies the culmination of a severe stylistic change that had its roots in the late nineteenth century, burgeoned in the early poetry not only of Pound and Eliot but also such poets as Pierre Reverdy, Gertrude Stein, and even the dadaists. One might say that the lineal style favored by alphabetic writing (hallmark of MacLuhan's Gutenberg galaxy) and scientific thought (predicated on Aristotelian logic) was giving way to the more holistic modes of thought being born of the electronic age. It is the style of simultaneous presentation seen also in the nonsensical juxtaposition of items on the page of a newspaper, or the insinuation of commercials for soap and weed-eaters into a radio or television broadcast of a Shakespeare play. We see it in our landscapes, where billboards loom out of farmlands and a jungle of modern tenements surrounds the splendor of the Acropolis. Cereal boxes tell stories in cartoons. Teeshirts stretch political slogans across the contours of delicious bosoms. Department stores and discount houses bring the most heterogeneous objects together into a bizarre caricature of metaphysical conceit. All this is part of the waste land of reality gone wild.

Because of the images in *The Waste Land*, it spoke directly to not only a decade but what has become a century of disillusionment. Whatever hope there was in the poem lay hidden under the shattered fragments of decadence and deterioration. And the images themselves were compelling. They had that vividness and felicity yoked to just the right turn from ordinary perspective to make them richly quotable, prickly to the imagination, difficult to forget. Time has not robbed them of these qualities.

Finally, in a sense readers did understand the poem: the understanding was not discursive but intuitive. They caught the mood of the poem, and they responded to the style. It had a definite impact that could be felt as a whole, though it could not be articulated in detail, line by line, in terms of a logical network of premises and conclusions. Even if taken descriptively, scenes are not related in the poem according to conventional logic. Connections in the poem are paralogical—some might say prelogical. Things progress as in a dream, jumping seemingly by discontinuities from context to context, with most of what comprises a context, frame, or episode distorted by motives extremely difficult to pin down. Consequently, what seems a firm overall impression disconcertingly crumbles away under logical analysis.

To remedy this uncomfortable situation—to resolve the uncertainties that were leading to variance and contentions—critics favorably disposed toward the poem ransacked the notes Eliot had appended to unearth clues to detailed meaning. They quickly picked up the deceptive leads Eliot had planted there to spike their guns, as he put it, and they were off and running to track down all the arcana of cartomancy (fortune telling by cards) and fertility rites revealed in Sir James Frazer's *Golden Bough* and Jessie L. Weston's *From Ritual to Romance.* Thus was born what has become the standard interpretation of the poem as an eccentric version of the Grail legend, with all the ancient connections of the legend to vegetation gods plotted by Weston and depicted in Frazer.

The difficulty of this interpretation is that, while it gives the impression of more firmly holding together the various episodes of the poem, it leaves the episodes as loosely strewn together as they might appear without the interpretation. In fine, the anthropological and mythological interpretation fails to penetrate the meaning of the poem to individual lines and images. Many details of the poem are hammered into the framework of the interpretation, a framework into which they simply do not naturally fit. Lines that cannot even be hammered into place are merely ignored. The Weston-Frazer interpretation, therefore, not only distorts the poem but leaves incomplete the very understanding it seeks to promote.

Moreover, Eliot stated flatly that the Weston-Frazer version of the poem was a wild goose chase on which he had purposely sent the critics, but by the time he admitted it, the literary establishment had vested such interest in the interpretation, having sold it to the public as the standard version, that there seemed no turning back. Critics and scholars scoffed over Eliot's avowal. They could not admit that they had been deceived.

So the Weston-Frazer interpretation stands. Grover Smith even adopts it uncritically in his otherwise authoritative and exhaustive treatment of Eliot's poems and plays. Yet anyone attempting to read *The Waste Land* as a version of the Grail legend cannot honestly deny that this approach still leaves a close reading of the poem a hollow guessing game that sheds little light on the appreciation and understanding of the whole taken line by line. Is Marie a fertility goddess? Once one knows that she is Marie Larisch, is one to place her in the Grail legend by a chain of reasoning that passes from the fact that King Ludwig was her uncle to the fact that he was also the patron of Wagner, and Wagner composed Parsifal, and Parsifal was based on the Grail legend? How about the woman or girl who says, "Bin gar keine Russin, stam' aus Litauen, echt deutsch"? Exactly what is she doing in the Hofgarten? Why is she juxtaposed to Marie Larisch? And Madame Sosostris: she is somehow identified with Bertrand Russell, the venerable philosopher who was somewhat of a rake, but is he really a convincing candidate for a vegetation god? No one tells who Belladonna is, nor why she is a lady of situations. Is it really satisfying to interpret the one-eyed merchant as Wotan, and the something he carries on his back as the mysteries of some ancient cult? Such far-fetched interpretations and blanks in the exegesis make the structure of the poem more tenuous and slipshod than it might even have appeared before the interpretation. It contributes to appreciation of the poem nothing but pedantic befuddlement. It adds a layer of obscurity rather than peels one away.

Alternatives to the standard interpretation have accomplished little more. Some have simply denounced the poem as a meaningless hodgepodge. If, as I intend to demonstrate in the exegetical portion of this book, the poem can be shown to have a coherence that indeed can be followed line by line, that is sufficient rebuttal to such radical criticism.

Hugh Kenner has recently suggested that The Waste Land began as an apostrophe to London. He concedes that it quickly grew into something else. I challenge the initial premise, but whether or not his thesis is accepted, it is not the sort of interpretation that can be expected to unravel the meaning of all the individual lines of the poem. At most, it would illuminate parts of what Kenner takes to be the original section— and here again I disagree and argue a contrary position—and would only tell something about the composition of the poem.

Most audacious among the heterodoxic interpretations of The Waste Land (and also most recent) is that of James E. Miller, Jr., who proposes that it is a homosexual lament for a dead lover. Miller probes many of the erotic subtleties of the poem and focuses long-overdue attention on the suppressed "Ode" from Ara Vos Prec. However, in the absence of sufficient biographical evidence, it is impossible either to deny or confirm that Eliot was a homosexual. I will show that the passages which Miller takes to be homosexual can more plausibly be read as heterosexual. And since he was unable, understandably enough, to find biographical support for his contention, there is no reason at this time to give it serious consideration.

Even if Miller were correct in his supposition, the homosexual angle still would not illuminate the fine grain of the poem. It would shed light only on certain passages. Where the poem strays from erotic considerations, it ceases to be illuminated by Miller's examination. Thus his interpretation is seriously flawed; it does not provide us with the key to unlock all the mysteries of the poem.

In this study the simplest approach has been followed: let the poem speak for itself. This involves tracking down the sources for the imagery, not strictly to discover allusions but to lay bare the network of psychological associations that must have guided Eliot consciously and unconsciously in the composition of the work. The implication is not that all such allusions were intentional in the sense, say, of establishing archetypical situations, echoing the style or import of another work, or fulfilling some preconceived scheme. Rather, I incline to think that most of the allusions operated for Eliot as those found by Lowes did for Coleridge in the writing of "Kubla Khan," as anchors for connotative meaning. After all, words mean to us what our experience with them has taught us about them. For an author like Eliot, reading was an important source of experience forming connotations of words and images. And in general, I shall deal more with expressions and images than with individual and separate words.

Of course, the enterprise of tracking down associations private to an author from his reading is fraught with perils, the most insidious of which is the temptation to find sources in works chosen almost at random or because they offer neat parallels that are supposed to prove their authenticity. There have been many instances of that in Eliot commentary. Such easy scholarship adds no more to the understanding of the poetry than the standard forced interpretations I have already reviewed; indeed, they equally mislead and obscure.

Many hitherto unnoted sources for The Waste Land are introduced here, but in every instance—save in a few cases clearly labeled speculative—I have sought to establish clearly that Eliot read them prior to writing the poem. Great care has been taken with authentication because the mass of new source material coupled with that already known form the major substance of this new interpretation. It is through this substratum that the poem is allowed to speak for itself.

Over a period of two decades, I collected these sources by reading what is known to have been read by Eliot before 1922, including all the books for which he wrote reviews. As the sources accumulated, some patterns began to emerge. I began to see images juxtaposed in The Waste Land associated not narratively but thematically and by emotions common to their contexts, like the elements in a stream-of-consciousness or dream progression. No forcing, no speculation was required to divine the patterns.

My supposition was that the poem had no preconceived plan to which it had to adhere. Not only did this seem reasonable in view of the inadequacy of the Weston-Frazer interpretation, but, when the facsimile of the original drafts of the poem were published, it was borne out by the evidence of the composition. All this is discussed in detail in the first chapter of this book.

All that was left, then, was the interrelatedness of the words and imagery of the poem itself to supply a structure from which coherent meaning could be generated. But to try to define that interrelatedness purely from examination of the surface of the work—which has already been done—again proves unsatisfactory. While a gut level response can inspire a feeling of coherence, it is too intuitive and amorphous to provide specific meanings and appropriate responses to the individual lines and episodes of the work. To articulate the meaning of the images, one must seek their origins and hope that within those origins lies the key to the interrelatedness of the poem.

What emerges from such an analysis of imagery, lines, and episodes is a fabric of experience decidedly different from the ordinary cloth of reality. It is not the rich tapestry of legend or fairytale, nor the jacquard of science fiction or fantasy. It is a weave directly from the loom of the mind, patterned after the woof and warp of the unconscious, guided by emotional continuity and thematic consistency achieved within a particular stylistic and philosophical framework. In short, it is an amalgam that could exist only within the tissue of literature itself.

If there is anything like a conventional unity to the poem, it stems from the philosophical considerations underlying its conception and its style. I shall not enter into any lengthy stylistic analysis of The Waste Land. Already legion are the studies of Eliot's stylistic debts; he himself chronicled them in his literary essays, which offer the most insightful treatment of those matters.

The opening chapter gives consideration to the overarching philosophical concerns of Eliot, which in his chosen resolutions lent metaphysical support to the principles of composition that he followed. Essentially the poetic world of Eliot exists in a framework of space, time, and causality radically different from that of the normal waking reality of the common man or woman. And the experiencing self in that world has been all but redefined, a legacy of Hume interpreted through Bradley and Eastern mysticism. Readers must have this new reality clearly outlined before them, if they are to map an intelligent route through The Waste Land.

The second chapter brings together what has been discovered through an examination of the genesis of the poem, its stylistic character, and its philosophical background and shows how all these things can be brought to bear upon a close reading and deeper appreciation of the poem. Eliot's approach to writing poetry, defined by his stylistic and philosophical proclivities, is placed in historical perspective so that his position and the significance of The Waste Land in twentieth-century literature may be properly evaluated. The themes he chose to explore in The Waste Land and elsewhere are summarized and discussed in relation to stylistic, philosophical, biographical, and emotional backgrounds. This latter discussion serves as an introduction to my actual reading of the text of the poem.

The exegetical section—which comprises the main body of this book—is arranged so that each section of the poem is introduced with appropriate background information, followed by a synopsis intended to acquaint the reader with themes and thematic relationships within the episodes that define the overall structural coherence of the section. This is to avoid confusion upon entering the allusive labyrinth of the text of the poem itself. Finally, using the lines of the poem as headings, each line is comprehensively discussed; its allusive complexities are spelled out plainly. Rather than merely citing sources, I have provided the full context of most allusions, quoted or described. Having all sources immediately at hand should also promote a more vivid sense of association, since few readers would be familiar with them all (an absurd supposition) or would take the trouble to look them all up (which, in certain cases, would be extremely troublesome).

The exegesis offered here incorporates a large body of allusions not previously catalogued. Some of these newly noted sources are admittedly minor, throwing light only on the associative processes underlying poetic inspiration. Many others, however, fill critical gaps and make it possible to discern for the first time the unbroken pattern of the poem from beginning to end. In fact, the fullness of the allusions yields not only an exegesis of the poem but a fascinating foundation for a study of the creative mind, certainly the creative mind of a single poet.

In general, most of the illumination shed in this study upon The Waste Land also clarifies our understanding of the remaining body of Eliot's work: poetry, plays, and criticism. One aspect of the unity of his work is the bearing of his critical theories on his poetics. And both are related intimately to his lifelong concern for his privacy, itself expressed philosophically through a continual preoccupation with the dilemmas of solipsism, a paramount theme traceable in his work to the very end, The Elder Statesman.

This adherence to solipsism, from which Eliot could see no philosophical escape, led ultimately to his infamous conversion. The complexity and subtleness of his religious conversion has rarely been appreciated and never fully explained. In a sense, The Waste Land represented a major step toward his conversion. It and his earlier poems show him teetering on the brink between metaphysical nihilism and religious mysticism, the distinction between the two being a tenuous one of perhaps temperament only. Oft repeated is the observation that the atheist and the blasphemer are sometimes closer to God than the so-called believer. They suffer the agony of being unable to affirm either God's existence or a significance in life and so constantly feel a divine presence through its absolute absence. Nowhere is the paradoxical split between belief and nonbelief more dramatically drawn than in the dilemma of personality and philosophy that culminated in Eliot's conversion, which was not a single event but a process that began early and continued to the end of his days.

Eliot's struggle with religious conviction helped to epitomize him as a poet and thinker peculiarly of this century. However we characterize the period (which can, of course, be extended into the nineteenth century), it is among other things a time of troubled faith in which traditional theology has lost much of its persuasiveness, at least for a significant number of intellectuals, while nothing has really established itself as an alternative. The call is not so much for a god as for a meaning to existence. That Eliot concerned himself so intensely with this struggle to find significance certainly was a key to his becoming, in the minds of many, the poet par excellence of the twentieth century.

For those who accept Eliot as modernist supreme, it may come somewhat as a surprise that his deepest poetic roots lay not in the French decadents but in the medieval figure of Dante. It was Dante, even more than St. John of the Cross, who gave him the unifying vision of a spiritual journey of the soul through which the elements of The Waste Land were brought together and made whole. From Dante he also learned the allusive method through which to assimilate the personal into the universal. And Eliot helped us to see Dante more clearly in our own age, demonstrating that not only can writers of the past influence those coming after them, but later writers can modify those who precede them. Both Dante and Eliot belong to the ideal order of history that is constantly shifting before our gaze. Eliot made his point on that score and, in a sense that perhaps not all can understand or accept, escaped the prison of time and space, leaving behind yet another trail from appearance to reality for future pilgrims of the soul to wonder at and try to follow, past the terror and glory of life to the other side of despair.

1

A Couple of Feelers
down at Tom's Place:
Genesis of *The Waste Land*

In early November 1919, Eliot was in the middle of writing a review of G. Gregory Smith's *Ben Jonson* for the *Times Literary Supplement*. "And when this is off," he wrote to his benefactor, John Quinn, "I hope to get started on a poem I have in mind."[1] That is the earliest reference we have to *The Waste Land*, though Eliot had undoubtedly discussed it with his wife and close friends even earlier. Actually the written trail of the evolution of the poem stretches back at least to 1914, when Eliot jotted down poetic fragments from which he drew in putting together the penultimate draft that he submitted to Ezra Pound for critical edition.

By 20 September 1920, he was still yearning for "a period of tranquility to do a poem I have in mind."[2] Sometime between then and May 1921 he found time to get the poem "partly on paper."[3] Both Grover Smith[4] and Hugh Kenner[5] speculate that "The Fire Sermon" was the first portion to be sketched out, and that "Death by Water" came shortly thereafter. Since the "Death by Water" section terminated in an English rendering of the closing of "Dans le Restaurant" (the only portion salvaged in the ultimate version of the poem), it seems precarious to place it second in chronology to "The Fire Sermon." At any rate, the question may be purely academic, since it relates only to the chronology of the existing early drafts of the poem, and not necessarily to the psychological gestation and literary exfoliation of it.

Quinn had extended himself on Eliot's behalf on a number of occasions, intervening with American publishers and offering financial assistance; in appreciation, Eliot sent the New York lawyer a packet containing the drafts of *The Waste Land* along with nine satellite poems, 23 October 1922. But there is no way of knowing whether these drafts comprised the entire work sheets, or whether certain early efforts were lost or suppressed. This alone makes dating the composition of the various sections of the poem tentative at best.

Still, in view of the evidence reviewed by Smith and Kenner, it seems reasonable to assume that parts three and four and the title page for the poem had probably been sketched out in London prior to May 1921, and that the remainder was done at Margate and Lausanne between mid-October and the end of the year. This division is sufficient to establish certain facts about Eliot's original conception of the work. Operating from the assumption that "The Fire Sermon" came first from Eliot's pen (or, in this case, typewriter), Kenner hypothesizes that the poem was initially conceived as an urban apocalypse inspired by Dryden's *Annus Mirabilis:* "London, perceived through various Augustan modes: that was 'The Fire Sermon' originally. It might have been entitled *London: a Poem,* or even *The Vanity of Human Wishes.*"[6] Kenner points out that at the time he was working on this early part of *The Waste Land,* Eliot was preparing a review of Mark Van Doren's *John Dryden* (which subsequently appeared in the *Times Literary Supplement* on 9 June 1921), a biography in which *Annus Mirabilis* was quoted and discussed in some detail. Kenner ties this in with Eliot's apostrophe to London, "O City city . . . ," which was much lengthier in the original draft. He sees this as the eye of the storm from which the inspiration of the poem spun out.

> The passage commences with a four-line stanza, set off by a space and rhymed *a b a b,* a stanza that just a little later in "The Fire Sermon" was repeated seventeen more times. This is an uncommon stanza, recognizable to most modern ears because Gray used it in his *Elegy.* Mark Van Doren . . . has something to say about its history, and about Dryden's persisting fascination with its "leisurely authority." Before Dryden, Spenser, Davies, Donne, and Ben Jonson had used it, and D'Avenant in *Gondibert.* Most pertinently, it is the stanza of *Annus Mirabilis,* which just here in "The Fire Sermon" it seems calculated to echo.[7]

This is a rather narrow assumption. About the time that he was entertaining the prospect of writing *The Waste Land,* Eliot was reading a book on Ben Jonson for review. Donne had long been one of his favorite poets, and he borrowed from him and from Spenser in writing the poem. It is, therefore, impossible to connect the particular iambic pentameter quatrain specifically with *Annus Mirabilis;* and this seems to be Kenner's key evidence for his hypothesis, since he notes no direct allusions to Dryden's poem in "The Fire Sermon" other than this supposed metric one. He cites a few parallels but nothing concrete enough to nail down his case. Actually there are allusions to the Dryden poem, but they appear in "The Burial of the Dead" and "What the Thunder Said." In any case, Kenner does not mention them.

Examining the Ur-text, we find that the London apostrophe was extremely tentative, even in the typed draft. If the line-struck phrases are totally removed, all semblance of meaning goes with them. What is left is not even evocative, as are fragmental passages in the final version of the poem. It is almost impossible to regard such a hodge-podge of half-formed ideas as the germinal seed from which the poem evolved. It is hopelessly incomplete, not fully thought out, aborted in conception. It is simply too uncertain in its final structure and semantic articulation. And it should not be overlooked that by far the more dominant episode in the section was the parody of *The Rape of the Lock*, which was subsequently removed. In fact, as originally conceived the section opened with this mannered scene.

All this is not to suggest that the urban apocalypse formed no part of Eliot's vision of *The Waste Land*. As Kenner observed, "He was always a city poet, not a country poet, his affinities rather with Baudelaire than with Wordsworth."[8] The urban background of his experience always found its way into his poems, from the yellow smoke of St. Louis to the crowds of London. But to assert that urban satire was the original main focus in *The Waste Land* is uncomfortably speculative, especially when more promising alternatives are evident.

In the mélange of "The Fire Sermon," either as originally drafted or in its final form, it seems futile to try to pinpoint one episode as genetically crucial, determinative of the whole poem. Rather, panoramically, it displays a Dantean complexion as personal experience becomes depersonalized and fuses with historical, literary, and mythical material. There can be no doubt that Dante was in Eliot's mind as he composed the poem. He was steeped in Dante. For a number of years during one period of his life, he carried a pocket edition of Dante with him.

Consider the circumstances under which Dante wrote his *Commedia*:

Whatever the precise date of its composition, most of the *Commedia* was written during a period of disappointment and disillusion. The death of the earthly Beatrice alone was enough for Dante to write, at the end of the *Vita Nuova* (about 1292), that he hoped to say of Beatrice "what was never said of any woman," in order to release his disgust with a world where every dream of happiness ends in a bitter disillusionment. Not only her death, but the reversal of all his hopes for reward of his study and his civic duties, had brought him to see how vain are the things of this world.

All that remained to him was a burning desire for a world where death and time did not exist. So forcefully did his feelings spur his imagination to create such a world that he condemned the whole of the world oppressing him. He felt himself commissioned to save others from the spiritual death he had so nearly suffered himself.[9]

Eliot approached the writing of *The Waste Land* in analogous circumstances. Henry Ware Eliot, his father, had died in January of 1919. Since leaving America, Eliot had felt estranged from his family. A visit from his mother, sister, and brother during the summer of 1921 did little to assuage the estrangement. The family had wanted him to return to the States and follow an academic career, something they regarded as more substantial than the precarious fortunes of being a writer. He thereafter felt that he had something to prove.

Meanwhile, his financial position left much to be desired. He was not always happy with the neighborhood in which he could afford to live. To remedy the situation, he worked himself to exhaustion, then went home to face a kind of private hell with his wife. His Beatrice had turned out to be a neurotic shrew. Oddly enough, when she was a child, after an operation for tuberculosis of the hand, she spent a lengthy convalescence at Margate, the very place where Eliot sought solace years later.

Aldous Huxley and Bertrand Russell saw Vivien Haigh-Wood Eliot as somewhat vulgar, though not without a certain grace and charm. Russell speculated that Eliot would quickly tire of her. It is possible that he helped precipitate a rift by having an affair with her. But this is idle speculation. Hope Mirrlees, a poet who, along with her parents and brother, enjoyed a long friendship with the Eliots, gives a telling description of Vivien:

> She gave the impression of absolute terror, of a person who's seen a hideous ghost, a goblin ghost, and who was always seeing a goblin in front of her. Her face was all drawn and white, with wild, frightened, angry eyes. An overintensity over nothing, you see. Supposing you would say to her, 'Oh, will you have some more cake?' she'd say, 'What's that? What do you mean? What did you say that for?' She was terrifying. At the end of an hour I was absolutely exhausted, sucked dry. And I said to myself, poor Tom, this is enough! But she was his muse all the same.[10]

She was the nemesis for whatever guilts he might have carried. Of Eliot, Herbert Read recalled that "I always felt that I was in the presence of a remorseful man, of one who had some secret sorrow or guilt."[11] Read attributed this sorrow or guilt not necessarily to any personal tragedy but perhaps to a larger sense of original sin. Whatever its origin, the feeling, otherwise perhaps nothing more than an aspect of character, was probably brought to a critical pitch by his circumstances, principally by his marriage.

Thus began Dante:

> Nel mezzo del cammin di nostra vita
> mi ritrovai per una selva oscura,
> che la diritta via era smarrita.
>
> Ahi quanto a dir qual era è cosa dura
> questa selva selvaggia ed aspra e forte,
> che nel pensier rinnova la paura!
>
> Tanto è amara, che poco più morte:
> ma per trattar del ben ch' i' vi trovai,
> diro dell' altre cose, ch' io v' ho scorte.
>
> I' non so ben ridir com' io v' entrai;
> tant' era pien di sonno in su quel punto,
> che la verace via abbondonai.

> [In the middle of the journey of our life
> I came to myself in a dark wood
> where the straight way was lost.
>
> Ah! what a hard thing it is to tell
> what a wild, rough and stubborn wood this was
> which in my thoughts brings fear anew!
>
> So bitter it is, that scarcely more is death:
> but to treat of the good that I found there,
> I will speak of the other things I discerned there.
>
> I cannot rightly retell how I entered there,
> so full of sleep was I at that moment
> when I abandoned the true way.][12]

It was spiritual crisis for Dante and for Eliot alike, a spiritual crisis precipitated by terrestrial misfortunes buffeting the inner conscience. As Dante felt for the political destiny of Florence, Eliot, in a time of larger political geography, agonized over the fate of Europe represented archetypically in the image of London. Disillusionment, at least for a small but growing elite of avante-gardists, was in the air. Ezra Pound wrote to William Carlos Williams, "Aristocracy is gone, its function was to select. Only those of us who know what civilization is, only those of us who want better literature, better art, can be expected to pay for it. No use waiting for masses to develop a finer taste, they aren't moving that way. . . . Darkness and confusion as in Middle Ages; no chance of general order or justice; we can only release an individual here or there."[13]

From the *Criterion* Eliot himself observed:

> I have always maintained what appears to be one of your capital tenets: that the standards of literature should be international. And personally, I am, as you know, an old-fashioned Tory. . . .
>
> The present age, a singularly stupid one, is the age of a mistaken nationalism and of an equally mistaken and artificial internationalism. I am all for empires. . . . But the more contact, the more free exchange, there can be between the small number of intelligent people of every race or nation, the more likelihood of general contribution to what we call Literature. . . . In England there do not seem to be any young writers. There is one advantage in living in England: one remains perpetually a very young writer. . . .[14]

And from the vantage point of 1934, he recalled that "younger generations can hardly realize the intellectual desert of England and America during the first decade and more of this century. . . . In America the desert extended, à *perte de vue*, without the least prospect of even desert vegetables."[15]

At first it was a question of intellectual purity, incisive perception, and the transmission of that perception through *les mots justes* conceived always concretely. Out of the slushy rhetoric of Georgian sentimentalism rose the gem-sharp speech of the Imagists. Pound and Eliot evolved poetically with that movement and then ascended beyond it. After technique came content. Eliot looked to the social matrix of literature and found only decay and sterility.

As Dante was exiled from Florence, Eliot was alienated spiritually and, in an ideological sense, politically from virtually the whole of Western Europe and his homeland. He was among the many who were disillusioned by the devastation of World War I; he allowed Herman Hesse to speak to this issue in the fragment from *Blick ins Chaos* quoted in the notes to *The Waste Land*.

Both Dante and Eliot approached their respective works, then, in quest of release to be gained by transmuting autobiographical detail into something beyond the individual and the particular through a special allegorical process. Pound outlined the layers of the allegory:

> . . . the *Commedia* is, in the literal sense, a description of Dante's vision of a journey through the realms inhabited by the spirits of men after death; in a further sense it is the journey of Dante's intelligence through the states of mind wherein dwell all sorts and conditions of men before death; beyond this, Dante or Dante's intelligence may

come to mean "Everyman" or "Mankind," whereas his journey becomes a symbol of mankind's struggle upward out of ignorance into the clear light of philosophy. In the second sense I give here, the journey is Dante's own mental and spiritual development. In the fourth sense, the *Commedia* is an expression of the laws of eternal justice; "il contrapasso," the counterpass, as Bertram calls it or the laws of Karma, if we are to use an Oriental term.[16]

With little modification, Pound's characterization of *The Commedia* would apply equally well to *The Waste Land*. Heaven and hell, in the modern poem, have given way to a more difficult to comprehend timeless metaphysical state, but, as it comprehends the workings of a kind of divine justice too, it functions in the same capacity as a unifying construct in the organization of the work. But no case can be made from such overarching parallels. More specific bonds connect *The Waste Land* as originally conceived with *The Commedia*.

Eliot's borrowings from Dante in *The Waste Land* and elsewhere are, for the most part, commonly recognized. They could be anticipated from the intimate familiarity that Eliot was known to have had with Dante's works. Even more to the point, he began those borrowings in "The Fire Sermon." He called attention to his Dantean debt in the notes to "Richmond and Kew / Undid me." Dantean imitation loomed even larger in the contemporaneous "Death by Water," although this imitation was obliterated from the final version by the collaborative editing of both Pound and Eliot.

"Death by Water" originally commenced with an eighty-four line narrative of a shipwreck off the New England coast. According to Valerie Eliot's commentary, this shipwreck was inspired by the tale told by Ulysses of the disastrous voyage in which he met his death, recorded in canto twenty-six of *The Inferno*. Eliot transmuted his recollections of sailing as a youth off the northeast coast of Cape Ann, Massachusetts, into a sea story the import of which is telescoped through its evocation of a classical myth reenacted in Dantean hell. However bewildering its layered complexity, it is in essence the method of composition used by Dante in *The Commedia* and taken over by Eliot for *The Waste Land*.

Most important here is the rather substantial reliance in this shipwreck episode on the Dantean model. To arrange it in proper perspective, it should be emphasized that, except for the Phlebas passage of a mere ten lines, this episode constituted the entire "Death by Water" as it was originally written. In other words, at this early stage of writing of *The Waste Land*, Dante must have been at the forefront of Eliot's mind. There is really nothing surprising in this fact, but it has not previously been sufficiently underscored nor utilized in bringing out the intent of the poem. At issue is not so much a matter of the so-called allusive method but, more important, the structured principles by which the poem is put together. This is not to speak of any overall plan of the work as a whole, something by which one section might be related to another through a discernable argument. Rather, what is now being considered is the inner structure of the individual episodes that together form the larger sectional units of the work. True, a certain unity of the whole derives from the inner texture of the episodes, but this is more formal than it is related to any continuity of content. Ernest Hatch Wilkins has singled out certain aspects of the structure of *The Commedia*:

> The whole poem, cathedral-like in its inexhaustible variety, is cathedral-like also in its architectonic unity—a unity based on its grand but never rigid symmetry and in the linking progress of the protagonist from the dread forest to the Empyrean. The sense of unity is reinforced in many ways: by anticipatory indications of experiences yet to come; by reminiscences of experiences that have already been narrated; by contrasting parallelisms between passages in successive canticles, as for instance between Charon's ferrying over the Acheron and the Angel's ferrying over the seas to the Mountain of Purgatory; and by summaries, or surveys, of past experience, or of space traversed.[17]

When these principles are carried over to a vastly shorter work, modifications are inevitable. *The Waste Land* lays no claim to the "cathedral-like" proportions of *The Commedia*, and so whatever symmetry it has must be of a less awesome character. Whereas in *The Commedia*, despite the allegorical method, the content is well articulated, in *The Waste Land*, partly because of the style and partly because of the extreme condensation employed in the imagery, the structure is more like that of a living organism with one thing growing out of another—not by a superimposed plan but more from sheer inner necessity. In that kind of structure, analogous to dream formation, it is often difficult if not downright impossible to separate parts analytically so that each stands out distinctly. In other words, the degree of interdependence (considering not only the surface meaning of an image, but also its personal, literary, historical, mythical, religious, and other implications) precludes clearly articulated dependence of parts so that they might all be perceived in an overall design of well-defined symmetry.

But the other artifices of unity are all there in forms similar to those in which they appear in Dante. The sybil, in the epigraph, condemned to live out as many years as the number of grains in a handful of sand, anticipates "fear in a handful of dust"; the "drowned Phoenician Sailor" presignifies Phlebas; "Unreal city," which appears at two points, presages "O City city," and so on. Likewise, the single word "Unreal" (376) looks back to "Unreal city"; the "empty chapel" of line 388 leads back to "*Et O ces voix d'enfants, chantant dans la coupole!,*" and "O swallow swallow" recalls the Philomel myth that appears at several places in the poem. "I see crowds of people, walking round in a ring; (56) parallels "A crowd flowed over London Bridge"; the boat of Elizabeth and Leicester parallels the responsive boat in "What the Thunder Said." Summaries are not found, of course, because the shortness of the poem does not necessitate them. But the structural parallels and similarities of method between *The Waste Land* and *The Commedia* go even beyond these, which after all are rather generic to all classic literature beyond the briefer poetic forms.

> While Dante is the privileged witness and faithful reporter of the events of the *Commedia,* he is also the central figure of the drama. In a sense, he is the drama. The *Commedia* is a very subjective poem, a confession and an autobiography, perhaps the first true autobiography of the middle ages. . . . A good deal of what Dante says about himself is straightforward: he tells of his exile, his friends, his masters, and his literary models from Virgil to Arnaut Daniel; but much is offered as allegory, usually but not always transparent.[18]

George Santayana, one of those from whom Eliot first learned about Dante—the others being Pound and C. H. Grandgent—elaborated the autobiographical approach employed by Dante. He wrote, in his *Three Philosophical Poets,* that "the sting of Dante's private wrongs, like the enthusiasm of his private loves, lent a wonderful warmth and clearness to the great objects of his imagination."[19] He called this process of inspiration the "Platonic expansion of emotion," explaining that "Dante had . . . the art of a Platonic lover: he could enlarge the object of his passion, and keep the warmth and ardour of it undiminished."[20]

Eliot has followed a similar procedure. He begins with some personal recollection, such as of Mary Institute, the establishment for girls in the house immediately adjoining his family residence in St. Louis. There was a wall closing off the school, or rather a fence with a gate through which entrance was forbidden while the girls were out at play. But young Eliot could look over at the girls, perhaps spot one particular girl, and dream. Perhaps there was a real incident with one of the girls. This may never be known for certain. At any rate, this recollection becomes transmuted and depersonalized into the young man and girl in the Hyacinth garden in "The Burial of the Dead." With sparse but deft imagery—wet hair, arms full of flowers, mute (perhaps sterile) ecstasy of mind—the scene retains the same "warmth and ardour" that it must have had in actual experience.

Depersonalization of the experience is achieved quite simply. There are no real names. The St. Louis background is absent. It is impossible to place the event in time; there is no date assigned to it. It is suspended in a frozen moment of eternity, like the figures in a Byzantine painting against a gold background that defines no real space or time. Autobiographical feeling is there, at least for the informed reader, but it is universalized in a peculiar manner.

Further, the event is expanded through layers of experience brought in through allusion. Eliot invokes his own poem "La Figlia che Piange," where there was "the smell of hyacinths across the garden," surrounding the garden with a Pre-Raphaelite aura. Capitalization of "Hyacinth" suggests some association with the Greek god of fertility, Hyacinthus, and vests the hyacinth girl with the role of one who officiates at some festival of regeneration. The loss of speech and the state somehow between living and dead recall the state of awe and fright suffered by Dante as he entered the last circle of hell. As the lover stares dumbly at his beloved, he stares at divinity, of which the blinding source of light is the symbol in Dante, but "the heart of light" is also the inversion of "the heart of darkness," and it was into the silence that Kurtz peered, in Joseph Conrad's *Heart of Darkness*, as he witnessed the "horror" of existence.

The episode is built up much like a sea-change, in which originally organic material is gradually replaced by mineral deposits that ultimately replicate the form of the living organism. Beginning with the living event, bits and pieces are replaced by fragments of other parallel events, real or imaginary, past or present, until what is left is a montage duplication of the original. Through this process the underlying form of the real occurrence remains, but the substance is totally different. And in this case it is always more transcendent, reaching as it does across space and time.

This, then, is the method of composition that originated in the writing of the germinal core of the poem. While it is in itself subtle enough, it is made still more complex and abstruse by the style of expression through which it functions and by the philosophical framework in which the whole is mounted.

Working from this compositional center established in "The Fire Sermon" and "Death by Water," inspired perhaps not exclusively but in large measure by Dante, Eliot proceeded with greater assurance to the remaining sections of the poem. Incidents changed but method did not. There was only one major false start, and that was in "The Burial of the Dead," which Eliot originally thought to commence with a protracted narration of a night on the town, probably recalling incidents from his college days. He even allowed himself the extravagance of using his own name for the narrator, certainly a bit of candor notable for its rarity. This unaccustomed slip is most telling.

Recall that Dante embarked upon his moral journey in a state of sleepiness; in the discarded first episode of "The Burial of the Dead," the narrator, presumably Eliot himself, leaves his companions at the break of dawn, ostensibly to watch the sunrise and then go home to sleep. Not perhaps literally but certainly metaphorically, Kurtz, in the epigraphic quotation, completes the parallelism by, uttering the words, "The Horror! the horror!", suggesting a kind of delirium, something akin to nightmare sleep in which the events of his life might be passing before him in a crazy, dreamlike manner.

The epigraph would have suggested a review of past life, a reliving of events, for some moral purpose or to some spiritual end, but in a kind of delirious vision. This idea would have been reinforced by the notion of Tom going home, drunk and half-asleep, to fall victim to hallucinations and hypnagogic phantasmagoria. Both devices would have been supported by the underlying and rather ubiquitous thread of the journey of Dante from the outer shores of hell to the empyrean, with nods to Aeneas's sojourn to the underworld—in other allusions throughout the poem—thrown in for good measure. That, at any rate, seems to have been Eliot's intention.

The allusive method of Dante, then, formed a cornerstone of Eliot's poetic practice, not only in *The Waste Land* but in the earlier poems from *Prufrock* on. He enriched this method by allying it with oneirism adopted as a modus operandi for poetic composition. In *The Waste Land* one is cued to this by the Dantean background and even more specifically by the epigraph borrowed from Conrad. A further cue would have come from the discarded opening episode of "The Burial of the Dead." Moreover, Eliot has inferred something like oneirism in his various accounts of the creative process in the writing of poetry.

Here is one of his more extended general accounts of the process:

I should say that the poet is tormented primarily by the need to write a poem—and so, I regret to find, are a legion of people who are not poets: so that the line between "need" to write and desire to write is by no means easy to draw. And what is the experience that the poet is so bursting to communicate? By the time it has settled down into a poem it may be so different from the original experience as to be hardly recognisable. The "experience" in question may be the result of a fusion of feelings so numerous, and ultimately so obscure in their origins, that even if there be communication of them, the poet may hardly be aware of what he is communicating, and what is there to be communicated was not in existence before the poem was completed. I will not say that there is not always some varying degree of communication taking place. There is room for very great individual variation in the motives of equally good individual poets.[21]

Much of this is echoed in "The Three Voices of Poetry":

> In a poem which is neither didactic nor narrative, and not ani-
> mated by any other social purpose, the poet may be concerned solely
> with expressing in verse—using all his resources of words, with their
> history, their connotations, their music—this obscure impulse. He
> does not know what he has to say until he has said it, and in the effort
> to say it he is not concerned with making other people understand
> anything. He is not concerned, at this stage, with other people at all:
> only with finding the right words or, anyhow, the least wrong words.
> He is not concerned whether anybody else will ever listen to them or
> not, or whether anybody else will ever understand them if he does.
> He is oppressed by a burden which he must bring to birth in order to
> obtain relief. Or, to change the figure of speech, he is haunted by a
> demon, a demon against which he feels powerless, because in its first
> manifestation it has no face, no name, nothing; and the words, the
> poem he makes, are a kind of form of exorcism of this demon. In other
> words again, he is going to all that trouble, not in order to communi-
> cate with anyone, but to gain relief from acute discomfort; and when
> the words are finally arranged in the right way—or in what he comes
> to accept as the best arrangement he can find—he may experience a
> moment of exhaustion, of appeasement, of absolution, and of some-
> thing very near annihilation, which is in itself indescribable.[22]

Further amplification of the scenario is given by Paul Valery who, Eliot
thought, "studied the workings of his own mind in the composition of a
poem more perseveringly than any other poet has done":[23]

> . . . the poetic state or emotion seems to me to consist in a dawning
> perception, a tendency toward perceiving a *world*, or a complete
> system of relations, in which beings, things, events, and acts, al-
> though they may resemble, *each to each*, those which fill and form
> the tangible world—the immediate world from which they are bor-
> rowed—stand, however, in an indefinable, but wonderfully accurate,
> relationship to the modes and laws of our general sensibility. So, the
> value of these well-known objects and beings is in some way altered.
> They respond to each other and combine quite otherwise than in
> ordinary conditions. They become—if you will allow the ex-
> pression—*musicalized*, somehow commensurable, echoing each
> other. The poetic universe defined in this way bears a strong analogy
> to the universe of dreams.[24]

Readers of *The Waste Land* should find Valery's last observation especially interesting because the poem displays something very much
like a dream structure. He wrote further that "a dream makes us see by a
common and frequent experience how our consciousness can be in-
vaded, filled, made up by an assembly of productions remarkably
different from the mind's ordinary reactions and perceptions. It gives us

the familiar example of a *closed world* where all *real* things can be represented, but where everything appears and is modified by the fluctuations of our deepest sensibility."[25]

All this must be placed within the context of what is known about the composition of *The Waste Land*. "What the Thunder Said" was written at one sitting in a kind of delirium, rather like automatic writing. Thus it would replicate a free-associational structure. This section differs from the others mainly in that it is broken up into shorter episodes, as is the last half of "The Fire Sermon." Otherwise the relation of each episode to that which follows it is as non sequitorial as that which prevails throughout the poem. And calling the relation non sequitorial is not meant to imply that the relationship is random but that it does not follow, on the surface, the norms of logic.

From this distinction emerges a crucial definition of the poetic structure that holds *The Waste Land* together: it is a fabric of free-associational relationships in which one thing is related to another through a complex of largely unconscious associations. If Eliot is to be believed, at least in "What the Thunder Said" the free-associational structure is genuine; whether in the rest of the poem it is also genuine or consciously reproduced is a moot question. However, in his interview in the *Paris Review* Eliot gave a clue that the whole poem did indeed come into being through something closely resembling a stream-of-consciousness process. Speaking of the evolution of his writing style, he noted that the writing of the plays *Murder in the Cathedral* and *The Family Reunion* had an effect on the writing of the *Four Quartets* in that "it led to a greater simplification of language and to speaking in a way which is more like conversing with your reader." He added that "in *The Waste Land*, I wasn't even bothering whether I understood what I was saying."[26] More extreme candor could hardly be expected.

This admission by Eliot also has serious implications for the supposed mythic framework of the poem. It is once again difficult to understand how Eliot could have dealt with the Grail legend and its ramifications through Frazer in any but a fragmentary and highly distorted way, when writing in such a free-associational style, not bothering to consider the logical meaning of what he was saying. That the material of Weston and Frazer could have entered the poem at various points in a prelogical way cannot be disputed; but in that manner, it would be just more grist for the mill. It would not have a determinative role in the structuring of the poem. The determinative force must have been Eliot's own psychological crisis experienced throughout the period in which the poem was gestated and written.

The notion of a free-associational structure of *The Waste Land* requires some careful qualification and elaboration before it can be useful in the analysis of the poem. David Foulkes provides a good preliminary definition of the free-associational process in dreaming. He says that "without the typical constraints placed upon the mind's activity by external-stimulus input and by a cathexis of external reality . . . thought processes tend toward incoherence of form (meaningless fragments of visual imagery) and disturbing intrapsychic content (anxieties, and socially unacceptable wishes or thoughts)."[27] By "cathexis of external reality" Foulkes is referring to the tendency of the waking mind automatically to compare or test its ideas and impressions against external reality to determine whether they are practically valid or distorted, unrealistic, misconstrued, or otherwise incongruent with the physically real. When the mind loses focus on external reality because of sleep, hypnagogia, drug intake, or deliberate realignment of attention (as in daydreaming, or automatic writing, or free association), the normal constraints of reality testing are diminished and the mind reverts to a kind of prelogical thought process. At those moments, the thought process "appears to express man's way of organizing life experience and his inner reflection of himself in a symbology which he quickly casts off" as soon as he returns to reality testing, or normal wakefulness. "Thus it does not lend itself to immediate logical operational inference. It can be seen, however, as a complex set of cues and signals which appear . . . primarily in pictorial form."[28]

Lewis R. Wolberg, drawing broadly on the literature of the topic, rather meticulously outlines the dynamics of dream formation—and it should be remembered that substantially the same applies to all of the free-associational processes. "The mind becomes contaminated with an archaic, prelogical kind of ideation that utilizes perseverations and stereotypes. There is a replacement of abstract conceptual, for concrete thinking, and an abandonment of accepted rules of time and space." In this context, a perseveration is a repeated response to the same question or situation.

> Certain distortions prevail in dreams, probably conditioned, first by a need to evade the psychic censorship which continues to operate in sleep, though to a lesser degree than in the waking state, and, second, by a primitive type of thinking that seems to be released by inhibition of the higher cortical centers. Inacceptable and repudiated aspects of the personality are, through distortions, made acceptable to the dreamer's ego.[29]

Finally Wolberg specifies the various mechanisms of distortion that seem to operate regularly in free-associational states: "Among the mechanisms serving the interests of distortion are symbolization, displacement, condensation, representation by multiples and opposites, secondary elaboration, and substitution for people of equated objects."[30]

A number of points need clarification and comment in relation to *The Waste Land*. First, the whole process of this prelogical stream of thought is initiated by a severance with external reality. Eliot has described how, in a state of ill health, he gave vent to a flood of subconscious material, at least in "What the Thunder Said." In fact, throughout the composition of the poem he was in a state of extreme anxiety, withdrawing into a sanitarium atmosphere. This state of mind, involving even a considered conversion to Buddhism, comprehended a disruption and reconsideration of values for Eliot; it necessarily would have been conducive to a long-term maintenance of a free-associational kind of inspiration.

Once this state of mind is achieved, there is a greater than normal breakthrough of disturbing material, mainly in concrete images, into consciousness. Possibly in no other of Eliot's long poems are there so many personal allusions, from the appearance of Pound as Stetson to that of Russell as Madame Sosostris, from snatches of his wife's speech to a remembered conversation with Marie Larisch, from a pleasant afternoon at the Hofgarten in Munich to a not-so-pleasant business luncheon at the Cannon Street Hotel. Only "Portrait of a Lady" comes close to matching it on this score, and there the material was less disparate and was welded into a logically more coherent whole.

Stereotypes and perseverations abound. The rock, the unreal city, the clairvoyante, the tarot characters, the typist and her lover, Tiresias, London Bridge, bats and rats—all are stereotypical or archetypical. As for perseverations or repetitive responses and utterances, there are the twitterings and juggings of birds, the drip drop dripping of water, the double crowing of the cock, the repeated cries of the Rhine maidens, and more. Consider the repetition of "HURRY UP PLEASE ITS TIME" and the farewell at the end of "The Burial of the Dead";

Goonight Bill. Goonight Lou. Goonight May. Goonight.
Ta Ta. Goonight. Goonight.
Good night, ladies, good night, sweet ladies, good night, good night.

There is the obsessive repetition of:

> If there were water
> And no rock
> If there were rock
> And also water
> And water
> A spring
> A pool among the rock

If there were the sound of water only
Not the cicada
And dry grass singing
But sound of water over rock
Where the hermit-thrush sings in the pine trees
Drip drop drip drop drop drop drop
But there is no water[31]

There is the nervous reiteration in his wife's conversations in "The Burial of the Dead," and finally "O O O O that Shakespeherian Rag."

Time and space are altered, brought together in impossible relationships in which events take place in an eternal simultaneity. Illustration of this hardly seems necessary. Not only are different historical events juxtaposed; often elements from various events or personages are fused into single ones. A prelogical space-time continuum underlies the entire structure of the poem, as if the four-dimensional relativistic universe were being considered from a five-dimensional point of view from which the time-line is static.

All the mechanisms of dream distortion also operate in the organization of *The Waste Land*. Some, such as symbolization, representation by multiples and opposites, condensation, and secondary elaboration are obvious; others, such as displacement and substitution of equated objects for people, are less evident.

Displacement, the transference of feelings toward one person to a second person, occurs on a number of occasions in the poem. It is usually part of a symbolization that is in turn intrinsic to the allusive method. That is, the identity of a real person is hidden behind that of a fictitious one so that by implication the affect associated with the first is displaced to the second. Already mentioned are the instances of Pound as Stetson and Russell as Madame Sosostris. Behind Phlebas probably hides Jean Verdenal, a young medical student with whom Eliot had shared a *pension* in Paris during his collegiate days. He and Eliot became close friends, but Verdenal died at the Dardenelles in 1915. Eliot dedicated his first volume of poetry to Verdenal. Of course, in addition to these displacements are others in which the identities of various personages, historical and fictional, are fused; but this is more complex than simple displacement.

Substitution of equated objects for people is, as would be expected, rarer, and where it does occur it is rather literal. Philomel, in the first episode of "A Game of Chess," appears in a painting. And the shadowy drowned person, variously Phlebas, the tarot character, the drowned Phoenician Sailor, and finally the father of Ferdinand (in *The Tempest*) alias perhaps Eliot's own recently deceased father (not to mention Jean Verdenal, and even the drowned god mentioned in Frazer), appears mineralized by a sea-change. This is a queer sort of transformation, but that is precisely the kind that should be expected in a free-associational process.

Symbolization in *The Waste Land* is so well recognized and established that further discussion to prove its presence is not required. However, certain aspects of it in regard to representation by multiples and opposites need to be explored briefly. Multiple identities have already been named for the drowned figure, and Eliot himself outlines a series of identity transformations for Tiresias in his notes (see the note for line 218). Opposites, as they occur in dream formations and related processes, are usually not precisely diametric; the opposition, like everything else, appears distorted. In other words, they are approximate. Those that appear in the poem are mostly between sacred and profane, or pure and impure, love. The hyacinth girl, for example, could be viewed in opposition to the typist; the regal lady in the first episode of "A Game of Chess," to the woman in the pub at the end of that section; Elizabeth, to the girl undone near Kew. Reversals of class are common in these oppositions.

Finally, condensation is a primary mechanism in *The Waste Land*. It is at the heart of the allusive method. In fact, the description of this psychological mechanism can be applied almost verbatim to poetic structure:

> Condensation is the compression of several latent meanings into a single manifest image. The simplest form of condensation is omission of some ideational elements and allowing a part to stand for the whole. Usually, however, condensation includes an active process in which meanings fuse and form a composite. For example, the image of a face may be a composite, in which the eyes are derived from one person, the hair from another, and the overall facial expression from still a third. Or, in another common type of condensation, ideas related to several persons can be relegated to a single person.[32]

This is analogous in every detail to the allusive method previously described. All that is required from that, and the attendant mechanisms, is that the various elements must be arranged into narrativelike episodes; this is what is implied in secondary elaboration. With secondary elaboration, the dream and the poem arrive at nearly identical completions.

In the preliminary definitions of the dream or free associational structure, emphasis was placed on the fact that the imagery involved is primarily visual and, in any case, highly concrete. This is interesting in view of the Dantean model proposed for *The Waste Land*, since Dante is known for his visual imagery, which in Eliot's poem is also striking not only by its quality but by its prominence. In his essay, "Dante," Eliot states unequivocally that "Dante's is a *visual* imagination" and that "allegory means *clear visual images*."[33]

This emphasis on the visual image in prelogical communication has important consequences:

> The pictorial quality of the dream raises a peculiarly significant problem with respect to translating the dream into language for purposes of interpretation. Visual representation, as Rapaport points out [in *Organization and Pathology of Thought*, New York, 1951], has the following real shortcomings in terms of logical verbal communication: (1) It is wanting in means to express relationships; (2) it is limited to either positing or not positing a content, and has only sparse means to qualify positing; (3) it lacks means to express abstractions; and (4) it is implicative or condensing, a quality which defies ordered verbal communication.[34]

One further amplification on this theme is telling: "The various syntactical connections which the interpreter supplies to define meanings of ideas in dream material are inferences arising from his response to the dream."[35] This is paralleled by certain processes of imagistic juxtaposition occurring in poetry, as noted by Eliot when he wrote of Saint-John Perse's *Anabasis* that "any obscurity of the poem, on first readings, is due to the suppression of 'links in the chain,' of explanatory and connecting matter, and not to incoherence, or to the love of cryptogram."[36] He could have said the same of *The Waste Land*.

The structure of the poem is prelogical, consisting of images and statements, pronouncements, juxtaposed without interconnecting logical syntax, just as in a dream. Precise meaning cannot be wrung from it because ambiguity is implicit within the structure. The ambiguity is not calculated; it is unavoidable and in a sense uncontrollable. Most of the potency of the poem lies in its imagery, which cannot be divorced from its symbolism; but the symbolism is not direct, in that the symbol does not stand in a clear one-to-one correspondence with some one thing symbolized. It is an evocative vehicle of ambiguous, often ambivalent, feelings, like the symbols in primitive religion and mythology that gather into themselves a plexus of meanings embodied in the ritual narratives revolving around them.

Given that the structure of *The Waste Land* is fundamentally oneiric, it can further be particularized by reference to the dominant literary devices and metaphysical assumptions adopted in its fabrication. As these devices and assumptions have received attention elsewhere in the corpus of Eliot studies, I need only cite them and briefly indicate, for the sake of completeness, in what way they qualify the mythic dreamscape of the poem.

Symbol formation and the linkage of imagery in *The Waste Land* are largely dictated by the practice of partial disclosure and the amalgamation of disparate materials. The former characterizes French symbolism, whereas the latter derives also from the conceit of the metaphysical poets. Mallarmé, whose poetry depended heavily on the oblique approach toward his subjects, explained partial disclosure:

> Nommer un objet, c'est supprimer les trois quarts de la jouissance du poème qui est faite de deviner peu à peu: le suggerer, voilà la rêve. C'est le parfait usage de ce mystère que constitue le symbole: évoquer petit à petit un objet pour montrer un état d'ame, ou, inversement, choisir un objet et en dégager un état d'âme par une série de déchiffrements. . . . Il doit y avoir toujours énigme en poésie, et c'est le but de la littérature—il n'y en a pas d'autres—d'évoquer les objets.

> [To name an object is to suppress three-quarters of the enjoyment of a poem, which is got by guessing little by little: to suggest it, therein is the dream quality. It is the perfect use of this mystery that the symbol constitutes: to evoke an object and to draw from it a state of mind through a series of decipherments. . . . There ought always to be an enigma in poetry, and it is the end of literature—there is none other—to evoke objects.][37]

As for the metaphysical conceit, Henry W. Wells, in his study of Donne, applies the term "radical imagery" to this metaphoric construction and defines it as that which "occurs where two terms of a metaphor meet on a limited ground, and are otherwise definitely incongruent. It makes daring excursions into the commonplace. The minor term promises little imaginative value. In a coldness to apparently incongruent suggestion this figure approaches the neutral comparison, while in ingenuity it approaches the conceit."[38] And Cleanth Brooks offers a perfect corollary: "we mistake matters grossly if we take the poem to be playing with opposed extremes, only to point the golden mean in a doctrine which, at the end, will correct the falsehood of extremes. The reconcilement of opposites which the poet characteristically makes is not that of a prudent splitting of the difference between antithetical overemphases."[39]

Eliot found the perfect rationale for this radical synthesis of disparate images in F. H. Bradley's concept of the Absolute. Bradley had said flatly that "our experience, where relational, is not true,"[40] and that "everything is experience, and also experience is one."[41] "Ultimate reality is such that it does not contradict itself."[42] Thus, according to this metaphysics, when disparate material is amalgamated the consequent experience brings us close to a feeling of the absolute unity that must lie behind the contradictions of appearance. This is akin to *sat-*

ori.[43] As such, it buttresses the religious implications of the oneirism implicit in *The Waste Land*. Finally, this heavy philosophical burden devolves back to the process of condensation in the dreamwork.

Also consonant with the primary processes of dream structure is the dissolution of spatial and temporal order in the Bradleyan Absolute.

> The past and future . . . are ideal constructions which extend the given present. And our present world itself is a construction based on feeling and perception, "construction" here meaning for us . . . a living outgrowth of the continuous reality. The past and future vary, and they have to vary, with the changes of the present, and, to any man whose eyes are open, such variation is no mere theory but is plain fact. But, though ideal, the past and future are also real, and, if they were otherwise, they could be nothing for judgement or knowledge. They are actual, but they must remain incomplete essentially.[44]

As Hugh Kenner points out in *The Invisible Poet*, herein lies the basis for much of Eliot's theory of tradition as expounded in "Tradition and the Individual Talent." Events in the Bradleyan universe are so arrayed that they can be set into a variety of orders, depending on the perspective and purposes of the observer.[45] It is only the human condition that places them into a linear sequence from past to future. A similar time scheme is suggested in the third chapter of Ecclesiastes, one of Eliot's favorite books of the Bible, where it is written "that which hath been is now; and that which is to be hath already been."

"Differences of time and of place," wrote Bradley, "do not count except so far as they themselves enter into the truth; or, again, the truth in its essence is unchanged however much places and times alter."[46] Space, no less than time, is effaced in the Absolute, because it subsists in relations and because it is internally inconsistent. "Events happen because of that which is beyond all happening and at once contains and subordinates its temporal order."[47] Likewise changes of place occur within that which is beyond all spatial relativity and which contains and subordinates spatial order within itself. So Eliot can invoke cities past and present in a single image:

> Falling towers
> Jerusalem Athens Alexandria
> Vienna London
> Unreal

unpunctuated to emphasize the sameness of all place and time; through allusion and condensation he can superimpose personages past and present to form an eternal composite figure.

I speak of *figures* rather than *persons* because the characters that populate *The Waste Land* are not, strictly speaking, people: they are Bradleyan finite centers, analogous to geometric points, loci without human boundaries. Hugh Kenner has aptly described them as "zones of consciousness" (though he was describing the characters in *Prufrock*). They are refugees from the world of Humean critique. Whereas Hume, looking inward for the self, always stumbled, as he said, "on some particular perception or other,"[48] for Bradley the self "is a construction which is made on and from the present feeling of a finite centre. The work of construction is performed by the finite centre and by the Universe in one, and the result depends for its origin and existence wholly on this active unity."[49] In other words, how the self splits off from the Absolute to assume an *apparent* autonomy is as ineffable as everything else about the Absolute. "In every finite centre . . . the Whole, immanent there, fails to be included in that centre. The content of the centre therefore is beyond itself, and the thing therefore is appearance and is so far what may be termed 'ideal.' "[50] Bradley—and following him, Eliot—departs from Hume, who concluded more directly that observation reveals no self, simply differing moments of awareness.

"My self," wrote Bradley, "is not the immediate, nor is it the ultimate, reality. Immediate reality is an experience either containing both self and not-self, or containing as yet neither."[51] Although he rarely alluded to it, Bradley was concerned with an essentially mystical experience, identical to *satori*. He claimed that "to find reality, we must betake ourselves to feeling" and that, whereas it is true that for the finite center experience is personal, that personal quality "does not exclude inclusion in a fuller totality. There may be a further experience immediate and direct, something that *is* my private feeling, and *also* much more."[52]

This viewpoint is identical with that of Hinduism and Buddhism:

> The self is really divine and transcends the whole of nature. It is the Supreme Self who is present in man's body as the witnessing and unmoving self. The self is not the limited ego in us which performs various acts and enjoys or suffers the consequences thereof. All activity belongs to nature or prakriti. It is only when the self is deluded by and identified with the ego that it thinks itself to be an agent, a doer, a sufferer, or an enjoyer. This means bondage and a consequent life of suffering for the self in this world. The self that is in bondage is liable to sin and suffering, birth and death.[53]

Eliot was much concerned with the relation of the knowing self to the nonself, objective reality, and that which might lie spiritually beyond. As he moved away from the Unitarianism of his family background, flirted with agnosticism under the tutelage of Bertrand Russell, and even considered becoming a Buddhist monk before ultimately converting to Anglo-Catholicism, the epistemological and spiritual problem of solipsism never ceased to preoccupy him. In religion he found no final solution to this nor apparently to any of his other more personal problems. Eliot's own testament precludes any reasonable supposition that he found any certainties in his faith—his acceptance of Bradleyan metaphysics made certainties unthinkable. Upon his well-publicized conversion, he wrote: "Most critics appear to think that my catholicism is merely an escape or an evasion, certainly a defeat. I acknowledge the difficulty of a positive Christianity nowadays; and I can only say that the dangers pointed out, and my own weaknesses, have been apparent to me long before my critics noticed them. But it [is] rather trying to be supposed to have settled oneself in an easy chair, when one has just begun a long journey afoot."[54] Ten months later he went even further in characterizing his faith:

> To me, religion has brought at least the perception of something above morals, and therefore extremely terrifying; it has brought me not happiness, but the sense of something above misery; the very dark night and the desert. To me, the phrase "to be damned for the glory of God" is sense and not paradox; I had far rather walk, as I do, in daily terror of eternity, than feel that this was only a children's game in which all the contestants would get equally worthless prizes in the end. . . . And I don't know whether this is to be labelled "Classicism" or "Romanticism": I only think that I have hold of the tip of the tail of something quite real, more real than morals, or than sweetness and light and culture.[55]

By following Bradley and the oriental mystics in loosening the boundaries between the self and the Absolute, Eliot placed the characters of *The Waste Land* into the context of his personal struggle as it mimicked that of primitive ritual reaching out through mythical narrative to a transcendent reality that can be symbolized but never known in human terms. Perhaps this was for Eliot the ultimate intellectual justification for universalizing his own inner turmoil. And it is fundamentally what transformed his poetic ruminations into what I have called a *mythic dreamscape*.

In summary, all the evidence pertaining to the genesis of *The Waste Land* renders untenable the notion that it somehow embodies the Grail Legend and its implications within ancient religion and mythology. Critics will undoubtedly persist in this interpretation simply because they have a prior investment in it, but such an alliance of critical conscience has little appeal here. From the drafts of the earliest written sections of the poem and the way in which it grew from them, from the

original title and the epigraph, from the role of Tiresias (loosely analogous to that of Virgil in *The Commedia*), from the work's initial conception as a sequence of poems rather than a unified whole, from Eliot's
own comments on the notes and other aspects of the poem, it is reasonably clear that Weston and Frazer were not his guides through *The
Waste Land*, though they might have held his hand for brief periods in
"What the Thunder Said." And from these pieces of evidence, as well as
from biographical details and other subsidiary considerations, it seems
equally clear that his guide in determining the compositional method—
a kind of autobiographical, allegorical approach—was primarily Dante;
from Dante, too, came the plan of the poem (probably existing as only a
subconscious motive) as a verbal embodiment or replication of the
search for significance.

Born into an era of psychological analysis—the era that gave us
psychoanalysis, the psychological novel, stream-of-consciousness writing, dadaism and surrealism—Eliot chose to pursue his spiritual quest
through a free-associative technique, second cousin to stream-of-consciousness, in which his symbolism partook of both dream and mythic
elements. His mythic dreamscape incorporated from his philosophical
background an order in which all points of time and space are eternally
present, persons past and present coalesce into single figures that are
little more than "zones of consciousness." The logic of the poem is that
of the primary processes, ideographic. And the mythic element, deriving only in part from Weston and Frazer, is not determinative; rather, it
is assimilated along with all the other material and on equal footing
with it, into the overall free-associative structure of the poem. In short,
there was never any preconceived scenario, no narrative of mythic
regeneration, no apostrophe to London, no critique of modern society,
to which the material of the poem had to conform, although all of these
things may have entered Eliot's mind consciously or subconsciously *off
and on* during the composition of various parts of the poem. The only
sustained formative force that ruled over the composition of *The Waste
Land* was the total life experience of its author, a critical turmoil of his
mind, and the consequent need to appease that turmoil in the way best
suited to him: by writing a poem *from* it.

2

Synthesis toward an Interpretation

AFTER unfolding the genesis and the design of *The Waste Land*, after tracing its literary and philosophical backgrounds, there still remains a formidable task in grappling with the poetic content in a close appreciative reading of the work. Innate complexities of the poem place it well beyond easy paraphrase. Meaning and intent are close to ineffable in certain respects and, as in most great literary works, they are layered. But, whereas in most other works, at least the classics, layering of meaning proceeds along rather forthright lines, in *The Waste Land* lamination is achieved through linkages that usually fall outside the sphere of logic, chronology, and causality. Thus there is a considerable challenge to synthesize what we experience and then to arrange and articulate it into more common modes of understanding.

Beginning with the very genesis of the poem, obscurantism entered with Eliot's penchant for obfuscating any traces of autobiography in his poetic works. Yet it seems that personal experiences gave him the seeds for some of his most powerful images. He worked from the elements of his own life, as most poets do, certainly most from the Romantic period onward, but he took extreme pains to cover his tracks, probably because the substance for his poetic visions was drawn from the most vulnerable moments of his life, touching upon sexual frustration and the sufferings of a temperament too much at odds with the crudities of existence as he found it.

Autobiographical obfuscation is not merely incidental to the poem, for obviously personal material makes up a good half of the whole. Leaving out of account the geographical background, the presence of London, direct and then often shadowy, there is still a tapestry of events related throughout the poem. For a full interpretation of these events, it is necessary to turn to the details of Eliot's own life. Opening with "The Burial of the Dead," the events begin in the Hofgarten and lead on to a meeting with Marie Larisch and later with Bertrand Russell.

Sandwiched between these meetings is the poignant encounter in the hyacinth garden. In "A Game of Chess" there are the many snatches of speech from Vivien Eliot and the conversation in the pub, related to

Eliot by Ellen Kellond, a maid that he and his wife employed. That section of the poem might almost be called domestic, in view of the origin of much of it. "The Fire Sermon" gives us a business engagement ending with "a weekend at the Metropole," one that Eliot assures us he kept; the sordid affair between the typist and the "young man carbuncular," that Eliot may have gathered from talk at the bank; and finally the sense of Eliot sitting at Margate, attempting to put together the pieces of his life. Memories of Jean Verdenal haunt "Death by Water." Reactions to a painting by Bosch, an indiscretion possibly related to the mysterious experience in the hyacinth garden, and reminiscences of sailing around the Dry Salvages are identifiably autobiographical elements in the final section of the poem. Undoubtedly there are other events of personal origin in the poem, ones that are missed for lack of biographical information.

In many cases the autobiographical incident is transmuted into something impersonal through the allusive allegorical method deriving largely from Dante. At other times the material is simply embedded in an allusive context: usually this is when the material does not touch so intimately upon the more vulnerable spots in Eliot's temperament. Such is the case with the business engagement recounted in the third section of the poem, "The Fire Sermon." It emerges out of the "unreal city" motif in which it takes on a microcosmic significance, mirroring that sort of transaction among the living dead in which the search for significance is lost to the more finite enterprise of seeking economic gain or some end equally without spiritual import.

Even when the superficial or narrative character of an incident in the poem can be clearly discerned, usually the feelings that it evokes are neither simple nor easily categorized. Eliot was by and large not interested in depicting simple emotions. He was most fascinated with those depths of feeling into which one cannot peer. More precisely, he concerned himself with clusters of feelings or with extraordinary emotions. Consider:

> In this decayed hole among the mountains
> In the faint moonlight, the grass is singing
> Over the tumbled graves, about the chapel
> There is the empty chapel, only the wind's home.
> It has no windows, and the door swings,
> Dry bones can harm no one.[1]

Without attempting to elucidate all of the pertinent allusions, readers recognize this as a graveyard scene. Overlaid upon this superficial descriptive skeleton is a reference to the Perilous Chapel, a place where significance, in the form of the holy grail, might be found. Life in the material sense ends here, but for those who believe it may mark the beginning of a fully spiritual existence, or it may represent simply a stage in the endless karmatic wheel. An allusion to Kipling's novel *Kim* helps to identify the mountains as the Himalayas, which is borne out several lines later by the reference to "Himavant." This brings in the Oriental aspect of the religious quest. And "dry bones" recalls the valley of death in Ezekiel and the promised awakening of the dead. Hence this graveyard is a place not only of death but also of possible rebirth. Opposite feelings are unified into an ambivalence typical to the poem. Here the feelings are clustered into a complex that, while it certainly relates to religious awe, cannot be labeled with the name of a simple, previously identified emotion.

Other complex emotions evoked in the poem are "fear in a handful of dust," the awe of "looking into the heart of light, the silence," the anxieties of attempting to read the future or even the design of the present in the tarot cards, the caged feeling in the opening episode of "A Game of Chess," the neurasthenic apprehension in the central portion of that section, the vague aesthetic reaction to the "inexplicable splendour" of Magnus Martyr, the frustration of being able to "connect / Nothing with nothing," the placid discomfort of contemplating Phlebas beneath the sea, the ineffable feelings of hallucination conjured in "What the Thunder Said," the solipsistic isolation of "each in his prison," and the near hysterical dissociation with which the poem ends. None of these feelings is simple or single, like the wish to kill someone or the desire to achieve some social end (which itself may have symbolic and therefore complex values). But here precisely is one of Eliot's key insights: emotions are rarely, if ever, simple. If analyzed, they spread out through the mind, and their ramifications become lost in the darkness of the unconscious. The search for motives behind emotions can never be complete.

Looked at from another angle, Eliot tried to capture emotions at that stage when they begin to become involved in associations, where all the symbolic overtones begin. Here, the superficial object of the emotion has vanished to give way to the deeper targets that the object only symbolized. The superficial objects are only vehicles for the more inscrutable feelings they invoke. That is why any semblance of narrative structure that they may form, as they are cast into a sequence of events, is virtually unimportant to an understanding of the intent of the poem. It is rather the associative structure of the invoked emotions that reveals the poem's ultimate intent.

From Bradleyan metaphysics as well as from his own study of oriental philosophy, Eliot had learned to regard the field of consciousness— what we are aware of at any given moment—as an organic whole the fragmentation of which belongs only to appearance, which is itself illusory. Emotion, therefore, ripped from the context of experience, is like a spot in a painting, totally meaningless unless surrounded by the rest of the canvas from which it is taken. Generally it is enough to know that the spot is from a maiden's hand or from a pitcher. Such information orients us sufficiently to proceed along our way. But Eliot wishes to place the spot in a larger context, so that we may see what the maiden's hand is doing, who else may be involved, what kind of maiden she is, or what the pitcher contains, where it is sitting, and so on. In effect, he wishes to bare the emotion to where its roots disappear in the ground of experience.

Take the birds in *The Waste Land*. Eliot was a bird watcher; to him birds would each have had quite a distinct character. So much for the superficialities. As vehicles for emotions, they carried overtones of exoticism, as birds tend to do in poetry, complicated by allusions to rape, and they blended in with the supernatural landscape, especially in "The Fire Sermon" and "What the Thunder Said," from which they derived an eerie quality, becoming disturbing presences that can be traced deep into the fabric of the poem. Nothing in the poem can be isolated from the whole without being killed in the process. That is probably what Gertrude Patterson meant when she wrote in *T. S. Eliot: Poems in the Making* that "having 'explained' each unit, which requires the reader to enter the world of connotation, it must then be sent back into the assembled structure which is the poem, and the whole poem viewed as an art form."[2]

Allusion, then, serves multiple purposes in *The Waste Land*. It enables Eliot to transmute personal experience into something of greater dimension while obscuring its autobiographical origins. Meanings can be fused and layered to express complex feelings and states of mind. Dream inversions and ambivalences can be conjured. Condensation in the extreme can be achieved. "Allusion in Mr. Eliot's hands is a technical device for compression. 'The Waste Land' is equivalent in content to an epic. Without this device twelve books would have been needed. But these allusions and the notes in which some of them are elucidated have made many a petulant reader turn down his thumb at once. Such a reader has not begun to understand what it is all about."[3] And finally, using allusion with the juxtaposition of superficially incongruent images, Eliot is able to depict emotions in their fuller complexity and subtleties by showing how they branch out through association into the depths of experience.

Considerable discretion must be exercised in tracking down allusions and assigning them their proper importance in the exegesis of the poem. Caveats obligatory to fair critical assay are not always observed.

Sources for a passage are sometimes named without any evidence that Eliot was familiar with them. Such a practice is to be deplored. Mere parallelism of phrase or idea proves nothing, only muddies the issue, unless one knows with reasonable certainty, and preferably by some testament of the poet himself, that Eliot was familiar with it before writing the poem. Thus, no matter how tempting a similarity may be, I do not use it to elucidate the poem unless I can establish that Eliot must at least have been exposed to it before completing The Waste Land. Doubtful instances are so labeled and, if too questionable and yet too suggestive to ignore, relegated to endnotes.

Having established a substantiable allusion, there remains the question of whether it was intended to contribute to the meaning of the poem. Thematic coherence is the only reliable criterion; it arises out of consideration of the whole work. Unconscious associations irrelevant to a central intent may nevertheless creep in fortuitously; these must be sorted out. Sometimes they suggest merely a grammatical or rhetorical form. Other times they are empty echoes stirred by some potent resonance. While the latter contribute nothing to an understanding of the meaning of the work, they may shed light on the creative process and so should duly be noted.

As for allusions supposed to be unconscious, I do not pretend to be able to discern them unerringly from witting references, nor do I hold such a distinction to be crucial. Words, in their fullest connotations, subsume for each individual a whole constellation of experiences. No one can be consciously aware of all the accreted experience that forms the idiosyncratic meanings of his or her words, the particular tones and angles of perception that they embody. John Livingston Lowes, in his Road to Xanadu, gives perhaps the most comprehensive study of the train of subconscious associations that accrue to the meanings of a poet's words. Modern psychological studies support the contention that words may express certain aspects of clusters of experience pivoted around some common point. Word association is one means by which these experience clusters can be ferreted out; this is a common method for exploring personal experience in psychotherapy. Related methods have been devised for the experimental exploration of the dimensions of meaning, apart from the therapeutic processes. All this research has shown that words do not symbolize single and simple referents but rather they evoke for each person complex memories that surround the denotative center with a web of feelings, moods, tones, colors, attitudes, textures, and other qualities of experience.[4]

It is likely, then, that certain usages of words and images, of grammatical forms and turns of phrase that a poet encounters will have a subtle effect on what they will mean to him. It thus becomes necessary to weigh all legitimate candidates for allusive sources of *The Waste Land* to determine whatever fraction each might lend to the total nuance of the passages in question. This is certainly in keeping with Eliot's general depiction of emotions and states of mind as highly complex and associative.

Closely related to the allusive method in both mechanics and intent is Eliot's use of symbolism. It is often through allusion, in fact, that his symbols are brought into being. Again the birds come to mind, with the nightingale and the swallow picking up their symbolic value from the Philomel myth. The "heart of light" equated with "the silence" become symbols of existential awe through references to Dante and Joseph Conrad. Belladonna symbolizes ill-fated love, echoing as she does from *Vanity Fair.* Allusion and symbolism are inseparable in the poetry of Eliot.

Symbolism, as well as allusion, is intended in *The Waste Land* to be evocative rather than to bring to mind a single, well-defined referent. An image of symbolic value is meant to enter the mind like a pebble cast into a pool, creating not one big splash but a widening ring of ripples, like a chain reaction of associations setting off clusters of feelings. This forces readers to participate in the recreation of the poetic vision, much as they must when reading the more succinct forms of Chinese or Japanese verse, such as the haiku. It is said that a haiku is like an open door, inviting readers to step through, discovering, by allowing their imaginations to work sympathetically upon the image, what lies on the other side. Eliot makes somewhat greater demands upon his readers.

In yoking together disparate aspects of experience, Eliot points symbolically toward the metaphysical Absolute. Here is where in his poetic practice the metaphysics of Bradley meets and dovetails with the theory of correspondences embraced by the French symbolists. Whereas the latter believed that everything displays mystical correspondences with other aspects of reality—colors with vowels, to name the most well known example—and that behind these correspondences lies an ultimate unity, Bradley claimed that all conflicts and contradictions exist only in appearance and are harmonized in the Absolute. Prompted undoubtedly by the practices of Baudelaire and Laforgue, Eliot saw in the Bradleyan metaphysics a rationale for the symbolist employment of irony. In the hands of Baudelaire, Laforgue, and Corbière, irony simply distorts reality, creating a peculiar kind of caricature. Sometimes it is like a clash of dissonance in music, an emotive coloristic device. But in the poetry of Eliot it indicates or almost evokes a hypothetical unity, an absolute in which the inner discord of the irony melts into sweet melody.

There is a counterpart in Bradley. Everywhere he suggests a conflict between practical reality, which he chooses usually to call appearance, and ideal reality, or the Absolute. That is, he recognizes and acknowledges the necessity of bowing to appearance, even though it is known through faith to be illusory. At one point he even says, echoing William James, that truth is simply what will work. By context it is plain that he means to define truth in that sense only within the realm of appearance, and he equates it elsewhere with the totality of the Absolute; those two definitions represent the opposition he perceives between appearance and reality.

Now, since all things within appearance—which means everything as we know it—contain within themselves some kind of contradiction, it is somewhat reasonable to suppose that only by pitting contradiction against contradiction can the whole house of cards finally be brought down. That is the path Eliot followed in his poetry. He juxtaposes the sacred and the profane, ideal and base or degraded love, the glorious and the squalid, often combining them through the allusive method into a single symbol or image in which, if the Absolute is not revealed, at least the facade of appearance begins to crumble away. What is left, unfortunately, is not the Absolute, for that is infinite and therefore beyond human knowledge. What is left is the dark night of the soul, which Eliot believed was a state of longing for the spiritual significance symbolized in religion, accompanied by the belief that the truth behind the symbolism could never be known or proved. There was possibly also the suspicion that somewhere in the dilemma of longing for significance that is impossible to find lay the answer to the eternal quest, perhaps a state of grace embodied within the terrible struggle to know and to live with the awareness that the struggle could not be resolved.

Irony, paradoxical contrasts, condensed allusive symbolism, dissolution of temporal, spatial, and causal order, and associative structure all contribute to the symbolic gesture toward the Absolute that constitutes the primary intent of *The Waste Land*. Reversing figure and ground, as it were, this intent could be seen as a poetic dismantling of appearance, not to glimpse the Absolute behind the illusion, but simply to remove the illusion and thus move that much closer to the real. Even though a poetic dismantling of appearance could not achieve spiritual revelation, it could provide a ritual symbolic of it. Therefore, the breakdown of appearance and the search for significance become, in this metaphysical perspective, virtually equivalent acts, certainly in so far as the poetic representation of either is concerned.

This equivalence is fortunate in as much as Eliot was born into an era in which progressive analysis had peeled away the veneer of appearance to reveal again not the Absolute but rather the peculiarly disjunctive progressions of the inner mind; the focus had shifted from the thing perceived to the psychological mechanics of perception itself. Reflections of such destructive analysis were seen in many literary quarters, not to mention the spheres of the other arts, and Eliot picked them up initially as part of the spirit of the times; he could not help but see how neatly his burgeoning poetics dovetailed with this idealistic brand of philosophy that he found so much to his liking. And, of course, the same temperament dictated both the poetic and the philosophical predilections, so one should not be surprised at their remarkable correlation.

Within this framework of literary history, from which also emerged the psychological novel with its many variants—including the Proustian examination of the laws of mental association, the Joycean recording of the thought process, and the close analysis of motives, character, emotions, and related psychological phenomena that pervaded the literature of the last decade of the 1800s and the first quarter of this century—it is hardly surprising that Eliot turned to a similar technique to present in some way the inner workings of the mind. From a kind of Laforguean caricature, an autocosmic miniature, in his early short poems, he seemed to sense the inward turning of such an approach and rather quickly moved in the longer poems toward a stringing-together of these subjective vignettes into a kind of stream-of-consciousness cinematic scenario. In fact, he noted in his essay "William Blake" that it is impossible to create a large poem without "splitting it up into various personalities."[5] Poetic insight is too pointedly focused to be telescoped much beyond the dimensions of a lyric without breaking down into a sequence of more or less autonomous images, each held within the sequence by some sustained concern that acts as a matrix from which the whole is generated.

Even had Eliot not familiarized himself with the English tradition of idealist philosophy and assimilated it to his poetics, his stream-of-consciousness technique would have led to a weakening of logical and chronological order in the presentation of his poetic works. As it was, idealism simply furnished a rationale for methodically and more wholeheartedly doing what he would have done anyway. Without this philosophical rationale, he might have employed a stream-of-consciousness technique only when it would plainly represent the workings of an individual mind, as Joyce did in Molly's soliloquy at the end of Ulysses. For, considered apart from any extraneous philosophical justification, Eliot's poetic method is blatantly romantic, subjective to the extreme, quite in conflict with the impersonal classicism to which he claimed allegiance. He really needed Bradleyan metaphysics, or something like it, to ease his conscience, as it were, in the pursuit of a poetics romantic at the core. Then, too, Bradleyan metaphysics added an important dimension of meaning to Eliot's literary style, and this auxiliary meaning realigned his poetic practices with the spirit of classicism, at least when seen in conjunction with his use of the literary past through the allusive method. Through the eyes of Bradley he was able to view the current literary trends—those in which he chose to participate—as something more than the dumb unfolding of everything that came before them. He could see how to use them in the conscious expression of his own needs as a poet. The philosophy of the French symbolists alone would not have sufficed; it was too sketchy.

Of course, his adapting the stream-of-consciousness technique to something other than a kind of tape-recording of the individual mind only made reading his poetry that much more difficult. Not that it is a gratuitous difficulty; it does evolve from the material and intent of the poetry. Eliot was not concerned with narration. Events for him were nothing more than vehicles for the expression of complex and extraordinary feelings and states of mind. They do not move through courses of conflict toward dramatic resolution. Instead, they linger in the mind like ghosts, taunting the imagination to extract their full significance. For poetry this represented a new form, one which in its many variants has come to dominate the mainstream of poetry in the twentieth century. It was born out of what Eliot called a classical moment, and "what is meant by a classical moment in literature is surely a moment of *stasis*, when the creative impulse finds a form which satisfies the best intellect of the time, a moment when a type is produced."[6]

This new type—a poetic form in which images representing events, objects, and states of mind are linked not by logical, causal, or chronological progression but by what may be called the associative law of imagination—has much in common with the world of dreams. Dreams are the best known form of altered-state-of-consciousness thinking. The words of John Butler Yeats are suggestive, though perhaps not wholly accurate: "Dream is the excuse of all art and poetry. It is the dream-world against the actual. Every man lives in the first, so far as he is governed by feeling: governed by intellect and practicality he enters the second."[8]

Giving in to the irrational upswellings of unconscious material is only one way to induce inspiration, and the inspiration so induced will be of a special kind unless it is rigorously reorganized to bring it back in line with common-sense modes of thought. Hardly, if ever, before the late nineteenth century did it occur to most writers to abandon themselves to a direct transcription of the unconscious mind, though certainly some rather raw material from that mental region went into the creation of myths. But in both fantasy and myth the subconscious material was still ordered into a common-sense narrative form, so that the semblance of everyday events was maintained. Eliot was inclined instead to abandon reality testing in favor of testing his feelings against the more inner states of his mind upon which those feelings seemed most deeply founded.

> [Conventional meaning may be used] to satisfy one habit of the reader, to keep his mind diverted and quiet while the poem does its work upon him: much as the imaginary burglar is always provided with a bit of nice meat for the house-dog. This is a normal situation of which I approve. But the minds of all poets do not work that way; some of them, assuming that there are other minds like our own, become impatient of this "meaning" which seems superfluous, and perceive possibilities of intensity through its elimination. I am not assuming that this situation is ideal; only that we must write our poetry as we can, and take it as we find it.[8]

This is essentially the contemporary parallel of mythopoeisis. Eliot was aware of this. In Wilhelm Wundt's *Elements of Folk Psychology*, which Eliot reviewed for the *International Journal of Ethics* (January 1917), he had read:

> Causality, in our sense of the word, does not exist for primitive man. If we would speak of causality at all on his level of experience, we may say only that he is governed by the causality of magic. This, however, receives its stamp, not from the laws that regulate the connection of ideas, but from the forces of emotion. The mythological causality of emotional magic is no less spasmodic and irregular than the logical causality arising out of the orderly sequence of perceptions and ideas is constant.[9]

Wundt argued that "it is not intelligence nor reflection as to the origin and interconnection of phenomena that gives rise to mythological thinking, but emotion: ideas are only the material which the latter elaborates."[10]

Interestingly enough, Eliot had earlier reviewed also for the *International Journal of Ethics* (October 1916) Clement C. J. Webb's *Group Theories of Religion and the Religion of the Individual*, which claimed that the elements of primitive mentality as described by Emil Durkheim and Levy Bruhl, such as participative magic, persist in modern thought so that they cannot be considered evidence that the religious impulse has become irrelevant to the needs of modern man. Magical thinking, closely allied to dreaming and other altered states of consciousness, could thus have been seen by Eliot as a viable alternative to the thought processes of normal waking consciousness, especially for approaching the essence of the religious impulse, the longing for significance. In making that approach he was forced by the exigencies of his philosophical convictions to deal with the relation between appearance and reality, of which he said that "we can never give an exact description or explanation of the relations of the real and the unreal."[11]

This circles back to the fact that his peculiar stream-of-consciousness style was particularly suited to his poetic intents, and it was suited in more ways than one. Not only did it permit him symbolically to dismantle appearance as a ritualistic approach to the Absolute, but it also carried him back to the mainsprings of spiritual experience and allowed him to project his inner turmoil in a therapeutic mimesis.

Stripped of considerations of literary and philosophical backgrounds, the form of The Waste Land could not have been much more personal without becoming nearly impossible for others to understand and appreciate. "Art," Eliot wrote, "reflects the transition as well as the permanent condition of the soul; we cannot measure the present by what the past has been, or by what we think the future ought to be."[12] The Waste Land reflected certain assumptions, permanent conditions of his soul, as they were being tested against the circumstances of his life, transitions of his soul. Some years after writing The Waste Land Eliot stated that "I should say that in one's prose reflexions one may be legitimately occupied with ideals, whereas in the writing of verse one can only deal with actuality."[13] As therapeutic mimesis, The Waste Land selectively replicated Eliot's inner rumination that must have reached its most poignant and anxious heights at Margate and Lausanne, when he was trying to recover from his nervous collapse. Even with all the strictures of philosophical exigencies and literary style, the poem probably resembled most a nearly literal transcription of Eliot's thoughts and feelings (in so far as the latter could be objectified in words) as he ruminated over matters that most pressed upon him at the time. The fragments he had written earlier were drawn into the ruminative process just as allusions to other writers were, or they were included later for a more calculated effect. It is, after all, part of the writing as well as the revision process to sustain an initial inspiration, amplify upon it, embellish it, and reinforce it, but always with an eye to realizing the initial potential, to see that it blossoms into whatever it promised to be.

One should view his debt to Frazer and Weston as part of this process of assimilation. They were merely more grist for the mill, not superstructures into which Eliot fit his material but simply sources from which to draw shadows to mingle with the shadowy presences enlisted from other times and other places and to mix their voices in the crossing whispers that together form the poem. These voices speak not according to logic; they are echoes of the mind listening to itself.

Of Baudelaire, Angelo Bertocci wrote in *From Symbolism to Baudelaire* that "he works as if the interweaving of an internal logic could by itself insure the poet's access to an objective realm, which is the real meaning of his faith in analogies and correspondences."[14] Turning inward to the logic of imagination was part of the literary and artistic temperament of the time. Serious poets who belonged to this stream of development no longer described the physical order of the world. Each took a separate path away from physical reality, but nearly all ended up listening to some aspect of the inner voice. As Symons commented on Gerard de Nerval:

> Gerard de Nerval, then, had divined, before all the world, that poetry should be a miracle; not a hymn to beauty, nor the description of beauty, nor beauty's mirror; but beauty itself, the colour, fragrance, and form of the imagined flower, as it blossoms again out of the page. Vision, the over-powering vision, had come to him beyond, if not against, his will; and he knew that vision is the root out of which the flower must grow. Vision had taught him symbol, and he knew that it is by symbol alone that the flower can take visible form. He knew that the whole mystery of beauty can never be comprehended by the crowd, and that while clearness is a virtue of style, perfect explicitness is not a necessary virtue.[15]

When Eliot was taking shape as a writer, poets, especially the French symbolists and then their English and American imitators, were progressing toward using images not to describe objective reality but as things in themselves, to be contemplated as points of attention, like colored stones, clouds, or sparkles on a pond. Words, hitherto always pointing toward the recreation of an idea or event, person or scene, were being gradually severed from their normal communicative function to stand as pure percepts, sounds dimly attached by association to referents. Each was to stand almost alone, in its own niche, not part of a semantic picture of anything palpably real but a montage possessing its own felt sense of order. Something of this is expressed in Eliot's statement that "the business of the poet is not to find new emotions, but to use the ordinary ones and, in working them up into poetry, to express feelings that are not in action emotions at all."[16] Artistic experience, he insisted, must be different from any other experience. If the artist is to hold the mirror up to nature, then for Eliot, and for many precursors to whom he had turned for instruction, the mirror had been turned to reflect not what lies before the eyes but what lies behind them.

In Eliot's preface to Saint-John Perse's *Anabasis* he stated that in that work "the reader has to allow the images to fall into his memory successively without questioning the reasonableness of each at the moment; so that, at the end, a total effect is produced." He continued:

> Such selection of a sequence of images and ideas has nothing chaotic about it. There is a logic of imagination as well as a logic of concepts. People who do not appreciate poetry always find it difficult to distinguish between order and chaos in the arrangement of images; and even those who are capable of appreciating poetry cannot depend upon first impressions. I was not convinced of Mr. Perse's imaginative order until I had read the poem five or six times. And if, as I suggest, such an arrangement of images requires just as much "fundamental brainwork" as the arrangement of an argument, it is to be expected that the reader of a poem should take at least as much trouble as a barrister reading an important decision on a complicated case.[17]

These observations certainly apply with equal validity to much of his own poetry, and certainly to *The Waste Land*. There the "logic of imagination" is the governing principle of order. Tracing this logic out in the dynamics of dreams and related free-associative mental states has already pinpointed many of the rules of order: symbolization, displacement, condensation, representation by multiples and opposites, secondary elaboration, and substitution of objects for people. However, while these mechanisms help to account for much of the individual dreamlike images and scenes in a poem such as *The Waste Land*, they do not fully account for the segues linking one image or scene with the next. A law of order is needed to explain the linkage, somewhat as the rules of the syllogism explain the sequences in deductive argumentation.

Unfortunately, few laws have been established that govern the operation of the mind unfettered from the constraints of reality testing. Interpretation of the empirical evidence has been mired in endless squabbling between competing schools of psychology. Instead of allowing the evidence to fall into its own pattern, researchers and theoreticians have attempted, for the most part unconvincingly, to hammer it into alignment with pet preconceived notions.

Nonetheless, research in the psychology of concept formation and problem-solving and the various theories of learning that have emerged from that research suggest one rather general nonpartisan observation that gives a considerable insight, albeit still preliminary, into the dynamics of the free-associative thought process. No matter in what terms the stages of concept formation and problem-solving are formulated, these actions proceed from some general condition to a strategy by which the variables are brought into relationships according to criteria that will best ensure the simplest and most consistent operations to attain the given end of the problem or task. Put more simply, when faced with certain variables, things with which we work for some particular purpose, we tend to perceive only their qualities that seem pertinent to the purpose at hand, and we group or segregate them largely on the basis of those qualities only. If presented the task of seating so many people with a limited number of furnishings—not only chairs and stools, but also boxes, cushions, piles of paper, and so on—at our disposal, we tend to narrow down a virtually unlimited gamut of characteristics to those that might make an object a suitable seat.

While all this may seem rather pedantic, it is really quite simple: in waking hours people tend to fix attention on things and aspects of things that will aid them in doing whatever it is they are doing. Basically, this is much of what is meant by reality testing. In a slightly larger perspective, it means that waking thought is constrained along certain, usually narrow, channels defined by the necessity of complying with the demands of the world immediately around us.

Take away that constraint, relieve the mind of complying with reality (that is, physical reality), and there is a broadening of possibilities by which things may fall into relation with one another. Formally speaking, the mind proceeds from a conjunctive to a disjunctive mode of thought, from relating things on the basis of practical exigencies to relating them according to criteria of a prevailing mood or concern, a feeling or an idée fixe. Cleanth Brooks, in The Well Wrought Urn, described the projection of disjunctive thought into the form of poetry: "The characteristic unity of a poem (even of those poems which may accidentally possess a logical unity as well as this poetic unity) lies in the unification of attitudes into a hierarchy subordinated to a total and governing attitude."[18] Naturally, the attitudes in the poem are conveyed through images and statements, so that in speaking of a hierarchy of attitudes we are also speaking identically of the verbal or semantic structure of the poem.

It may appear that the concept of disjunctive association has not advanced us much beyond the recognition of linkages that are either random (there is no discernible logic) or, because of the obscurity of their origin, inexplicable; but such is not the case. Constraints of reality are merely replaced by a state of mind to which the genesis of images and the progression of thought must respond. While it is true that this constraint leads to a kind of indeterminancy, in that it is next to impossible to predict any idea following another, the indeterminancy may fairly well be resolved in the opposite time sequence by tracing back and explaining why a certain thought ensued from the previous one.

Furthermore, from a purely formal point of view, the difference between conjunctive and disjunctive thought may be justly construed as quantitative rather than qualitative. When we proceed from one thought to another in a waking context, the possibilities are greatly limited by the practical demands that must be met with the means at hand in only a limited number of ways. In addition, waking reality presents us mostly with situations nearly identical to previous ones (washing, eating, driving a car, playing a phonograph, and so forth), so that reactions to them are that much more foreseeable. On the other hand, in a free-associative state of consciousness novel situations are always arising, since thoughts may come together for so many nonpractical reasons. To take just one example, if I may be reading the newspaper when the doorbell rings and subsequently, perhaps only for an instant, I doze off, in that hypnagogic moment somehow I am reading the doorbell as the newspaper rings. This strange situation has never occurred before and is fraught with possibilities, especially since other fortuitous factors may enter, not because they are germane but because they happen to be present at the time. If this train of free-associative events is allowed to progress, its general direction will be dominated by whatever intense feelings, attitudes, moods, or ideas happen to be uppermost in mind at the time. Only in retrospect could the logic of it be traced back, given sufficient information.

In the case of *The Waste Land*, one must look for not some kind of narrative or argumentative thread or progression but a vacillation around certain central concerns. One must look past the superficial descriptive meaning of the symbols and allusions, images and statements, to their evocative import. Although it may not be possible to gather this import from each element of the poem, the secret is resolved when they are taken together as a whole; the resulting key to the poem is verified time and time again by the contexts from which many of the allusions are drawn. Not that it cannot be verified within the poem itself, but that verification would be, without the allusive substantiation, little more than subjective speculation.

Briefly here I shall set forth the themes of the poem, leaving for the exegesis a close examination of how they are realized and interconnected in the text. I shall for the moment offer only such examples as may help to clarify the issues.

Thematically central to the poem is the spiritual quest, which is difficult to define precisely because its nature is revealed gradually in the process of taking it on and trying to carry it out. One can discern its origins in the feeling, which plagued both Bradley and apparently Eliot, that there must be something more, something more coherent, behind the welter of contradictions in appearance that we call reality. At first neither a philosophical nor a religious conviction, it begins as a simple need that reaches into so many veins of experience that it cannot be escaped. It grows into a dogma probably more as a defense than a consequence of pure reason.

For Eliot, nurtured on Bradleyan metaphysics, the full satisfaction of this spiritual need necessarily lay beyond possibility. A finite mind can conceive the infinite, or the undifferentiated whole of existence, only in symbolic form, which is not in any sense direct knowledge. Faith can sustain the belief that the Absolute must exist, but neither reason nor faith can prove it. Thus one of the results of the quest is the uncomfortable realization that it is part of the human condition not to be spiritually fulfilled; at the same time, this very unfulfillment is what keeps humans spiritually active. True enlightenment can spell only the dissolution of the individual into the Absolute, after which there is no longer a human question.

Nevertheless, such an awareness cannot quench the need for significance, the need to see how things, particularly the vicissitudes of one's own life, come together beyond contradiction so that it all may be seen to have been worthwhile. Further exactness is out of the question, since it is meaningless to fix on a specific desired meaning when any absolute meaning could not be comprehended in human terms. There is in this situation much of the animal chasing its own tail.

This spiritual quest must inevitably devolve into considerations of the particularities of life. Kept completely impersonal, the quest is arid and meaningless, for the pattern of the individual must somehow interweave with the whole, the Absolute. So it is with Eliot in The Waste Land: he said that one thing he was trying to do in that work was to bring together the strands of disparate religions. Other than a common ethic, different religions have in common only their intent to solve the human spiritual riddle. Again the intent of the poem seems aligned with this spiritual pursuit. M. L. Rosenthal recognizes something of this when he writes that "the poem derives its strength from the way its implied Christian, pagan, and private motives cast light on one another and from the ensuing fusion of symbols," but he does not develop this insight in any detail.[19]

Innermost to Eliot, as a devolution of the wider spiritual dilemma to more personal circumstances, was the solipsistic problem expressed in terms of the difficulty, if not implausibility, of communication between individuals. I have already noted how substantial a place this occupied in his early poetry—which is not to suggest that it disappeared from his later poetic and dramatic works. Of course, I am not speaking of the simple transmission of facts; that is not where irremediable difficulty is likely to occur. Communication fails in the attempted sharing of attitudes, moods, emotions, and ways of perceiving and valuing things. "The Love Song of J. Alfred Prufrock" and "Portrait of a Lady" both concern themselves with the discomforts of failed communication.

In *The Waste Land* one first encounters failed communication in "Bin gar keine Russin, stamm' aus Litauen, echt deutch" [I am not Russian, come from Lithuania, pure German]. From there on, instances are multiplied. There is the failure of humans to understand the message of the prophet: "Son of man, / You cannot say, or guess, for you know only / A heap of broken images." In the hyacinth garden there is failure of speech, and Madame Sosostris can give a reading of the cards no more understandable than the oracular pronouncements from Delphi. The cry of the nightingale is not understood: a mixture of pain and beauty. Incessantly the ghost voice of Vivien carries out an inquisition upon an unresponsive partner. Lil and Albert obviously do not see eye to eye. Nymphs departed, the poet sings his song only to the sweet Thames. He weeps by the waters of Leman, not in anyone's presence. The typist and the carbuncular young man enact intimacies in which they exchange nothing of themselves save physical contact. Eliot himself, albeit in disguise, "On Margate Sands / . . . can connect / Nothing with nothing," cannot read the design of his life. This is a failure of knowing, inextricably associated with the failure to communicate. In the end, we return to our room, locked in, made a prisoner by ourselves. Solipsism and the unshakeable conviction that there *are* others out there with whom it should be possible to communicate remain to the end unreconciled.

If one cannot communicate neither can one love, even though one must do both. Nowhere in *The Waste Land* is love fulfilled, not in the hyacinth garden, not in the longing of the sailor for his "Irisch Kind," not in the dying moments of Tristan, not between the neurasthenic lady and her silent partner, and certainly not between the typist and her suitor or between Lil and Albert. Rape and seduction complete the depiction of sexual relations, except for the promise of something unachieved in the hyacinth garden and the recollected "awful daring of a moment's surrender" that, by the context, was frustratingly evanescent.

Love in *The Waste Land* seems to offer a kind of redemption, being the closest supposed rapprochement between individuals, the actuality of which solipsism denies. Yet it is necessary as part of the struggle to discover or to create meaning. Absence of love takes many forms: bickering, assault, mechanization of feeling, sterility, emotional death. All these possibilities are explored in the poem, much as they might be turned over in the mind, each an alley down which to run in the endless search, each an inevitable blind wall presented at the end of the chase.

Eliot calls specifically upon the redemptive love theme in his early allusion to Wagner's opera *Tristan and Isolde*, a split allusion that brackets the scene in the hyacinth garden, where the redemptive efficacy of love is felt but not actually named. Ambiguously the promise of love is both realized and unachieved, an ambiguity that commentators on the poem have failed to appreciate. Failure of speech and "looking into the heart of light, the silence" characterize both mindless unresponsiveness and enlightenment. Double values of meaning in which opposite denotations are merged into a single image or scene occur routinely throughout the poem, and are common to the free-associative thought process.

These duplex symbols and images are fundamental to the intent of the poem. They are not there merely to confuse the unwary. Not only do they highlight the contradictory nature of appearance, but they also convey the tension within the dilemma of needing to search for something that cannot be found. Thus, while the person in the garden might well have failed the promise of love, the vision of achievement must simultaneously be present, otherwise the possibility of redemption is lost.

It should be repeated and kept in mind that it is the process of searching for meaning, not the hypothetical attainment of it, that is important. So long as we spiritually try, we stay alive in the fullest human sense of the word. Humans, the spiritual or psychological beings, differ from other animals and from computers and machines in that they seek to transcend the limitations of the given moment, to reach out for what is not immediately there, to try to become what they are not, to understand something more than may be evident. If we project that tendency, as a mathematician may indefinitely extend a line, at infinity is the end result that we may call the Absolute, and it is toward that end that we take upon ourselves the spiritual struggle; indeed that *is* the spiritual struggle.

Another way to understand the search for meaning is to construe it as a direction. We move westward not to arrive at west; that would be nonsensical. Generally we travel in a specific direction to arrive at a chosen destination, but in this case the destination is beyond our ability to reach. This must be seen against the other alternatives. We may not move at all: this is vegetation, virtual death. We may move about in random fashion, not caring in what direction we are heading at any moment. This, according to Eliot, is how most people conduct themselves. The trouble is that there can be no sense of purpose to such randomness; even if not everyone needs purpose—I leave that a moot question—thinking persons of a certain temperament most assuredly do. And Eliot was one of the latter. He would say that it is better to do evil than to do nothing, for at least that way one exists in a special sense of the word. Consciousness, the highest quality of life, is thus carried to a higher point. For those who agree, that is what it takes to be most human—even in a perverse sense.

Those who fail to search are the living dead in The Waste Land. On his way to work at the bank, Eliot woefully watched the crowd of people flowing across London Bridge: "I had not thought death had undone so many." Most of them shuffle through the daily routine like robots, rarely questioning, never searching. It is not, as some critics seem to insist, that they have forgotten God; they simply have no care about the impulses to which in certain cases belief in God may respond. As Eliot once wrote, it is not that twentieth-century humans have ceased to believe in God; more critically, they no longer understand the motives that gave rise to a belief in God in the first place.

Crowds of people appear throughout the poem always in association with death. In the first section, they are identified with the crowds that Dante witnessed walking in circles in hell. "Hooded hordes swarming / Over endless plains" remain the damned of hell, but as we can see from the Ur-text they are also the fallen people of Poland, routed from their homes under the devastations of war. By way of Dryden, there is even a hint that they belong too to the throng dispersed by the Great Fire of London. At any rate, they bespeak another devolution from the main theme, the archetypical death and rebirth motif encountered widely in ancient myths of fertility explaining the seasons in terms of the ritual death and rebirth of the fertility god.

Death and rebirth are treated as all other images and themes in the poem, as vehicles for the evocation of feelings. They relate back to the central theme of the search for significance. Death is a fact; rebirth is a symbolic possibility that can help to motivate spiritual action. It is never treated as anything more. To be reborn sometimes carries connotations of something approaching enlightenment. Neither rebirth nor enlightenment is attained within the poem. It closes with the closing words of a prayer or invocation, not with the enunciation of a revelation.

Such are the themes of The Waste Land. They supply the emotional glue by which the whole is held together. Passing in succession, they move in and out of focus as attention falls first on one and then the other, exactly as several preoccupations of the mind take turns dominating the moment of awareness. As each gains ascendance it is objectified in an image, a symbol, a scene, or a declaration, after which there is a retreat from which renewed contemplation of some other possibility of the themes is essayed.

A physical background against which successive contemplation of the thematic concerns takes place resolves itself and dissolves, as occasion demands, like a changing picture fading in and out of clear vision. Aspects of London and Paris are prominent, but other places and other times sometimes merge into the setting. By and large, the setting is foreboding of death, spiritual and actual, with barren rocks, dead trees, hot sun, desert dryness, cracked earth, but always the vague promise of rain. Rats crawl through the mud; bones lie scattered in the valley of death. Inside, the rooms are closed, heavy with perfume, suffocating, harboring anxiety and boredom.

There is a tendency to read the poem as a pessimistic condemnation of the modern world. It is true that Eliot was much disgruntled with Europe when he wrote *The Waste Land* and that undeniably entered the poem. It would not be too much to say that his discontent with the state of civilization helped to generate the poem. Nevertheless, the strong philosophical rationale that gave intellectual shape to the central intent of the work also dictated that both sides of the coin should appear. Some commentators have viewed the negative background as pivotal and have interpreted all contrasting settings as foils against which the bleakest aspects of the work are enhanced. Although the very title of the poem suggests the world is an oppressive delusion, this interpretation nevertheless errs in deferring uncritically to the extreme.

Whether by religious conviction, Bradleyan metaphysics, or the doctrines of French symbolism, no matter how dismal the world there must linger a counterbalancing vision, something by which the contradictions of appearance may be brought into a transcendent harmony, in the human sense a redemptive possibility. It is in *The Waste Land* but it does not win out. Neither side wins. They coexist, as they do in actuality.

There is a shower of rain, which comes with summer over the Starnbergersee, and thunder echoes with portent several times later on, delivering once more at the end a "damp gust / Bringing rain." Moments of poignant beauty flash across the memory, crumbling away the dark vision of life with which they alternate throughout the changing scenes. A pleasant chat in the Hofgarten, the feeling of freedom in the mountains, the shipman yearning for his beloved, the experience in the garden, the "inexplicable splendour" of Magnus Martyr, remembrance of the joy of the sailboat, are all cracks in the mundane to infernal canvas that stretches across the eternity of the poem. In number they are fewer than the darker visions, but perhaps not more so than in actual life.

Hope in *The Waste Land* is glimpsed through a veil of despair, a faithful reflection of Eliot's state of mind as he lived through the events that took him to Margate. "It is part of damnation," he observed, "to experience desires that we can no longer gratify."[20] And so he began his unique spiritual odyssey, "mixing / Memory and desire," projecting and transmuting the elements of his personal torments into a peregrination through idiosyncratic and archetypical anxieties spinning off from the center of a solipsistic soul seeking not only escape from its own prison but some hint of the design into which the predicament of existence could be fit. *The Waste Land* is a religious statement in the sense that "statements expressing religious knowledge are more than just speculative fabrication removed from religious activity; they, to the contrary, reflect the inner struggle of man as *homo religiosus* to understand himself and the existence of which he is part."[21]

Readers must approach it not for any message that it contains but for the portrait that it gives of a civilized and sensitive mind examining its own troubled state through a series of poetic images. The effect is much like piecing together the inside of a mansion by peering through this window and that, juxtaposing partial views of connected rooms but not in any really systematic order. Consistency of mood and concern determines the tenuous unity found there, as the actuality of the interior of the mansion ensures that the windows all give in upon the same space. That *The Waste Land* troubles so many readers and yet commands the attention of an equal legion should tell us that we have encountered a new form and a new monument in the ideal order of art.

3

The Burial of the Dead

THIS chapter begins a line-by-line exegesis of *The Waste Land* aimed at delineating the various strands of associational meaning and the disjunctive linkages by which they are woven into the structure of the poem. I shall trace the progress of the poem not through any supposed narrative argument but rather through a development much like that of a polythematic musical composition in which attention drifts back and forth from one theme to another rhapsodically, with no order preordained by the exigencies of plot.

For each section of the poem, preliminary background will illuminate such matters as overall inspirational sources, compositional complexities, and peculiarities: in general, any issues that bear upon the import of the section as a whole, opposed to particularities of individual lines and passages. Following that, a synoptic overview will map out main themes and gross structural details, affording a global framework in which the finer details of the section may more readily be assimilated and appreciated.

Eliot had not originally intended to use "The Waste Land" as the title for his poem; instead, he considered calling it *He Do the Police in Different Voices*. This was a reference to a statement of Betty Higden in Charles Dickens's *Our Mutual Friend*. Old Mrs. Higden has taken in a dim-witted foundling by the name of Sloppy. "You mightn't think it," she says, "but Sloppy is a beautiful reader of a newspaper. He do the police in different voices."[1] Within the novel itself, this quotation has no deep significance. To understand Eliot's adoption of it, one need only turn to a brief and seemingly unnoteworthy statement in his essay "William Blake": "You cannot create a very large poem without introducing a more impersonal point of view, or splitting it up into various personalities."[2] By alluding to a reading of the newspaper, Eliot perhaps underlined his preoccupation in the poem with contemporary events, central to the Dantean method he was pursuing. Whereas the events were contemporary, they were to be unified by being voiced through a single person. In *Our Mutual Friend* that person was Sloppy;

in *The Waste Land* it was Eliot himself in the guise of the narrator, though in the Notes he chooses to identify this role with Tiresias.

In the case of "The Burial of the Dead," an important generative source is the life of Marie Larisch, a source first revealed over two decades ago by George L. K. Morris.[3] Unfortunately Morris did little more than outline some salient features of the life of Countess Larisch and call attention to certain parallels between her autobiography, *My Past* (1913), and *The Waste Land*, expressing hope that future commentators on the poem might give due attention to the matter, a hope that has never been realized. Nor was his case helped by Valerie Eliot's remark in the facsimile edition of the poem:

> Writing in the *Partisan Review* (vol. xxi, No. 2, 1954), Mr. G. K. L. Morris [sic] drew attention to similarities between parts of *The Waste Land* and the reminiscences of Countess Marie Larisch, *My Past* (London, 1913). The assumption was that Eliot must have read the book, but in fact he had met the author (when and where is not known), and his description of the sledding, for example, was taken verbatim from a conversation he had with this niece and confidante of the Austrian Empress Elizabeth.[4]

Such a carefully worded and ambiguous disclaimer is worthy of Eliot himself; while it seems to discredit Morris's assumption, it does not in fact state that Eliot had not read the autobiography of Marie Larisch. It singles out one bit of information as derived from a conversation with the countess, implying that all the information pertaining to her life came from the same source. That is possible, of course, but it does seem unlikely that Eliot would not have bothered to read the autobiography of one whom he had met and in whom his interest was sufficient to incorporate her into his poetry. Moreover, in view of the large number of verbal and incidental parallels between *My Past* and *The Waste Land*— all of which will be documented in the exegesis at the appropriate passages—it seems merely academic whether Eliot picked up his details firsthand or from the book. Close parallels in wording and the sheer likelihood that he would have pursued his subject into the printed page lead me to accept Morris's assumption, while remaining thankful for the additional, though equivocal, information donated by Valerie Eliot.

Marie Larisch was the niece of Elizabeth, empress of Austria and queen of Hungary (1837–98), and of the mad king Ludwig II of Bavaria (1845–86), patron of Richard Wagner. Rudolph (1858–89), the crown prince of Austria, cousin to Countess Larisch, is the figure who appears in the sledding episode in lines 13–18 of the poem. He is singled out in the countess's autobiography as her nemesis. He brought about her downfall by enlisting her aid as a go-between of himself and one of his mistresses, Marie Vetsera, whom the countess had met through Elizabeth, the archduke's mother. Countess Larisch brought Baroness Vetsera to a clandestine meeting with Rudolph, who subsequently abducted her to his hunting lodge at Mayerling, where the two were found shot, apparently the victims of a suicide pact. Nearly a year earlier he had proposed such a pact to his then mistress, the actress Mitzi Kaspar, who turned him down.

Discovered on the morning of 30 January 1889, this double suicide was one of the great scandals of the day. According to Countess Larisch as well as recent historians, Rudolph brought this calamity upon himself through fear that his dealings with the Hungarian opposition were about to be exposed. Apparently he had schemed to have himself crowned king of Hungary and to resuscitate the kingdom of Poland. Marie Vetsera, at that time an impressionable girl of only seventeen, entertained a long infatuation for the archduke and fell in willingly with his despondent plans for self-destruction.

Her part in the affair exposed by a note of gratitude left behind by Baroness Vetsera, Countess Marie Larisch was suddenly cut off from her aunt Elizabeth, for whom she had an inordinate devotion from the days of young womanhood to the time of the disaster. It would hardly be an exaggeration to say that the countess lived for and through her aunt, who personified a kind of ruthless and self-indulgent perfection. So far did her devotion extend that she even married a man chosen by her aunt, a man for whom she had no love but whose apparent weakness of character she thought would allow her to remain ever in the company of beloved "Aunt Cissi."

Eliot must have found the countess at once a sympathetic character, for her husband, George Larisch, was in many respects the counterpart of Vivien Eliot. Before the countess married him his cousin Heinrich warned her that "George is queer, his temper is uncertain, and he is obstinate."[5] And she wrote further:

> My husband was haunted by the fear of developing signs of his father's madness, and in his gentler moods he would beg me never to desert him if he ever showed symptoms of insanity, and above all, never to consign him to a *Maison de santé*. I could not understand this fear, perhaps because I had become a fatalist in madness through seeing how unexpectedly it attacked the Hapsburgs, and my own near relations of the Bavarian Royal House.[6]

Soon after the marriage, the admonitions of Heinrich were borne out, as the countess records: "I was quite prepared not to be happy, but I was not prepared to be made uncomfortable, and in those early days George displayed many of the peculiarities against which I had been warned by his cousin Heinrich."[7]

This vein of madness that ran through the life of Marie Larisch could hardly have failed to capture Eliot's interest at this difficult period of his own life, when he was desperately attempting to deal with Vivien's mental deterioration as well as the mental anguish that it, with a constellation of other things, had brought to him, the anguish that took him to Margate and to the writing of The Waste Land itself. He must have been drawn to her story as to an amplified reflection of his own concerns. Beyond this, many other details made her story suitable for incorporation into the poem. For example, after receiving the good counsel from Heinrich, she said that "when George proposed to me that very day, I accepted him, but as he kissed me I felt like a dead creature."[8] Nothing could be more propitious for a future inhabitant of the waste land.

Another quality that suited her as a model for Eliot's poetic inspiration was her moral culpability. Hubris ultimately brought her down, as in a Greek tragedy. Quite dramatically, as she made a last-ditch effort to thwart Rudolph from abducting Marie Vetsera, he accused her of moral turpitude:

> The Crown Prince glanced at me with mingled cruelty and cynicism. "Since when, may I ask, Marie, have you been considered fit to play the saint? You are a fine one to talk of honour or loyalty. You have been a go-between for my mother since you were a girl. And yet you dare to mention morality to me, when you have not scrupled to stand by and see my father deceived."[9]

Though she naturally presents her role in the Mayerling affair in the best possible light, she leaves no room for doubt about her final guilt. Nor does she attempt to deny Rudolph's allegations.

Yet it is not so much Marie Larisch whose presence haunts The Waste Land, dominating "The Burial of the Dead," as that of her aunt Elizabeth, to whom she was a virtual slave. My Past is as much the story of Empress Elizabeth as it is the autobiography of Countess Larisch. From the time when she was a young lady, the countess was infatuated with her aunt, stayed in her company whenever possible, gloried in the older woman's beauty, and subjugated herself to the dictates of the empress. All through her book, she paints a running portrait of Empress Elizabeth as one devoted to her own physical beauty and to prolonging her youthfulness and amorous appeal to men. This portrait makes Elizabeth a perfect figure for Eliot to convert into a kind of mythic archetype:

Elizabeth was in love with love because it represented the colour of life to her. She regarded the excitement of being adored as a tribute which her beauty had a right to demand; but her fancies never lasted long, probably because she was too artistic ever to become sensual, and the lover who shattered her conception of him as an ideal was constantly dismissed. "Tout lasse, tout casse, tout passe" [All become tiresome, all break, all pass] might have been Elizabeth's motto throughout a life which was full of disappointments, and she was one of those women who are predestined to suffer through their affections. Her real place was with the Immortals; she should have been wooed upon the fragrant slopes of Parnassus, or yielded, like Leda or Semele, to an all-conquering Jove. The grossness of life repelled the Empress just as much as its beauty attracted her, and I believe she was far happier when her eccentricities developed and she communed with ghosts in a world of shadows, or talked with the spirit of Heine, who, she imagined, inspired her compositions. Her shyness was solely due to the morbid dread that she would be thought less beautiful as she passed down the vale of years; and only those who, like Elizabeth, value their beauty because it attracts love can understand what she felt. The ordinary mind will deem her a vain and shallow woman, and reflect that true happiness can be found in one's children's children, but such people have not the artistic temperament which the Empress possessed.[10]

Elizabeth, as she appears in various guises throughout the poem, symbolizes adherence to appearance through vanity, while Marie Larisch is a satellite figure enmeshed in the vainglorious world of which her aunt was queen. Marie in a real sense made herself the foil for her aunt, and as such she can merge easily into the transmutations of Elizabeth scattered throughout this section and the rest of the poem. Fragments from the lives of the two women and splinters intersecting with the lives of others with whom they were associated form much of the substance of "The Burial of the Dead." It is almost their tragedy projected through remnant chips of civilization strewn across a floor of memory suddenly ruptured by the clutch of insanity, incipient, dissolving into despair the barely glimpsed shores of the future.

Synopsis: "The Burial of the Dead"

This section is devoted largely to ruminations about spiritual death and the difficulties of rising from it—symbolically in the sense of being reborn and practically in the sense of gaining insight into the design of reality. Of course, such an insight is impossible except through resignation into faith; this is shown in the failed understanding in the hyacinth garden and in the dubious, or perhaps more accurately, the incomplete knowledge of Madame Sosostris. Actually, contrary to the usual critical reading, Madame Sosostris is a charlatan only on one level. On another level, she succeeds in foretelling the design of reality by naming the themes of death and redemption. Her meaning is obscure; it cannot be deciphered clearly, but the very nature of things dictate that this must be so, for the truth can be hinted at, no more. She hints at it through the use of archetypical images and cryptic symbology, as would any other oracle, but this cartomancy is further obscured by being disjunctively elaborated as in a dream.

Redemption is seen as possible through love (in the garden), knowledge (in the fortune-telling), and faith (in the symbols of the rock and the buried corpse). These are all means by which spiritual life can be sustained in the face of widespread spiritual death, because each is an effort to transcend the moment. Whether or not they succeed by achieving perfect understanding is not the question, for it is determined at the onset that such understanding is not possible, except symbolically. Symbolically the insight can be no more than suggestive, and that much is attained here. Possibility hovers throughout the section.

Physically the background of "The Burial of the Dead" is literally a waste land superimposed over London and Munich, drawing its substance from the Bible and *The Divine Comedy*, with ghostly memories of Gloucester, Massachusetts, and possibly even of St. Louis. Although each place appears separately, except for the blendings with hell, they belong together in the eternal moment of the poem in which, following the Bradleyan model, all time is simultaneous and all space present at a single point of consciousness.

Episodic development, within single scenes and in the movement from one scene to another, proceeds from personal recollections intertwined with remembered events from the lives of Marie Larisch and her aunt. It appears that the Larisch material acted as a kind of generative framework upon which to build the remaining structure through disjunctive association and allusive elaboration. In other words, as Eliot wrote this section he was centrally absorbed with what he knew of Countess Larisch, and from events surrounding her life he associated personal and allusive material thematically related to compose it.

MOTTO: "NAM SIBYLLAM QUIDEM CUMIS EGO IPSE OCULIS MEIS VIDI IN AMPULLA PENDERE, ET CUM ILLI PUERI DICERENT: Σιβυλλα τι θελεις: RESPONDEBAT ILLA: ἀποθανεῖν θέλω."

[FOR, WITH MY OWN EYES I SAW THE CUMEAN SIBYL SUSPENDED IN A BOTTLE, AND WHEN THE BOYS ASKED HER, "SIBYL, WHAT DO YOU WANT?" SHE REPLIED, "I WANT TO DIE."]

This account of the fate of the Cumaean sibyl is given by Trimalchio in the forty-eighth chapter of the *Satyricon* by Petronius Arbiter, Roman statesman and writer of the first century A.D. Trimalchio scoffs at this ancient seer who, when granted one wish by Apollo, wished for as many years as grains in a handful of sand. She got her wish but unfortunately she had neglected to ask also for prolonged youth and so she withered into a creature shrunken small enough to fit into a large bottle.

This epigraph belongs properly not to "The Burial of the Dead" but to *The Waste Land* as a whole. It sets a certain preliminary tone for the work. The sibyl is one who understands the design of reality. She carried to Tarquinius Superbus, the last king of Rome, the fabled Sibylline Books outlining in oracular form the future of Rome. Originally there were nine books, but the king refused her price two times, and each time she burned three of the books. Finally he bought the remaining three books, paying the price originally asked.

In the fate of the sibyl is distilled the agony of those who seek the truth, who attempt to pierce the veil of appearance to glimpse the reality behind. This unquenchable impulse to understand hurtles such people headlong into a search the utter futility of which somehow proves their redemption, for salvation comes not in the attainment of the supreme end but in the striving after it. All this is borne out in the character of Celia in *The Cocktail Party*. As she confides to Sir Henry Harcourt-Reilly, she suffers from solipsistic anxiety, the feeling that "one always is alone"[11] and the uneasy conviction that her usual perception that "everything seemed so right" is all a mistake.[12] Thus she is almost unwittingly forced into a nameless quest, which carries her as a missionary to Kinkanja, a fictional island apparently off the coast of Africa. There, while assisting in averting a potential plague, she is caught up in an insurrection of the natives and killed, crucified near an anthill and possibly even cannibalized. Reilly accepts her terrible fate as somehow inevitable, part of the divine plan according to which, because she was more aware than others, Celia had to suffer more to be released. It is interesting that Eliot has her explain part of her psychological discomfort as a "sense of sin,"[13] since he suffered from the same burden. And she defines it metaphysically as an awareness that what seems right is in fact not, or in other words, that appearance is not reality. Thus, in this respect the sibyl, as seer and seeker, must have had a special identification for Eliot, surely one of the reasons he chose the passage from Petronius to lead into his poem.

Further, the sibyl is one for whom life shows all its monotonous redundancy because the span of her years encompasses generations, generations that enact before her eyes the same rituals over and over

again. She shares this affinity with Tiresias, who has "foresuffered all /
Enacted on this same divan or bed." Both were seers.

The similarity does not end there. In *The Odyssey* Tiresias is consulted by Odysseus in Hades, where the old man walks among the lost
souls. Aeneas likewise seeks out the Cumaean sibyl in her cave and
persuades her to conduct him across the river Lethe into Hades, where
he meets the shade Dido, and on to the Elysian fields where he embraces his dead father. Of course, in this she shares the roles of Virgil
and Beatrice in *The Divine Comedy*.

It is probably as a guide through the hell and heaven of the soul that
the sibyl stands most properly at the head of *The Waste Land*, supplant-
ing Kurtz, who made a more mysterious and less universalized journey
through the same territory. Something in both characters led to a vision
filled with horror and glory, rooted perhaps in hell but stretching ever
heavenward.

Prophecy accounts for a web of allusions in the poem, many biblical,
tracing back to Ecclesiastes and Revelation. The Cumaean sibyl and
Tiresias form part of that web, in which they are also associated with
Madame Sosostris, an association that ties in with Empress Elizabeth,
who had notable experience with cartomancy. Further, the sibyl's fate
was what Elizabeth so much feared, that of having her beauty dese-
crated by age, a parallel so underscored by Marie Larisch that Eliot
could hardly have been unaware of it.

Before leaving the topic of the epigraph, it would be profitable to give
detailed attention to what Eliot first considered using, that tantalizing
bit from Conrad's *Heart of Darkness* that describes Kurtz on the door-
step of death:

> Did he live his life again in every detail of desire, temptation, and
> surrender during this supreme moment of complete knowledge? He
> cried in a whisper at some image, at some vision,—he cried out twice,
> a cry that was no more than a breath—
> 'The Horror! the horror!'[14]

As has been recounted many times, Eliot said that he thought the
citation "somewhat elucidative," but Pound contended that Conrad was
not "weighty enough" for Eliot, who subsequently discarded the epigraph and replaced it with the one from Petronius that appears in the
published version of *The Waste Land*. Eliot did not specify in what way
the Conrad quotation is elucidative but it is not hard to guess, considering its context. Kurtz journeyed to the forests of the African savage,
married a native woman, became one with the primitive mentality; he
saw what civilized men had never glimpsed, but died at the threshold
of the vision.

Two other significant passages in the story amplify on the substance and feeling of the horror that Kurtz glimpsed. One, quite brief, finds Marlow waiting "before a mahogany door," waiting to deliver a packet of letters to Kurtz's woman: "While I waited he seemed to stare at me out of the glassy panel—stare with that wide and immense stare embracing, condemning, loathing all the universe. I seemed to hear the whispered cry, 'The horror! The Horror!' "[15] The other, more elaborate, occurs as Marlow begins to tell of the aftermath of his adventure:

> . . . as you see, I did not go to join Kurtz there and then. I did not. I remained to dream the nightmare out to the end, and to show my loyalty to Kurtz once more. Destiny. My destiny! Droll thing life is— that mysterious arrangement of merciless logic for a futile purpose. The most you can hope from it is some knowledge of yourself—that comes too late—a crop of unextinguishable regrets. I have wrestled with death. It is the most unexciting contest you can imagine. It takes place in an impalpable grayness, with nothing underfoot, with nothing around, without spectators, without clamour, without glory, without the great desire of victory, without the great fear of defeat, in a sickly atmosphere of tepid scepticism, without much belief in your own right, and still less in that of your adversary. If such is the form of ultimate wisdom, then life is a greater riddle than some of us think it to be. I was within a hair's breadth of the last opportunity for pronouncement, and I found with humiliation that probably I would have had nothing to say. This is the reason why I affirm that Kurtz was a remarkable man. He had something to say. He said it. Since I had peeped over the edge myself, I understand better the meaning of his stare, that could not see the flame of the candle, but was wide enough to embrace the whole universe, piercing enough to penetrate all the hearts that beat in the darkness. He had summed up—he had judged. 'The horror!' He was a remarkable man. After all, this was the expression of some sort of belief; it had candour, it had conviction, it had a vibrating note of revolt in its whisper, it had the appalling face of a glimpsed truth—the strange commingling of desire and hate. And it is not my own extremity I remember best—a vision of grayness without form filled with physical pain, and a careless contempt for the evanescence of all things—even of this pain itself! No! It is his extremity that I seem to have lived through. True, he had made that last stride, he had stepped over the edge, while I had been permitted to draw back my hesitating foot. And perhaps in this is the whole difference; perhaps all the wisdom, and all the truth, and all sincerity, are just compressed into that inappreciable moment of time in which we step over the threshold of the invisible. Perhaps! I like to think my summing-up would not have been a word of careless contempt. Better his cry—much better. It was an affirmation, a moral victory paid for by innumerable defeats by abominable terrors, by abominable satisfactions. But it was a victory![16]

Here is the ignominy of life—that so little really matters, that the struggle cannot be proved with any finality to be worthwhile. And the most that can be hoped for is a little knowledge of the self, a knowledge that, if gained at all, comes at the end of the journey when it is no longer of any use. Any answer that comes is bound within human finitude, so that it never really satisfies. This wisdom, this insight wrested from existence just as the soul passes from existence, can reach toward completeness only by being contradictory, bringing the opposite faces of reality into a coincidence that, to the human mind, must in the end be nonsensical. William York Tindall expressed it beautifully:

> The heart of Conrad's darkness is presented in the forest, which, assisted by peripheral devices, embodies suggestions of our unconscious and primitives selves, of all that Kurtz succumbs to and responsible Marlow rejects. In this great image, at once limited and expanded by its context of smaller images, discourse, character, and action, Conrad has gathered all that man adores and fears.[17]

Quite succinctly, in "all that man adores and fears" is the idea of the holy, which comprises the uncanny, the thrill of awe or reverence, the sense of dependence, impotence, unworthiness, or, conversely, exaltation, sublimity, ecstasy. It is the most primitive basis of religious experience. In choosing some introductory evocation to The Waste Land, it was to Conrad's invocation of the holy, in its full dimensions, that Eliot turned. The shadow of it is cast fully across the poem, and it will help illuminate the intent of the poem. For the moment, it is necessary to turn to a more superficial aspect of the Conrad epigraph.

Recall that Dante embarked upon his moral journey in a state of sleep or, more precisely, sleepiness. In the discarded first episode of "The Burial of the Dead" the narrator, presumably Eliot in this case, leaves his companions at the break of dawn, ostensibly to watch the sunrise and then go home to sleep. Not perhaps literally but certainly metaphorically, Kurtz, in the epigraphic quotation, completes the parallelism in that he appears to be in a kind of delirium, something akin to nightmare sleep, in which the events of his life might pass before him in a crazy, dreamlike manner.

The epigraph would have suggested a review of past life, a reliving of events for some moral purpose or to some spiritual end, but in a kind of delirious vision. This idea would have been reinforced by the scene of Tom going home, drunk and half-asleep, to fall victim to hallucinations, hypnagogic phantasmagoria. Both elucidative devices would have been supported by the underlying and rather ubiquitous thread of the journey of Dante from the outer shores of hell to the empyrean, with nods to

Aeneas's sojourn to the underworld in other allusions throughout the poem. That, at any rate, seems to have been Eliot's intention.

THE BURIAL OF THE DEAD

The title refers to the Anglican service for the dead, which derives at least in part from the fifteenth chapter of the first book of Corinthians, dealing with the resurrection of Christ and with the subsequent resurrection of the baptized dead. Burial of the body is likened to the sowing of a seed, an analogy that comes into play in the last lines of the section. It is said that "the dead shall be raised incorruptible, and we shall be changed."[18] To be raised at all they must be baptized into the faith, which introduces the symbol of water, the purifying agent.

Behind this archetype lies another burial, that of the star-crossed Marie Vetsera, told with great feeling by Countess Larisch in her autobiography. Because her affair with the archduke was not to be made public, the corpse of the poor girl had to be prepared hastily by her uncle, ushered out between two men, propped up with a walking-stick down her back to hold her erect so that she would appear to be alive, packed into a coach, and buried in a plain wood casket in the Cistercian Abbey of Heiligenkreuz, where her grave would remain unseen. While she received this demeaning burial, the archduke was accorded a service of great pomp, a mourning whose echo is heard elsewhere in "What the Thunder Said."

Of course, still fresh in Eliot's mind were the recent deaths of his father and of his friend in youth, Jean Verdenal. But evidences at different points in the poem suggest that Eliot built mostly upon the twin but differing burials of Archduke Rudolph and his hapless mistress.

APRIL IS THE CRUELLEST MONTH, BREEDING
LILACS OUT OF THE DEAD LAND, MIXING
MEMORY AND DESIRE, STIRRING
DULL ROOTS WITH SPRING RAIN.

With no preliminary introduction, we are thrust into the poem's central conflict between spiritual death and the ambivalent agony of rebirth, enlightenment, insight. April is cruel because it threatens us with new life, something which, on the symbolic level, is both wanted and feared. April is the traditional month of Easter, time of the resurrection of Christ, time also in ancient cultures of the rebirth of the vegetation gods, for which the lilac is a tangible symbol.

This is also the time for pilgrimages, when Dante strayed into the forest ultimately to meet Virgil, to be guided into the lower depths, peer into the horrors of the godless, then rise into the empyrean bliss. If April represents the season of spring, it is not too far-fetched to relate it to the time at which the hero in *The Roman de la Rose* commences his quest for the rose, symbol of both carnal and divine love, though strictly speaking that was in May. Other considerations than time, however, make this association plausible. In the words of the quester:

> I became aware that it was May, five years or more ago; I dreamed that I was filled with joy in May, the amorous month, when everything rejoices, when one sees no bush or hedge that does not wish to adorn itself with new leaves. The woods, dry during the winter, recover their verdure, and the very earth glories in the dew which waters it and forgets the poverty in which the winter was passed.

This scene of rebirth unfolds as the earth assumes "a robe so ornate that there are a hundred pairs of colors in it" and more significantly "the birds, silent while they were cold and the weather hard and bitter, became so gay in May, in the serene weather, that their hearts are filled with joy until they must sing or burst."[19] It is not certain how familiar Eliot was with *The Roman de la Rose*; it seems improbable that he ever digested the entirety of it. But his later extensive use of the rose motif suggests he had a nodding acquaintance with this work.

This likelihood grows when the hero of the *Roman* enters a rose garden, such as that which seems to have haunted Eliot, reminding him of the forbidden garden next to his home where as a youth he caught fleeting glimpses of the girls at play, perhaps even of some special girl, a childhood Beatrice. The possible association grows as readers are shortly led into another archetypical garden, the hyacinth garden.

In commencing a pilgrimage, however, April with it stirring of dull roots with spring rain points most immediately to the opening of the prologue of *The Canterbury Tales*:

> Whan that Aprill with his shoures soote
> The drogte of March hath perced to the roote,
> And bathed every veyne in swich licour
> Of which vertu engendred is the fluor;
> Whan Zephirus eek with his sweete breeth
> Inspired hath in every holt and heeth
> The tendre croppes, and the yonge sonne
> Hath in the Ram his halve cours yronne,
> And smale foweles maken melodye,
> That slepen al the nyght with open ye
> (So priketh hem nature in hir corages);
> Thanne longen folk to goon on pilgramages,

And palmeres for to seken straunge strondes,
To ferne halwes, kowthe in sondry londes;
And specially from every shires ende
Of Engelond to Canterbury they wende,
The hooly blisful martir for to seke,
That hem hath holpen whan that they were seeke.[20]

Eliot was not the first to pick up from these lines. Shakespeare, too, must have recalled them when he had Anthony say of Cleopatra, "The April's in her eyes; it is love's spring, and these the showers to bring it on."[21] There can be no doubt that Eliot read these lines of Shakespeare, though they add little but extra force to the Chaucerian allusion. However, they link curiously with a description given in the Larisch autobiography.

Marie Vetsera had so quarreled with her mother over her infatuation with Archduke Rudolph that she ran away to seek refuge with the countess. Meanwhile, Rudolph had also visited the countess, persuading her to bring Baroness Vetsera to a secret rendezvous with him. Countess Larisch relates that when she confided this to the young girl, "her April mood was upon her; she uttered a little cry of joy, and smiles succeeded her tears."[22] Thus "April is the cruellest month" takes on a more concrete reference, and the Larisch architecture continues to be built from the epigraph and from the section title.

These opening four lines establish several themes that are repeated throughout the poem. First, April is the month of rebirth, vegetative and spiritual. It is also the time of love, "love's spring," simply another aspect of rebirth. These are presented ambivalently, as a joy and as a threat. And, finally, all occurs within the context of a journey or quest.

Another aspect of this complex is held in the phrase "mixing / Memory and desire," which comes from a novel much cherished by Eliot in his younger days, *Bubu of Montparnasse* by Charles-Louis Philippe. In the preface that he wrote for the English translation of it, Eliot records that he first read it when he arrived in Paris in 1910, and that it had always been for him "a symbol of Paris at that time." The novel deals with the seamier side of Parisian life, the world of the pimp and prostitute, much in keeping with the early poems that Eliot wrote in those collegiate days. That world definitely belonged within the waste land. But even out of context the passage that inspired Eliot's phrase is meaningful enough on its own: "A man walks carrying with him all the properties of his life, and they churn about in his head. Something he sees awakens them, something else excites them. For our flesh has retained all our memories, and we mingle them with our desires."[23]

Indeed, the journey into which Eliot launched himself here was precisely an introspective odyssey in which "all the properties of his life," which is to say his memories, were to "churn about in his head." As his mind fixed upon one impression, another was awakened, and all these memories were tinged with desire, aimed usually toward the completion of things. Overarching was the desire to understand all the disturbing fragments cast upon the shore of memory.

Literary echoes die out tenuously in "stirring / Dull roots with spring rain," with overtones not only from Chaucer and Shakespeare but also perhaps from John Day. More than once throughout *The Waste Land* Eliot borrowed from Day's *The Parliament of Bees*, especially from character three. But here he may have recalled, albeit unconsciously, some remarks made by Oberon in the section devoted to character eleven. Oberon speaks of "April deluge and May frosts" (27) then, returning the salutations of the Vintager, he says:

> May thy grapes thrive
> In autumn, and the roots survive
> In churlish winter . . .

> (58–60)

No change of meaning would derive from this; it would only reinforce the basic significance found in Chaucer, Shakespeare, and Guillaume de Lorris, author of the first part of *The Roman de la Rose*, insofar as it relates to the traditional romantic notions built around the spring season.

A last recollection sounding in these lines might be from a volume of poetry, *In the Valley of Vision* by Geoffrey Faber, which Eliot reviewed for the *Egoist* in 1918. It is a slim allusion, but one that makes sense in the light of the hyacinth garden scene. It is to a long poem called "Loyalty," in which a lady laments a lover who had spurned her. Love personified is addressed as "cruellest tyrant" for having "whetted the edge of my heart" and having proffered the "hope of April, and all the despair of November." Yet she pursues Love and through him her lover, willing, as she says, to "strain my eyes, if perchance afar I may view him, / And know all my life will be nought beside that moment of seeing."[24]

Certainly there is little in the quality of the verse that could etch it into Eliot's memory, but the sentiment that it depicts is so appropriate to that found in the garden scene and, to a lesser degree, in the vignette of the girl left upon the shore, near the end of "What the Thunder Said" in the original draft, that it could not help but leave a vestigial imprint on Eliot's feelings about April. Phrases lurking in the verse that could act as almost accidental determinants of association are "cruellest tyrant" linking with "cruellest month," and "that moment of seeing" with

"Looking into the heart of light," itself jostling ever so slightly "the edge of my heart." I do not wish to lay any great critical stress upon these similarities, except to note that such are often the fortuities of inspiration and creation. And at any rate, this poem of Faber is an interesting lament from the vantage point of the hyacinth girl.

Departing from purely literary allusions, one could speculate, with James E. Miller, Jr., that these opening lines of "The Burial of the Dead" carried deep personal meaning for Eliot, relating to the loss of his friend Jean Verdenal.[25] George Watson, tracking down the meager facts known about Verdenal, found that the young man died 2 May 1915 while dressing a wounded man on the battlefield.[26] This would make April, in a sense, the eve of his death. Certainly, dying as he had in early May, Verdenal might have become associated in Eliot's mind with the fertility gods of Frazer and mythology, gods who died perennially only to be reborn in the spring, while Verdenal would remain forever dead. Therein was a cruelty.

In this scenario, "breeding / Lilacs out of the dead land" ties in with Eliot's only published reminiscence of Verdenal. After reading a book about Paris in the days he had spent there as a student, Eliot wrote: "I am willing to admit that my own retrospect is touched by a sentimental sunset, the memory of a friend coming across the Luxembourg Gardens in the late afternoon, waving a branch of lilac, a friend who was later (so far as I could find out) to be mixed with the mud of Gallipoli."[27] This citation gives further credence to the possibility that Eliot learned of the death well after the fact.

Whether or not there were erotic aspects to the relationship between Eliot and Verdenal, this recollected image would lead to "mixing / Memory and desire." We can even go on, as Miller does, and interpret "stirring / Dull roots with spring rain" as a metaphorical reference to "the stirring of the older poet's arrested or paralyzed sexuality,"[28] but an interpretation perhaps more in keeping with the text of the poem suggests (while not contradicting the sexual interpretation) a yearning to be released from the general malaise with which Eliot was then plagued.

WINTER KEPT US WARM, COVERING
EARTH IN FORGETFUL SNOW, FEEDING
A LITTLE LIFE WITH DRIED TUBERS.

So far, the landscape of the waste land remains in the foreground, with this continuation of the straightforward description. The mood of ambivalence is maintained with the nostalgia of winter, the dead season, mitigating the restlessness of spring, which begins anew the pangs of the quest as spiritually alive individuals reach out to transcend the moment. One new theme enters surreptitiously through two lines from James Thomson's "To our ladies of death" from *The City of Dreadful Night*:

> Our Mother feedeth thus our little life,
> That we in turn may feed her with our death.

This series of poems by Thomson is built around a city in spiritual ruins, whose people have committed themselves to an atheistic pessimism. The poems sustain the theme of the living dead; their image of the corpse nurturing the earth foreshadows "That corpse you planted last year in your garden." Even more significant, the motif of the city, indeed the "Unreal city," is for the first time invoked, though on the subconscious level. That is to say, the motif has been introduced into the strata of dreamlike associations like a seed planted to bloom later into consciousness.

SUMMER SURPRISED US, COMING OVER THE STARNBERGERSEE
WITH A SHOWER OF RAIN;

Attention lingers on the mood, on the conflicts that acted as catalysts in setting off the chain of rumination until, perhaps taking off from the undercurrent of urbanity hidden in the Thomson allusion, the frame shifts to a concrete memory. The scene is Munich, where Eliot had spent some pleasant days. Storm clouds roll over the Starnbergersee, a lakeside resort just outside town. Bathing, boating, dancing, and other recreations abound there. In the first draft of these lines, Eliot described the Konigsee, a similar lakeside area, rather than Starnbergersee, which he later chose undoubtedly for the rich associations it bore. Also Starnbergersee rounds the line with a fuller and more satisfying cadence.

Strictly speaking, this is where the reference to Marie Larisch finally becomes explicit. She lived in a castle on the Starnbergersee; on its banks, too, was one of Ludwig's extravagant castles. Further, the mad king drowned in that lake. Likely it was here, or nearby, that Eliot met with Countess Larisch, making it the perfect spot from which to depart on his voyage of memories.

The shower of rain contradicts the standard contention that the inhabitants of the waste land, mirroring the Grail legend, wait in vain for life-giving rain. This is not in any sense a narrative structure. Rain is merely another archetypical symbol that evokes possibilities of regeneration.

> WE STOPPED IN THE COLONNADE
> AND WENT ON IN SUNLIGHT, INTO THE HOFGARTEN,
> AND DRANK COFFEE, AND TALKED FOR AN HOUR.

An interesting spatial transition in the Bradleyan mode, the scene begins on the shores of the Starnbergersee and proceeds directly into the Hofgarten, a public park in Munich proper, just as scenes might in a dream. Just as suddenly as the location changes, the storm is gone. It may have been here, in the famous beer tavern, that Eliot encountered Marie Larisch. Whether it was here or at Starnbergersee makes little difference; the associations remain the same.

BIN GAR KEINE RUSSIN, STAMM' AUS LITAUEN, ECHT DEUTSCH.

[I'M NO RUSSIAN, COME FROM LITHUANIA, PURE GERMAN.]

An unidentified voice intervenes briefly, as if from the next table or from another corner of the beer tavern. This artifice introduces the theme of the disintegration of Europe, something much on Eliot's mind at the time—something, indeed, that the intelligent person of that era could hardly ignore. Most particularly, in this poem Eliot seemed to concentrate on the fate of the smaller nations vainly seeking their independences. He returned to this problem again in "What the Thunder Said," where at lines 369–70 he described the "hooded hordes swarming / Over endless plains," plains that were Polish in the Ur-text.

Poland and Lithuania, of course, shared intertwined destinies for two centuries. First dominated by Russia, then coveted by Nazi Germany, each had enjoyed but a brief hour of independence before capitulating to the swastika. Several ephemeral cabinet governments were established and dissolved in Lithuania. Most of the leaders were German. Poland and Lithuania even became involved in mutual conflict over the city of Vilna.

Thus, this intrusive fragment of conversation evokes the political disintegration then overtaking Europe, amplified later in the lines to which Eliot appended the note containing an extract from Hess's *Blick ins Chaos* (*Glimpse into Chaos*). The fragment also implies the difficulty of communication, in that whatever may theoretically have preceded it in the conversation evidently called for a protesting clarification.

This line may owe something to a scene in Wyndham Lewis's novel *Tarr*, which Eliot reviewed in the September 1918 issue of the *Egoist*:

Tarr asked Fräulein Vasek from what part of Germany she came.

'My parents are russian. I was born in Berlin and brought up in America. We live in Vienna,' she answered. 'I am a typical Russian.'

So she accounted for her jarring on his maudlin german reveries.

'Lots of russian families have settled latterly in Germany haven't they?' he asked.

'Russians are still rather savage: the more bourgeois a place or thing is the more it attracts them. German watering places, musical centers and so on, they like about as well as anything. Often they settle there if they can afford to.'

'Do you regard yourself as a Russian or a German?'

'Oh a Russian. I'm thoroughly russian.'[29]

"Echt deutsch" is equivalent to "thoroughly German," and other details of the conversation, with German substituted for Russian, dovetail with Eliot's line.

AND WHEN WE WERE CHILDREN, STAYING AT THE ARCHDUKE'S,
MY COUSIN'S, HE TOOK ME OUT ON A SLED,
AND I WAS FRIGHTENED. HE SAID, MARIE,
MARIE, HOLD ON TIGHT. AND DOWN WE WENT.

Here is the incident to which Valerie Eliot referred in her notes to the Ur-text, pointing out that Eliot had gleaned it from a conversation with Countess Larisch. It presages the downfall to which both she and her cousin, Archduke Rudolph, were brought in the Mayerling affair. Also, the fear that the sled ride instilled in Marie suggests the early warning she received and the uneasiness she felt about the role that Rudolph might play in her life.

Mixed with the Larisch background may be a tenuous reference to a passage in one of Eliot's favorite books of the Bible, Ecclesiastes 12:5: "Yea, they shall be afraid of that which is high." This refers to the fear of the aged, who no longer dare such things as ascents to high mountain tops. It would provide an ironic contrast with the next line.

IN THE MOUNTAINS, THERE YOU FEEL FREE.

Yet those who fear high places will not ascend to this feeling of freedom. And those who do are apt to be vacationers, not questers for truth. This is brought out immediately in the following line.

I READ, MUCH OF THE NIGHT, AND GO SOUTH IN THE WINTER.

This and related stereotypes of tourism seem to have held a special significance for Eliot. In "The Rock" he writes, "If the weather is foul we stay at home and read the papers."[30] He returns to this motif even more specifically in *The Family Reunion*, where he echoes the words used in *The Waste Land*:

> *Ivy.* I have always told Amy she should go south in the winter.
>   Were I in Amy's position, I would go south in the winter.
>   I would follow the sun, not wait for the sun to come here.
>   I would go south in the winter, if I could afford it,
>   Not freeze, as I do, in Bayswater, by a gas-fire counting shillings.
> *Violet.* Go south! to the English circulating libraries,
>   To the military widows and the English chaplains,
>   To the chilly deck-chair and the strong cold tea—
>   The strong cold stewed ban Indian tea.

Charles agrees, saying that the family is "country-bred" and that it would not be Amy's style to leave the country in winter. There is no point going south, avers Violet, "[s]imply to see the vulgarest people"; besides, the tourists "bathe in the absolute minimum of clothes."[31] And Charles continues on the decadence of the younger generation. From this it is pretty clear what Eliot had in mind when he spoke about going south in the winter. He wished to evoke the empty glitter and slavish materialism of the tourist meccas, another aspect of spiritual death. Something of this feeling, though more subdued and less pretentious, may be found in a letter that Edward Fitzgerald wrote to Bernard Barton in 1842. It is quoted in A. C. Benson's *Edward Fitzgerald*, from which it is recognized that Eliot borrowed some phrases for *Gerontion*.

> In this big London, all full of intellect and pleasure and business, I feel pleasure in dipping down into the country, and rubbing my hand over a cool dew upon the pastures, as it were. I know very few people here: and care for fewer; I believe I should like to live in a small house just outside a pleasant English town all the days of my life, making myself useful in a humble way, reading my books, and playing a rubber of whist at night. But England cannot expect long such a reign of inward quiet as to suffer men to dwell so easily to themselves. But time will tell us:
> 'Come what come may,
> Time and the Hour runs through the roughest day.'[32]

There are good reasons that the life of Fitzgerald might intrude into this line of willful indolence. He dedicated himself to the quest for gentle pleasures, never trying very hard to accomplish anything, never deeply questioning. Of difficult periods in his life, Benson wrote:

... he lived as best he could. In such current conceptions of religion he could not rest. He could but say with a wistful affectation of cynicism:—

> 'Qu'est-ce que cela fait si je m'amuse?'
> [What matter does it make if I enjoy myself?]

And in the presence of hopeless failure and grief—"I do not know; I cannot help: and I distress myself as little as I can."[33]

Further, Fitzgerald lived apparently less in reality than in the insubstantial fabric of memory:

> I imagine that Fitzgerald's one haunting thought was regret. An impersonal regret for all the beauty and charm of the world that flowered only to die; and a more personal regret that he had not been able to put out his powers to do and to be. He was overshadowed by a constant sense of the brevity, the fleeting swiftness of time, the steady, irrevocable lapsing of life to death. Melancholy takes many forms; in some it finds its materials in anxious and gloomy forebodings of what the future may bring or take away; with some the present seems irremediably dreary. But Fitzgerald lived in a wistful regret for the beautiful hours that were gone, the days that are no more.[34]

Such a person has much in common with that modern offshoot of Hamlet, J. Alfred Prufrock (who also walks nameless through "Portrait of a Lady"), frozen into inaction because he has analyzed away all purpose and does not believe in the efficacy of attempting something purely as an affirmation of life, humanity, or spiritual transcendence.

Before leaving this line, it should be noted that Countess Larisch liked to go south in the winter, and so there is no departure here from the framework of her story.

WHAT ARE THE ROOTS THAT CLUTCH, WHAT BRANCHES GROW
OUT OF THIS STONY RUBBISH?

Again there is a return to the waste land description, the geography of desolation that is sustained like a basso continuo throughout the poem. This time it has biblical derivations.

> Can papyrus grow where there is no marsh? Can reeds flourish where there is no water? While yet in flower and not cut down, they wither before any other plant. Such are the paths of all who forget God; the hope of the hypocrite shall perish. . . . He thrives before the sun, and his shoots spread over his garden. His roots twine about the stoneheap; he lives among the rocks.[35]

Although it is the hypocrite who lives among the rocks, the poem makes plain in the final line of "The Burial of the Dead" that the hypocrite is everyman. In this sense, the waste land can be found everywhere. It is symbolic of the world at large.

SON OF MAN,

YOU CANNOT SAY, OR GUESS, FOR YOU KNOW ONLY

A HEAP OF BROKEN IMAGES, WHERE THE SUN BEATS

Once into biblical sources, Eliot forms a pastiche from them. "Son of man" is the epithet by which God always addresses Ezekiel; if taken in opposition to "son of God," it is once again tantamount to everyman, while retaining a dreamlike ambiguity.

There are numerous references in the Bible to the breaking of graven images, the subduing of pagan religions, and the reaffirmation of the true God of the Hebrews. To turn again to one of Eliot's favorite books, Ezekiel 6:4 tells of the Lord's judgement of Israel for idolatry: "And your altars shall be desolate, and your images shall be broken; and I will cast down your slain men before your idols." Eliot had only to interfuse this with Isaiah 25:2: "For thou hast made of a city an heap; of a defenced city a ruin: a palace of strangers to be no city; it shall never be built." Typically, two opposing significances come together, first the judgement then the defence, but in both cases the key words carry connotations of faithlessness and the desolation that comes from it.

Symbols, idols, are all that humans can know of the Absolute, and so they cannot really answer questions of moment. They must realize that action is the only real answer to such questions. They must dare in the face of symbolic meaninglessness.

Eliot explored further in *The Family Reunion* the setting he erects here. In part two, at the close of the second scene, Harry sets himself that mysterious task of salvation:

> Where does one go from a world of insanity?
> Somewhere on the other side of despair.
> To the worship in the desert, the thirst and deprivation,
> A stony sanctuary and a primitive altar,
> The heat of the sun and the icy vigil,
> A care over lives of humble people,
> The lesson of ignorance, of incurable diseases.
> Such things are possible. It is love and terror
> Of what waits and wants me, and will not let me fall.
> Let the cricket chirp. John shall be the master.
> All I have is his. No harm can come to him.
> What would destroy me will be life for John,
> I am responsible for him. Why I have this election

I do not understand. It must have been preparing always,
And I see it was what I always wanted. Strength demanded
That seems too much, is just strength enough given.
I must follow the bright angels.[36]

It is salvation through paradox, therefore nothing more than faith in
poetic form. A landscape of despair is where this paradox must be
worked out, in the agonizing dark night of the soul, where the master is
St. John of the Cross and the St. John to whom the revelation of the Last
Judgment appeared in the book of Revelation. Hence the stony waste
land of the hypocrite everyman, who "thrives before the sun," is the
same place of desolation where questers must work out their faith, a
place where "the sun beats."

AND THE DEAD TREE GIVES NO SHELTER, THE CRICKET NO RELIEF,

Some commentators have cited Isaiah 56:3 as a source for this line:
"Neither let the son of the stranger, that hath joined himself to the Lord,
speak, saying, The Lord hath utterly separated me from his people:
Neither let the eunuch say, Behold, I am a dry tree." God promises even
the eunuch salvation. Since Eliot was so fond of this book, I cannot
exclude this reference, but there is another that seems more primary.
Numerous passages in the Bible refer to a divine source of salvation as
the tree of life. In Revelation it is symbolically equated with Christ.
Consider Revelation 2:7–10:

> He that hath an ear, let him hear what the Spirit saith unto the
> churches: To him that overcometh will I give to eat of the tree of life,
> which is in the midst of the paradise of God.
>   And unto the angel of the church in Smyrna write; these things
> saith the first and the last, which was dead, and is alive;
>   I know thy works, and tribulation, and poverty, (but thou art rich)
> and I know the blasphemy of them which say they are Jews, and are
> not, but are the synagogue of Satan.
>   Fear none of these things which thou shalt suffer: behold, the devil
> shall cast some of you into prison, that ye may be tried; and ye shall
> have tribulation ten days: be thou faithful unto death, and I will give
> thee a crown of life.

From this it makes perfect sense to say that "the dead tree gives no
shelter," for, if the tree of life is denied, it is dead as a source of
salvation. God is seen as a shelter, as in Psalms 56:3: "For thou hast
been a shelter for me, and a strong tower from the enemy." That is, of
course, for the faithful. So for the faithless or the indifferent, God,
through Christ symbolized by the tree of life, can give no shelter.

Likewise, the cricket, ancient harbinger of rain, prophet of death in some lore, can give no relief to those who "thrive before the sun," for rain as a symbol of rebirth holds only fear for them, and they who are dead cannot die again. In other words, the living dead cannot bring themselves to begin with a comprehending or keenly aware fear of death as an approach to spiritual enlightenment. In *The Family Reunion*, Harry says that the cricket chirps in the dark night of the soul that he envisaged. There Eliot assures us that it is to the superstitious lore of the cricket that he turns to derive his symbolism in this case. The cricket appears with similar connotation in one of Eliot's favorite plays, *The Duchess of Malfi*:

> How superstitiously we mind our evils!
> The throwing down salt, or crossing of a hare,
> Bleeding at nose, stumbling of a horse,
> Or singing of a cricket are of power
> To daunt whole man in us.[37]

AND THE DRY STONE NO SOUND OF WATER

Immediately to mind comes the famous story of Moses bringing forth water from the rock by smiting it with his rod. Only there is no miracle in the waste land. Lack of water becomes an obsessive motif in "What the Thunder Said."

ONLY

THERE IS SHADOW UNDER THIS RED ROCK
(COME IN UNDER THE SHADOW OF THIS RED ROCK)

In the Ur-text the rock was originally gray, suggesting that Eliot shifted to "red rock" for its richer associations. Within its context of biblical allusions the rock must be conceived foremost as a symbol of God, a common identification made in many parts of the scripture, and also of Christ, as in Isaiah 32:1–2: "Behold, a King shall reign in righteousness, and princes shall rule in judgement. And a man shall be as a hiding place from the wind, and a covert from the tempest; as rivers of water in a dry place, as the shadow of a great rock in a weary land."

Rocks and stones have been associated with various magic potencies in ancient folklore. Large rocks or rock formations, because of their size, have inspired religious awe in many ancient peoples. Frazer, in a passage that Eliot likely read, described the approach to the center of worship of one of the fertility gods in Asia Minor as a road running through a range of mountains "torn here and there by impassable ravines, or broken into prodigious precipices of red and grey rock."[38] It was located "at the mouth of a deep ravine enclosed by great precipices of red rock."[39] Such rocks must have inspired awe in those who made their way beneath them, great shadows spread before them, wending their path to a religious ritual.

But Eliot did not have to turn to any literary sources for this image; he had lived it along the New England coast. Around Gloucester rise cliffs of granite red and grey. In fact, right in his own childhood yard there was an outcrop of rock around which he must have played. As a child he too must have experienced some awe at the rocks that overlooked the mysterious ocean.

Much in line with his youthful experiences of the rocky topography in New England is a picture painted in the third canto of the purgatory section in *The Divine Comedy*, from which Eliot apparently derived some facet of this image. There Virgil urges Dante, newly arrived in purgatory, to move along toward a distant mountain, the symbolic meaning of which is left undefined. It is, appropriately enough for Eliot's purposes, ominous and yet ambiguous:

> Le sol, che retro fiammegiava roggio,
> rotto m'era dinanzi, alla figura
> ch'aveva in me de suoi raggi l'appoggio.

> [The sun, that behind us was flaming red,
> was broken before me, in the figure
> in which its beams were stayed by me.][40]

Dante does not describe the mountain as red; rather, it must be supposed red by implication. Since this canto also contains comments on Dante's shadow and Virgil's lack of one, which certainly pertain to the subsequent three lines of *The Waste Land*, we must conclude that Eliot's decision to change his rock from gray to red may have been influenced by the red sunlight against the mountain described in the passage just quoted. This conclusion is reinforced by the fact that, in his last speech at the close of *Murder in the Cathedral*, the Third Priest tells the "weak sad men" of Canterbury to "Go where the sunset reddens the last grey rock." In any case, this reference does not substantially alter the import of the rock as a symbol of religious awe; it might merely add depth to it.

Perhaps more suggestive than any of these allusions, however, may be one to the Cumaean sibyl whom Virgil described as "insanem vatem, quae canit fata sub ima rupe,"[41] an inspired prophetess who reveals the fates under a rock (that is, at the mouth of a cave situated below a sea cliff). This allusion is tantalizing because the resolution of this episode—"I will show you fear in a handful of dust"—leads back to the grains in a handful of sand the number of which spelled the years of life to which the sibyl was sentenced. Invoking the sibyl at this point would give major structural advantages.

First, it associates the implied biblical prophet speaking these lines with a seer of classical civilization, the type of alloying that Eliot pursues throughout the poem. Second, it subsumes this episode into the quest theme by reminding us of Aeneas's quest for a new homeland for the Trojans, tying immediately into *"Frisch weht der Wind / Der Heimat zu."* And it reflects forward a further dimension of identity to "the Lady of the Rocks." In view of all these links and Eliot's familiarity with and favoritism toward *The Aeneid,* one can hardly dismiss this key to the passage.

Finally, still another source for the image, suggested by Grover Smith, is the "roche de Sanguin" in Chrétien de Troyes's *Perceval.* This is the red castle, where Perceval slew Partinans who in turn had by guile killed the brother of the Fisher King. On beholding the severed head of Partinans, the Fisher King was cured of his malady, told Perceval he was his uncle, and made him his heir. If this is indeed a source for the red rock, it is certainly a peripheral one that, in itself, adds nothing to our understanding of the poem. However, it does induce certain potentially interesting implications.

The "roche de Sanguin" might belong to a constellation of associations woven around the image of the Grail Castle. Many such castles were built by the mad king Ludwig. He had an inordinate interest in medieval literature, an interest that doubtlessly had something to do with his favorable disposition toward Wagner, who drew upon medieval literary sources for his music dramas. Marie Larisch narrates in her autobiography that the servants of the king staged unusual dinners for him, one of which included actors portraying figures from the past, such as the minnesinger Wolfram von Eschenbach, author of *Parzeval* and also of an early version of the legend of Tristan and Isolde.[42] In his opera *Tannhauser* Wagner makes Wolfram play the role of generous opponent of Tannhauser and admirer of Elizabeth.

It is said that King Ludwig took Monsalvat, the Grail Castle in Wagner's *Parsifal,* as inspiration for his Schloss Neuschwanstein, about forty miles south of the Starnbergersee:

> At the time when Eliot visited Bavaria, the legend of King Ludwig was much more alive than it is today. Some of the people still around Starnberg and near the castles remembered the King; others had heard his story first-hand from their parents. Besides, anybody interested in it could study it in the accounts of recent Bavarian history and in the numerous biographies which then had already reached a peak of popularity. It is an attractive thought that when he was in the Alps, Eliot visited not only the Starnbergersee but also Schloss Neu-

schwanstein. The castle is a major goal of tourist pilgrimage, and it takes only a few hours' ride to get there from Munich past Starnberg. Visitors with historical interest, traveling from Munich to the Starnbergersee, usually make a point of going on to Schloss Neuschwanstein, as it is historically so closely linked with Starnberg. Assuming that Eliot did make this trip, it is interesting to note that at the back of the castle there is a mass of reddish rocks and debris which tumbled down when the foundation for the huge construction was leveled off. It is also remarkable—and probably symbolic of the color of the Grail—that one element of this castle, the three-story building around the entrance gate, is red, creating a striking contrast to the white marble of the rest of the castle.[43]

This setting may also be reflected in the "stony rubbish" of line 20 and the "dry stone" of line 24.

AND I WILL SHOW YOU SOMETHING DIFFERENT FROM EITHER
YOUR SHADOW AT MORNING STRIDING BEHIND YOU
OR YOUR SHADOW AT EVENING RISING TO MEET YOU

This whole segment having to do with the red rock and the shadows came almost completely from "The Death of St. Narcissus," a poem Eliot wrote, by his own dating, probably in 1915. He was inspired for certain ideas in the early poem by Ezra Pound's "A Girl" and T. E. Hulme's "Conversion," but neither bore upon the section in question here. In the first draft the present lines were embedded in a portrait of a martyr whom the protagonist puts before us with his "bloody cloth," "green limbs," and lips blue in death. In the fair copy the lines appear clipped of these macabre details, much in the form they kept in The Waste Land.[44]

At that time Eliot was laboring under the influence of imagism, so that his images were more evocative than allusive, although he seems to have been wedded partially to the allusive method from the beginning. St. Narcissus is obviously a transformation of Christ, as, in a sense, every martyr is. His sources of inspiration are plainly biblical—the "bloody cloth" is unmistakable. There is a hint of Plato in the image of the shadow cast upon the red rock by the light of a fire. This recalls the analogy of the cave, used by Plato in book 7 of The Republic to illustrate his conception of reality as it appears to humans. We are asked to imagine men living in a cave, chained with their backs to the entrance. Behind them is a fire. Between them and the fire is a road, and a wall built along the road hides the people who walk along it. However, the light of the fire casts a shadow of objects the people carry on their heads and the shadow falls upon the wall of the cave. This shadow of things is

like the appearance humans perceive with their senses, an appearance
that Plato considered but a poor copy of ideal reality.

In the context of "The Death of St. Narcissus," the first shadow seems
to be the ordinary one seen by a man walking across the desert sands,
while the second at least suggests not simply the ordinary shadow cast
by a camp fire but, beyond that, the shape of appearance by which the
senses deceive the mind from comprehending through noesis the true
nature of reality. Noesis, rational-intuitive perception in Platonism,
Eliot would undoubtedly have construed as Bradleyan vision out of the
unification of disparate perceptions.

As transplanted into The Waste Land the meaning of the shadows is
further complicated. Since in the morning the shadow falls behind the
observer and at evening it falls before him, he must be travelling east,
which implies a possible pilgrimage toward Mecca or, more broadly,
toward some religious goal (if we take Mecca symbolically). A further
dimension of this derives from the third canto of the purgatory section
of The Divine Comedy, to which allusion seems to be made in the
previous lines. There Dante sees that he casts a shadow because he is
still of this life, whereas Virgil does not, because he is of the spiritual
realm. It seems that Eliot had in mind that a shadow symbolizes material as opposed to spiritual existence. Interpreted in this way, not to be
shown your shadow is to be turned away from this existence toward
something either spiritual or diabolic, if indeed any distinction can be
drawn between divinity and damnation in the metaphysics of Eliot. He
saw damnation as simply an approach to divinity.

Such an interpretation is buttressed by the formal source of these
lines, a passage from Philaster, 3.2, of Beaumont and Fletcher, railing at
the treachery of woman:

> . . . how that foolish man
> That reads the story of a woman's face
> And dies believing it, is lost forever;
> How all the good you have is but a shadow,
> I' the morning with you, and at night behind you
> Past and forgotten . . .

One can scarcely keep from associating "all the good you have is but a
shadow" with the line from Bubu of Montparnasse (to which allusion
was already made at line 3), "A man walks carrying with him all the
properties of his life, and they churn about in his head," and the famous
remark of Macbeth that "Life's but a walking shadow." All these associations simply weave together in support of the shadow representing the
insubstantiality of appearance, leading back to the Bradleyan theme of
appearance versus reality.

The thread of the Beaumont and Fletcher passage might also imply that the following line can be perceived within the framework of the life of Empress Elizabeth, a woman whose face evidently betrayed many a man, for that is what she lived for, to betray them in a kind of love that could never survive because it demanded perfection. As we shall see, there is a larger consideration that assists the transition into the Larisch association.

I WILL SHOW YOU FEAR IN A HANDFUL OF DUST.

Immediately one thinks of the Cumaean sibyl, condemned to live out as many years as the number of grains in a handful of sand. Even though Eliot chose the Petronius epigraph after he wrote the poem, he was certainly aware of the parallel between it and this line, and it probably formed part of his conscious intention. Dust, moreover, has always been linked with death and destruction. Turn once more to Isaiah; this time the fifth verse of book twenty-six: "For he bringeth them down that dwell on high; the lofty city, he layeth it low; he layeth it low, even to the ground, he bringeth it even to the dust." And everyone knows the expression, "Earth to earth, ashes to ashes, dust to dust," which continues, "in sure and certain hope of the Resurrection unto eternal life," from "The Burial of the Dead" in *The Book of Common Prayer*, containing the liturgy appointed for use in the Church of England. Most particularly, Eliot found his image in John Donne's *Devotions upon Emergent Occasions, Meditation IV*:

What's become of man's great extent and proportion, when himself shrinks from himself, and consumes himself to a handful of dust? What's become of his soaring thoughts, his compassing thoughts, when himself brings himself to the ignorance, to the thoughtlessness of the Grave? His diseases are his own, but the Physician is not; he hath them at home, but he must send for the Physician.[45]

"Fear in a handful of dust," then, means fear at the clear perception of death, already seen as a starting point for spiritual rebirth in that it is one of the historical and psychological roots of the religious impulse.

Another side of this image has to do with Empress Elizabeth, whose greatest fear, we recall, was that in growing old she would lose her beauty. Her niece remarks in *My Past* that Elizabeth "communed with ghosts in a world of shadow."[46] More tellingly, she fantasized living after death in a great rock, an association exploited more pointedly in "the Lady of the Rocks." Here the allusion to Elizabeth introduces the theme of vanity as a form of delusion by appearance.

FRISCH WEHT DER WIND
DER HEIMAT ZU
MEIN IRISCH KIND,
WO WEILEST DU

[FRESH BLOWS THE WIND
TO THE HOMELAND;
MY IRISH CHILD,
WHY DO YOU TARRY?]

This is sung by a happy sailor up high in the mast of the ship in the first act of Wagner's *Tristan und Isolde.* He is recalling a maiden whom he has left back on shore. The ship, captained by Tristan, is bringing Isolde from Ireland to be the bride of King Marke of Cornwall, Tristan's uncle. She deeply resents this, for she is in love with Tristan and the king is an old man whose affections she does not covet.

Daughter of a line of sorcerers, Isolde was famed for her powers to heal; knowing this, Tristan had sought her out after having been wounded in a duel. In that duel he had beheaded Morold, an Irish lord to whom Isolde was betrothed. When she learned whom Tristan had slain, she vowed to slay him in turn. Instead she was transfixed by his gaze and fell in love with him.

However, Tristan, remaining true to his friend King Marke, keeps himself aloof from Isolde so as not to succumb to her charms. Angered by this inattention, she asks her maidservant to bring her a vial of poison and prepare a cup of peace from which she and Tristan are to drink. The maidservant substitutes a love potion, so that when the two drink of it, they fall passionately in love.

Tristan und Isolde premiered six years after its completion, in 1865, before young king Ludwig of Bavaria and an audience of notables. Subsequently Wagnerian opera became part of the flavor of the German scene. In fact, as F. O. Mathiessen pointed out in *The Achievement of T. S. Eliot,* the typicality of much of the material in the first two segments of "The Burial of the Dead" is testified to in the following passage from *Letters from America* (published in 1916) in which the author Rupert Brooke describes "the first shocked impression made upon one of his friends by the announcement, 'We're at war with Germany'"[47]

My friend ate and drank, and then climbed a hill of gorse, and sat alone, looking at the sea. His mind was full of confused images, and the sense of strain. In answer to the word 'Germany,' a train of vague thoughts dragged across his brain. The pompous middle-class vulgarity of the buildings of Berlin; the wide and restful beauty of Munich; the taste of beer; innumerable quiet, glittering cafes; the

Ring; the swish of evening air in the face, as one skis down past the pines; a certain angle of the eyes in the face; long nights of drinking and singing and laughter . . . certain friends; some tunes; the quiet length of evening over the Starnbergersee.[48]

It is interesting to note that Marie Larisch had met Wagner when she was young, a meeting that she relates in her autobiography.

"YOU GAVE ME HYACINTHS FIRST A YEAR AGO;
"THEY CALLED ME THE HYACINTH GIRL."

Here begins a situation almost identical to the one depicted in "La Figlia che Piange," a poem ostensibly inspired by a stele of the same name seen by Eliot in 1911 in a museum somewhere in northern Italy.[49] Grover Smith argues that in his poem the poet and the lover are one, namely Eliot himself.[50] Certainly this would fit in with the obsessive recurrence of the love-in-the-garden motif encountered throughout Eliot's poetical and dramatic works. Especially consider the last stanza of "La Figlia che Piange":

> She turned away, but with the autumn weather
> Compelled my imagination many days,
> Many days and many hours:
> Her hair over her arms and her arms full of flowers.
> And I wonder how they should have been together!
> I should have lost a gesture and a pose.
> Sometimes these cogitations still amaze
> The troubled midnight and the moon's repose.

The poet-lover gropes for some reasonable way to part from one with a "fugitive resentment" in her eyes. This is the theme of failed understanding through failed love (as it is a fact undoubtedly of failed love through failed understanding); that is, failed love is an instance of the inability to solve the quandary of solipsism. That it had a basis in Eliot's personal experience I have already speculated but cannot prove. The scene is evoked again in "Portrait of a Lady":

> I remain self-possessed
> Except when a street piano, mechanical and tired
> Reiterates some worn-out common song
> With the smell of hyacinths across the garden
> Recalling things that other people have desired.
> Are these things right or wrong?

Many years later, in the opening section of Burnt Norton, the scene returned, this time with the early hyacinth being converted into the Christian symbol of the rose:

Footfalls echo in the memory
Down the passage which we did not take
Towards the door we never opened
Into the rose-garden. My words echo
Thus, in your mind.

As such it was elaborated in *The Family Reunion*. Leonard Unger has published an exhaustive study of this motif, and his study should be consulted for further examples and details.[51]

Walter J. Ong has ingeniously traced this garden imagery definitively back to Eliot's boyhood experiences with Mary Institute, the girls' school that his grandfather William Greenleaf Eliot founded adjoining the family home on Locust Street, between Jefferson Avenue and Beaumont Street in St. Louis.[52] Ong displays an exacting correlation between the crucial lines in *Burnt Norton* and Eliot's brief account of youthful reminiscences about the institute in a speech proffered for the institute's centennial on 11 November 1958. Eliot remembered once entering the school yard before the last girl had left. Peering into one of the school windows, he met the gaze of one who peered back at him, and he left hastily. Despite being so close by the girls, he said, he remained shy of them. This leaves us to conjecture that this incident played out so many times in his poetry occurred nowhere other than in his youthful and undoubtedly wishful mind.

T. E. Hulme's "Conversion," which influenced "The Death of St. Narcissus," may have inspired Eliot to use the image of the hyacinth. The first two lines read: "Light-hearted I walked into the valley wood / In the time of hyacinths." There the poet is stifled by beauty "like a scented cloth / Cast over."

—YET WHEN WE CAME BACK, LATE, FROM THE HYACINTH GARDEN,
YOUR ARMS FULL, AND YOUR HAIR WET,

In the Ur-text, Eliot had not capitalized hyacinth, indicating once more that he did not initially have in mind any connection of his poem with the vegetative gods myths. Subsequently he brought in through the capitalization a parallel with the garden of Hyacinthus, Greek god of fertility, suggesting further an interpretation of the hyacinth girl as the grail-bearer who, according to Weston, comes from a place of water and flowers, bringing regeneration. On a more personal level, the scene continues from "La Figlia che Piange" with some hint of the story recounted by the garçon in "Dans le Restaurant." At the age of seven, he had attempted sexual relation with a girl even younger than he when the two had taken refuge from a downpour by ducking under some willows. A passing dog frightened him and put an end to his squalid adventure. All that passed over from this poem written in French was the notion of amorous activities in association with being wet. Round about this garden scene, too, is a Pre-Raphaelite aura borrowing mostly in tone from Rossetti's "The Blessed Damozel." The tenuous relationship with "Dans le Restaurant" was probably unconscious and not meant to overlay the idyllic quality of the passage with any patina of decadence.

I COULD NOT
SPEAK, AND MY EYES FAILED, I WAS NEITHER
LIVING NOR DEAD, AND I KNEW NOTHING,

This ambiguous state of being is identical to that described by Dante as he entered the lowest circle of hell:

> Com' io divenni allor gelato e fioco
>   nol domandar, lettor, ch' io non lo scrivo,
>   pero ch' ogni parlar sarebbe poco.

> Io non morii, e non rimasi vivo:
>   pensa oramai per te, s' hai fior d'ingegno,
>   qual io divenni, d'uno e d'altro privo.

> [How icy chill and hoarse I then became
>   ask not, reader, for I write it not,
>   because all speech would be to little avail.

> I did not die, and I did not remain alive:
>   think now for yourself, if you have any grain of ingenuity,
>   what I became, deprived of both the one and the other.][53]

It is a state akin to death, when the mind is extinguished, which also occurs at the moment of enlightenment, especially as represented by the concept of nirvana, which literally means extinction (of self and individual consciousness). Thus it is an ambiguous state in which opposites—death and the fullest consciousness—meet.

Eliot expanded upon this state of mind in *East Coker* 3.18–23:

> Or as, when an underground train, in the tube,
>   stops too long between stations
> And the conversations rises and slowly fades into silence
> And you see behind every face the mental emptiness deepen
> Leaving only the growing terror of nothing to think about:
> Or when, under ether, the mind is conscious but conscious
>   of nothing—
> I said to my soul, be still, and wait without hope.

In his own mind, Eliot seemed to have brought together all states in which the mind is suddenly emptied of all specific content: nirvana, narcosis, and death. Each is in a way a conquest of appearance. Each is transcendental. And in their unexpected identity surely lies some mystery, touched from the side of reason by Bradleyan metaphysics and from the side of faith by religion.

An added dimension, embracing transfiguration, is gained by the passage from Marie Larisch's account of how she returned Marie Vetsera to her home after the girl had come to her seeking asylum and assistance in arranging a rendezvous with Rudolph. She reconciled the girl with her mother, then literally put her to bed:

> I kissed her tenderly, and thought how lovely she looked as she lay back on her pillows. I often think of Mary as I saw her that night—the last she was destined to spend under her mother's roof. She was to know a bitter-sweet hour of love, to drink the wine of passion, and to pass tragically from those on earth. For Mary Vetsera and Another were soon to be numbered with those who "know not anything."[54]

Lingering in Eliot's mind as he wrote this garden scene might have been some lines from the long poem "Loyalty" in Geoffrey Faber's In the Valley of Vision. The poem describes England at war, a picture of gloom interrupted by a romantic glimpse of night that is immediately labeled a "bewitching lie":

> The air is heavy with the scent of may [sic].
> Scarce fifty paces hence,
> Beneath the yellowing moon, a nightingale
> Almost as in the passionate yesterday
> Richens the dark. Almost my senses fail
> For the sound hath sweetness so intense.
> Almost it seems as though again I lay
> In boyish ecstasy,
> Dreaming the unimaginable near,
> Dreaming the whole world dear,
> Dreaming of men as gods, and life as liberty.[55]

"Such spells as these," the poet says ruefully, are "weak ghosts of old enchantment" that "have no power." And finally he avers: "The times do mock such spells."

Poetry of this caliber hardly deserves to be revived, yet there are reasons for this poem to have surfaced in Eliot's memory at this point in the composition of "The Burial of the Dead." It dealt with a subject of deep concern to him, the decline of Europe through warfare and political chaos. In the fragment of "Loyalty" quoted, there are similarities in intent between these words and Eliot's. Both poets dwell upon the nostalgia of a youthful moment. A nightingale sings in "Loyalty" and likewise later in *The Waste Land*. But most specifically, in Faber's poem the protagonist listens to the song of the nightingale on an evening in May and, as he says, "my senses fail," while the poet-lover in the hyacinth garden on an evening in April looks into the face of his beloved and, as he says, "my eyes failed." Such similarities cannot be ignored; they enhance the vaguely mystical character of the garden scene.

There is also peculiar use of the word *nothing* in the context of the poem, here and in "A Game of Chess." Borrowing from Marie Larisch's phrase, "know not anything," "I knew nothing" takes on connotations of transfigurative death. In Buddhistic conceptualizations, the expression means to look into the Void to attain enlightenment. By contrast, in "A Game of Chess," the shrew asks in repetition, "Do / You know nothing? Do you see nothing? Do you remember / Nothing?" Then later she continues her inquest with "Are you alive, or not? Is there nothing in your head?" *Nothing* assumes a sarcastic cast, implying that the target of her nagging has withdrawn into a disturbed silence, another aspect of the Void, the silence of the inner world suddenly thrust into the full impact of solipsistic isolation, the realization that communication is, after all, not taking place.

In any case, knowledge in the poems and plays of Eliot is always incomplete because it is intrinsic to knowledge to be so; that is part of the human condition, and it is impossible, by the very nature of things, to advance a true explanation for this circumstance. That, too, is part of the human condition. We are all pieces to a puzzle designed so that it cannot be solved, and the major spiritual task of humans is somehow to learn to live with that understanding. Whatever resolution may be found can be no more than apparent, or practical; there can be no final solution. Such a solution can only be the object of faith, formulated symbolically, with any transcendental awareness of it confined to the ineffable, the domain of Bradleyan *feeling*.

Like Bradley, Eliot hovered between the real and the practical, agonizing over his inability to find a rapprochement between the two. Truth in the Bradleyan universe is, like all other concepts, a self-contradictory fragment of appearance. "Truth is the whole Universe realizing itself in one aspect."[56] That is real truth, tantamount to the felt Whole. Then there is practical or apparent truth: "there is in the end no truth for us save that of working ideas."[57] The truths cannot meet, except insofar as apparent truth must be subsumed in real truth. If Eliot had been able to abandon these convictions to which Bradley had led him, he might have been able to adopt Catholic dogmas as literal truth; but he never repudiated the Bradleyan position.

LOOKING INTO THE HEART OF LIGHT, THE SILENCE.

Most immediately striking here is the dreamlike inversion of heart of darkness into heart of light, as if to denote the illuminative aspect of Kurtz's terrible and glorious vision. The inversion undoubtedly took place under the influence of the passage from *The Divine Comedy*:

> del cor dell' una delle luci nuove
> si mosse voce, che l'ago alla stella
> parer mi fece in volgermi al suo dove
>
> [from the heart of one of the new lights
> there moved a voice, which seemed to make me
> the needle of a star in turning me to where it was][58]

As in hell voices were emitted from the tip of a flame, so in paradise they come from points of light, a device biblical in origin, since in the Bible the voice of God emerges often from a brightness in the sky. In Dante, too, the voice of God, as well as his immediate presence, is presented from a sphere of bright light.

One should bear in mind, in contemplating this fusion of dark knowledge and illuminative vision, that Eliot has always presented spiritual experience as embracing both the horrible and the sublime. Bradleyan metaphysics demands that opposites be united in the Absolute. Such a synthesis is integral to Eliot's philosophical and religious convictions.

"The silence" holds the same kind of ambiguous fusion. Harry, in *The Family Reunion*, looks back on the day his father died and says, "I remember the silence."[59] Conrad expands this feeling into a broader articulation in *Heart of Darkness*:

> There were moments when one's past came back to one, as it will sometimes when you have not a moment to spare to yourself; but it came in the shape of an unresentful and noisy dream, remembered with wonder amongst the overwhelming realities of the strange world of plants, and water, and silence. And this stillness of life did not in the least resemble a peace. It was the stillness of an implacable force brooding over an inscrutable intention. It looked at you with a vengeful aspect.[60]

Paradoxically the silence holds within it an urgency, beyond ken and yet demanding to be answered, part of that base of human feeling that can move the mind toward some transcendent act, ending in what Eliot described in *Burnt Norton* as a "release . . . surrounded / By a grace of sense, a white light still and moving." This recalls the disturbing feelings that underlie the religious impulse embodied, for example, in the concept of the holy, uniting dread with reverence.

A more positive aspect of this bivalent line may be reclaimed from "Days," a poem by Joseph Campbell in his *Earth of Cualann*, reviewed by Eliot in the *Egoist*, December 1917. There "the silence" is one of enchantment, befitting the idyllic and nostalgic aspect of the garden scene. It is framed by the refrain, "The days of my life / Come and go," which begins and ends the poem. One of these days is "a moon," another "a cloud of gulls." But the first of these days of his life he describes thus:

> One is a black valley
> Rising to blue goat-parks
> On the crowns of distant hills.
> I hear the falling of water
> And the whisper of ferns' tongues.
> And, still more, I hear
> The silence.[61]

Eliot must have been caught somewhat by the economy and crisp imagery of this poem. Campbell is almost Laforguean in his depiction of the moon. And before "the silence" there is the sound of water, paralleling line 356 in "What the Thunder Said." Insofar as this insinuated itself into the recesses of Eliot's mind, the ambience of the poem in which "I hear / The silence" is embedded brought not so much any exact denotation to the meaning that *silence* had for Eliot as a kind of tone.

OED' UND LEER DAS MEER.

[DESOLATE AND EMPTY THE SEA.]

One evening, at the castle of King Marke, Tristan and Isolde are discovered in an embrace, and Melot, one of the king's courtiers, hurtles himself on Tristan, who allows his adversary to stab him. His men take the wounded Tristan back to Kareol, his castle in Brittany, where he awaits Isolde to come and once more heal him. A lookout posted to report any sign of Isolde's approaching ship sings out "Oed' und leer das Meer." Ultimately Isolde does arrive, but too late; Tristan dies in her arms, and she joins him in transfiguration. The king has learned the truth about the switch of the love potion for the death potion and in forgiveness has come to grant Isolde to Tristan, but death has been a swifter traveler.

It is interesting to note that the garden scene, bracketed by the quotations from *Tristan und Isolde*, was originally slated by Eliot to be moved to come between the opening segment of "The Burial of the Dead" and the lines immediately preceding it, beginning "What are the roots that clutch, what branches grow." This would have tightened the Larisch framework, making "I read, much of the night, and go south in the winter" lead right into the first Wagnerian fragment. Perhaps from Eliot's viewpoint the Larisch angle would then have been uncomfortably evident. The intervention of the rock motif, much more obscure within the context of the countess's story, makes the link much less visible. Undoubtedly other matters went into his decision to retain the present order as well, elusive matters hinging on felt continuity, contrast, and other details of taste too elusive to be confidently identified.

MADAME SOSOSTRIS, FAMOUS CLAIRVOYANTE,
HAD A BAD COLD, NEVERTHELESS
IS KNOWN TO BE THE WISEST WOMAN IN EUROPE,
WITH A WICKED PACK OF CARDS.

The mood has shifted from nostalgia, which held a contemplation of past fears and regrets (including moments when sudden knowledge and death seemed almost to come together), to a phantasmagorical sequence evolving around an oblique attempt to read the design of reality. The mechanisms of dream-formation are employed to the utmost. Beginning with the tarot pack as a touchstone from everyday waking reality, bogus cards intrude, fabricated from allusive associations that together help to characterize the whole fortune-telling scene as involving disparate events drawn from every corner of existence. Seen through this distorted perspective, the task of Madame Sosostris is to achieve Bradleyan synthesis through the focus of her cards.

Fortune-telling, as another facet of the quest for significance, is introduced at the very onset of the poem through the figure of the Cumaean sibyl and is carried on by Tiresias. It is intrinsic to the original plan of the poem. Doubtful is it that Eliot needed any single outside source to prompt him in this; it is a natural part of what he was trying to do. Nevertheless, there is a significant parallel with the Larisch framework.

Countess Larisch explains that her aunt Elizabeth was given to certain superstitions and once consulted a "card woman." After the consultation Elizabeth refused to divulge what the woman had told her, except to say that she foretold that the empress would not die in her bed. Elizabeth seemed quite concerned with the manner of her death. Upon experiencing what she took as an actual visitation of King Ludwig after his drowning, she inquired of him also how she would die. He told her that it would be quick and painless.

Eliot named his cartomancer after a make-believe fortune-teller in Aldous Huxley's novel *Crome Yellow*, a light-hearted comedy of manners revolving around the employees at a bank. Eliot read an advance copy of the book at the time he was working on *The Waste Land*. His eye was caught by the act of Mr. Scogan, the manager of the bank, who set up a fortune-telling booth, under the name of Madame Sosostris, at a bazaar sponsored by the bank. At one point, Mr. Scogan expresses himself on religion, recalling that in his youth he was always striving to achieve the proper religious and aesthetic feelings. These are, he says, important for a fuller life. Yet, when he read the mystics, he found their words by and large "claptrap," acknowledging that this must inevitably be the case for anyone not empathetic with the feelings of the mystics. "The written work is simply an attempt to express emotion, which is in itself inexpressible, in terms of intellect and logic. The mystic objectifies a rich feeling in the pit of the stomach into a cosmology. For other mystics that cosmology is a symbol of the rich feeling. For the unreligious it is a symbol of nothing, and so appears merely grotesque. A melancholy fact!"[62] Eliot could scarcely have found a better rationale for his cartomantic episode. Each of the tarot cards is "a symbol of the rich feeling" that a mystic may have "in the pit of the stomach," embodying part of a "cosmology." Abstracted from the cloister of the faithful, these symbolic cards appear "merely grotesque," and this appearance is further enhanced through distortion, a kind of stream-of-consciousness caricature.

To help along the caricature of fortune-telling, *Crome Yellow* had more to offer Eliot than the little speech of Mr. Scogan. It had Priscilla Wimbush, mistress of Crome, a fine country estate. She appears first as she is doing her horoscopes. "Wonderful, isn't it?" she exclaims. "Everything is in the Stars."[63] Mrs. Wimbush was an inveterate gambler, particularly wont to wager on horses and sporting events. "Most of Priscilla's days were spent in casting the horoscopes of horses, and she invested her money scientifically, as the stars dictated."[64] Football is another focus of her astrological wagering, and she imagines the fate of a game entailing "a conflict in the heavens so vast and so complicated" that it was little wonder her predictions were not always correct. She badgers Denis, the narrator, for not believing in such things: "you don't know what it's like to have faith. You've no idea how amusing and exciting life becomes when you do believe. All that happens means something; nothing you do is ever insignificant. It makes life so jolly, you know."[65] Mrs. Wimbush and her weakness for the races did not escape the mesh of Eliot's poetic mind; before he finished this bout with Madame Sosostris, he saw to it that the lady gambler would be enshrined, however invisibly, in his poem.

Grover Smith has pointed out that the double sex of Madame Sosostris, stemming from the assumption of a female name by Mr.

Scogan, ties her on another level to Tiresias, also a seer who enjoyed the identity of both sexes. And, as if that did not make things complicated enough, recently Marion Montgomery revealed an identification of Mr. Scogan with Bertrand Russell, an identification known to Eliot; in fact, Eliot annotated the identification in his copy of the novel. Russell himself assumed that he was the one after whom the character of Mr. Scogan was modeled, although Huxley stated in an interview that the character was based on Norman Douglas.[66] What is important here is what Eliot believed—that he took Mr. Scogan to be Russell.

In his recording of *The Waste Land* Eliot pronounces *clairvoyante* in the french manner, for in French the word means simply one who has a penetrating mind, one who is perspicacious, which is certainly an apt description of Russell, known even then as one of the wisest men in Europe. As for his bad cold, a personal joke might have been involved between Eliot and Russell, but it is known that, according to Marie Larisch, after Rudolph and his young mistress spent a night of passion at Mayerling, the next morning, to evade going out on the hunt with friends who had arrived, he "pleaded a bad cold, did not go out with the guns, and that evening he sat at table with his throat muffled in a silk handkerchief."[67] Whether this possible association of Russell with Rudolph points to any suspected wrongdoing of the former with Vivien Eliot, it may never be known. It would help to explain the otherwise provisional "nevertheless" following "Had a bad cold," as well as place a literal meaning on "wicked." But this is pure speculation; nothing more. An alternative possibility is that Eliot was jibing Russell, at least in his own mind, for his rather notorious philandering.

HERE, SAID SHE,

IS YOUR CARD, THE DROWNED PHOENICIAN SAILOR,

(THOSE ARE PEARLS THAT WERE HIS EYES. LOOK!)

As in a horror film, the first card drawn is that of his dead comrade Jean Verdenal, who perished in the Dardanelles in 1915. He appears later as the ill-fated Phlebas in "Death by Water." He belonged to that youthful world spent in France and Germany contemplated in this whole first section of the poem. Natural, too, that Eliot should be musing on those gone, since he had been informed of his father's death in a telegram received 8 January 1919, which explains the Shakespearean allusion.

In *The Tempest* 1.2.396–404, appears the song from which Eliot quotes. Prospero has sent the airy spirit Ariel to lure Ferdinand, prince of Naples, to his abode, where he is to fall in love with Prospero's daughter Miranda. Through the spirits who attend Prospero, the ship

carrying Ferdinand and his father the king is brought to wreck upon the
shore, and Ferdinand believes his father drowned. Thus Ariel, who is
invisible, sings:

> Full fathom five thy father lies;
>   Of his bones are coral made;
> Those were pearls that were his eyes;
>   Nothing of him that doth fade
> But doth suffer a sea-change
> Into something rich and strange,
> Sea nymphs hourly ring his knell:
>   Burden: Ding-dong.
> Hark! Now I hear them,—ding-dong, bell.

In this the deaths of Jean Verdenal and Eliot's father merge into a single
image, conjuring not simply loss but a material transformation, counterpart to spiritual transfiguration. Grover Smith suggests that Eliot may
have at that time been familiar with Colin Still's *Shakespeare's Mystery
Play: A Study of "The Tempest"* (London, 1921), which tentatively
relates the play to a pagan initiation mystery. I incline to regard this as a
fortuitous circumstance, difficult to fit meaningfully into the context of
the poem in which the line from the play is quoted. Certainly the direct
content of Ariel's song would have been sufficient to motivate reference
to it at this point.

HERE IS BELLADONNA, THE LADY OF THE ROCKS,
THE LADY OF SITUATIONS.

The identity of Belladonna has baffled critics since the first appearance of the poem. Much guessing has been done, much grasping at
thin straws. She has been associated with the deadly plant belladonna,
as well as with the cosmetic made from it and used in ancient times.
More plausibly, she has been identified as the madonna in Da Vinci's
Virgin of the Rocks, wherein the Blessed Mother sits presiding over the
Apocryphal meeting between the Christ child and the infant St. John.
Presumably this makes her a lady of situations, but in fact there is only
one situation, and that hardly substantial enough to warrant the epithet.

Actually, Eliot would have come across the name in Thackery's *Vanity Fair*. Madame de Belladonna, a distinctly minor character never
mentioned in any summarial treatment of the novel, follows Becky
Sharp as mistress to Lord Steyne. She appears only in two chapters of
the book. But in the end she inherits considerable valuables from old
Lord Steyne, among them some jewels, including the "Jew's-eye dia-

mond" that he wore on his forefinger. It is difficult to believe that Eliot would, on that account, stoop to a pun so bad as "the Lady of the Rocks," yet, if he recalled the name as he employed it, he may have chuckled at the ludicrous possibility. Madame de Belladonna was a lady of situations, but again the situations were not really germane to Eliot's intents. It is fairly certain only that *Vanity Fair* first planted the name in his mind.

To find the true identity of Belladonna, one need only turn back to Marie Larisch's autobiography. As she describes her aunt Elizabeth:

> Her life's task was to keep young, and she was always thinking about the best methods by which she could preserve her beauty.
>
> Elizabeth was not a believer in any special face treatment. Sometimes she only used a simple toilet cream; occasionally at night she wore a kind of mask "lined" inside with raw veal; and in the strawberry season she smeared her face and neck with the crushed fruit.
>
> The Empress took warm baths of olive oil, which she believed helped to preserve the suppleness of her figure, but on one occasion the oil was nearly boiling and she narrowly escaped the horrible death associated with many Christian martyrs. She often slept with wet towels around her waist in order to keep its proportions slender, and drank a horrible decoction composed of the whites of five or six eggs mixed with salt for the same purpose.
>
> Once a month Elizabeth's heavy chestnut tresses were washed with raw egg and brandy, and afterwards rinsed with some "disinfectant," as she termed it.
>
> When the actual washing was over, the Empress put on a long waterproof silk wrapper and walked up and down until her hair was dry. The woman who acted as her coiffeuse was hardly ever seen without gloves, which she even wore during the night; her nails were cut close; rings were forbidden her; the sleeves of her white gown were quite short; and it may be almost truthfully asserted that the hairs of Aunt Cissi's head were all numbered.[68]

Elizabeth had made of her beauty an obsession: "Sometimes she became a prey to an unnatural hatred for her children. 'Children are the curse of a woman, for when they come, they drive away Beauty, which is the best gift of the gods,' she once said to me."[69]

Many times Countess Larisch extols the beauty of her aunt, even going into details about her undergarments. Certainly here is a belladonna, a beautiful lady (as the name translates from Italian) *par excellence*. That she qualifies as "the Lady of the Rocks" one may perhaps infer from the following comment she once made to her niece:

> Marie, sometimes I believe that I'm enchanted, and that after my death I shall turn into a sea-gull and live on the great spaces of the ocean, or shelter in the crevice of some frowning rock; then I, the

fettered Elizabeth, shall be free at last, for my soul shall have known the way of escape. If ever I am destined to become old, nobody shall see my face. When once I have been kissed by Time I shall veil myself and people will speak of me as 'The woman who was.'[70]

I have already noted that Elizabeth virtually ruled the life of her niece, even dictating her marriage, making her "The lady of situations"— archetypically one who controls the fates of others.

Why should she appear at this particular point in the cartomancy? One might reasonably expect her to appear somewhere in the proceedings, since they are linked with her having actually consulted a card-woman. Even without this specific connection, she would likely turn up in one guise or another because her presence, along with that of her niece, dominates this whole section. But there is a cue for her entrance in "Those are pearls that were his eyes." "Her fingers were always destitute of rings," Countess Larisch tells us, "but she wore certain ones on a chain round her neck. My aunt adored pearls, of which she possessed quantities of rare and beautiful specimens, and she frequently gave them the "sea treatment" which is supposed to preserve their purity and lustre."[71] Other than the dominant link by subject, there is the one of "sea-change" in Ariel's song and "sea treatment," altogether enough to bring her into the tarot after the "drowned Phoenecian Sailor." One cannot discount the further possibility that the meeting between Eliot and Countess Larisch may have occurred around the time when Jean Verdenal drowned, which would provide additional significance to her card following his.

HERE IS THE MAN WITH THREE STAYES,

Emerging from cards built on private reveries, this is the first real tarot, the three of wands. In his notes to *The Waste Land* Eliot admits that he is "not familiar with the exact constitution of the Tarot pack of cards, from which I have obviously departed to suit my own convenience." Gertrude Moakley has convincingly argued that Eliot familiarized himself with this aspect of cartomancy through Arthur Edward Waite's *The Pictorial Key to the Tarot*.[72] From that book comes the following description of the three of wands:

A calm, stately personage, with his back turned, looking from a cliff's edge at ships passing over the sea. Three staves are planted in the ground, and he leans slightly on one of them.
Divinatory Meanings: He symbolizes established strength, enterprise, effort, trade, commerce, discovery; those are his ships, bearing his merchandise, which are sailing over the sea. The card also signifies able co-operation in business, as if the successful merchant

prince were looking from his side towards yours with a view to help you.[73]

Eliot states in his notes that he associates this personage "quite arbitrarily, with the Fisher King himself," which clarifies virtually nothing. Read traditionally, this card could pertain to Eliot's position at the bank.

AND HERE THE WHEEL

This is, of course, the wheel of fortune, tied by Waite to the vision of the wheel in Ezekiel, "as it were a wheel in the middle of a wheel," apparently four wheels concentrically arranged. The biblical symbolism is obscure but, in general, the wheel in many systems of ancient mythology symbolizes eternity through the idea of a never-ending line, thus either the eternalness of the divine or the endless round of birth, death, and rebirth, as in Hinduism.

Of the divinatory meaning of this tarot card, Waite says that "behind the general notion expressed in the symbol there lies the denial of chance and the fatality which is implied therein"[74] Appearing between "the man with three staves" and "the one-eyed merchant," this card might be interpreted as indicating a continued commitment to commercial enterprise—which for Eliot would have meant continuing on in his job at the bank, another aspect of his concern in those days, for the fatigue from it had helped to bring about his collapse.

AND HERE IS THE ONE-EYED MERCHANT,

Herbert Knust has suggested that this is Wotan, who bartered one of his eyes for a drink from the fountain of life and wisdom, after which the fountain ran dry, portending the fall of the gods.[75] This would, of course, fall in with the other Wagnerian references in "The Burial of the Dead," but alone the allusion is incomplete and almost out of place. Every other pseudotarot figure represents someone within Eliot's personal acquaintance or concern. He seems to have created them specifically to embody his more personal involvements, as part of his Dantean scheme. Wotan by himself does not belong in this gallery.

Looking at it that way, it is not too difficult to identify "the one-eyed merchant" as James Joyce, with whom Eliot was beginning to form a friendship. Joyce had a history of poor eyesight, and, even before 1920, when he began having attacks of irisitis, he was differentiating between his "good" eye and his "bad" one. Soon he was wearing a patch or a black lens over one eye.

Further, Joyce was at that time engaged in a very troublesome matter of marketing his novel *Ulysses*. Eliot had read the first part of it and had helped in the efforts to get it into print. But publishers were afraid of it. Attempts to serialize the work in the *Little Review* resulted in copies being confiscated and booksellers prosecuted. Bluenosers could not comprehend the work's literary innovations. Eliot, however, not only recognized them but saw in *Ulysses* something akin to what he was attempting in poetry, especially in *The Waste Land*: what he characterized in his appreciative essay "*Ulysses*, Order, and Myth" as "a continuous parallel between contemporaneity and antiquity."[76] Plainly, then, the *Ulysses* scandal was of immediate concern to Eliot and was fresh in his mind as he was shaping *The Waste Land*.

Finally, it was generally known, and Eliot was definitely aware, that Joyce had recently suffered a collapse similar to his own, and that he was likewise plagued with financial problems. This alone might have been enough to form a common bond between the two; with all the other considerations, one can imagine that Eliot was sufficiently concerned with Joyce that he might reserve a tarot for him.

AND THIS CARD,
WHICH IS BLANK, IS SOMETHING HE CARRIES ON HIS BACK,
WHICH I AM FORBIDDEN TO SEE.

If Wotan serves as a mythological vehicle for the allusive presentation of Joyce, both come together in being conspicuous for their curiosity and great learning. It was the insatiable thirst for knowledge that caused Wotan to barter away one of his eyes for a magic drink that would ensure him acumen. As for Joyce, his encyclopedic mind was displayed conspicuously in *Ulysses* with its polyglot vocabulary, obscure allusions, and passing references to arcane lore.

On the shoulders of Wotan perch his two ravens, Hugin (thought) and Munin (memory), who whisper in his ears all that they have witnessed in their daily flight over the world. Ostensibly they are what "he carries on his back," and they cannot be seen by Eliot because he "can connect / Nothing with nothing." It was his own thoughts and memories that were troubling him, that he was struggling to put into order.

Metaphorically, Joyce carried on his back the burden of getting his novel published and vindicating his reputation. It was something that Eliot, and everyone else, was "forbidden to see" because censorship forbade its appearance. Perhaps the "blank" card was chosen to symbolize the blank pages left to receive the imprint of the book when it finally would break into print.

A deeper, more tenuous, and doubtlessly unconscious web of associations might also have identified Joyce with the "one-eyed merchant," commencing with Matthew 6:22: "The light of thy body is the eye: if therefore thine eye be single, thy whole body shall be full of light." This might have recalled a passage from the early portion of *Ulysses* that Eliot read:

> —A merchant, Stephen said, is one who buys cheap and sells dear, jew or gentile, is he not?
> —They sinned against the light, Mr. Deasy said gravely. And you can see the darkness in their eyes. And that is why they are wanderers on the earth to this day.[77]

Further evidence that this passage may have influenced Eliot is the appearance in reverse of "jew or gentile" in "Gentile or jew / O you who turn the wheel and look to windward" in "Death by Water." While it would be too much to imply that such a reference was planned, it perhaps was operative on a certain level of the mind.

I DO NOT FIND

THE HANGED MAN.

In the tarot the Hanged Man is the lamed Greek god Hephestus, god of fire, especially of volcanic fire and of fire for forging and smithing. It is interesting to note, though probably fortuitous to the text, that he was assisted in his smithing by the Cyclopes. Eliot says in his notes that he associates the Hanged Man arbitrarily with the god sacrificed by hanging described by Frazer in his study of the fertility myths; hence, he says, he is also associated with the Fisher King. This would be in keeping with Waite's account of the role of the Hanged Man in the tarot pack:

> This is the symbol which is supposed to represent Prudence, and Eliphas Levi says, in his most shallow and plausible manner, that it is the adept bound by his engagements. The figure of a man is suspended head-downwards from a gibbet, to which he is attached by a rope about one of his ankles. The arms are bound behind him, and one leg is crossed over the other. According to another, and indeed the prevailing interpretation, he signifies sacrifice, but all current meanings attributed to this card are cartomancists' intuitions, apart from any real value on the symbolic side.[78]

Then again, Waite denied these interpretations, saying that "we may exhaust all published interpretations and find only vanity," adding that "I will say very simply on my own part that it expresses the relation, in one of its aspects, between the Divine and the Universe."[79] No statement could have been better calculated to appeal to Eliot's innate fascination with the ambiguous. Still, Waite rather tipped his hand in the end by stating that "He who can understand that the story of his higher nature is imbedded in this symbolism will receive intimations concerning a great awakening that is possible, and will know that after the sacred Mystery of Death there is a glorious Mystery of Resurrection."[80]

One need not be more specific than Waite—indeed, cannot be—to comprehend how the Hanged Man fits into the cartomancy scene. He augurs spiritual rebirth, or enlightenment. That he is not found in the deal suggests that full enlightenment is not forthcoming. Nothing in this contradicts the other possible interpretations that Waite records. If the card represents sacrifice, it means that the observer or protagonist has not made the sacrifices necessary for spiritual awakening. Even as an omen of prudence, it could be read as part of Eliot's self-questioning: certainly he felt that many of his decisions and situations into which he had allowed himself to fall indicated a lack of prudence on his part.

Thus he had played out his short game of fortune, consisting in a partial review of issues and people who mattered greatly to him at that particular time. If his wife did not appear more overtly in the game, it was probably because her identity was absorbed into that of Empress Elizabeth. Eliot would also have been careful about how he would present his wife, since she would be a close reader of the text, intimate enough with the details to spot any derogatory representations—as, indeed, she did, when she had Eliot remove the line, "The ivory men make company between us," in "A Game of Chess."

FEAR DEATH BY WATER.

By making "Death by Water" the title of the Phlebas section of the poem, Eliot showed that the phase related, at least in his mind, to the death of his friend Jean Verdenal. That it carried those personal connotations can hardly be denied. But it was part of the method of the poem to universalize the personal; accordingly, there is the usual ambiguous layering of meaning here.

First, there is the sacrificial aspect. Drowning was one of the methods used to make the ritual sacrifice for fertility, as described by Frazer. Frequently an effigy of the fertility god was cast into the river to ensure life-giving spring rains for the following year. Water was one of the most ancient symbols of life. Symbolic drowning of the god was therefore like sending the spirit back to the source to renew itself or, conversely, to infuse the water with life-giving force.

Second, there is the purifying aspect. Water has always been regarded as the universal cleansing agent. It has been part of many rituals of purification from ancient to modern times. Baptism is perhaps the most conspicuous example. Those who are baptized have their sins washed away and can then be reborn pure on the Day of Judgement.

In both these aspects, water has within it the agency of life, whether material or spiritual. To fear death by water is thus to fear rebirth, but it is not simply that the inhabitants wish not to be reborn; they are in awe of it because, for Eliot, it entails both horror and glory—it is a terrible ordeal. From a consideration of the vicissitudes to which he had been subjected, Eliot, on the personal level of the poem, emerges with the tarot fortune: Fear the ordeal of enlightenment and salvation, for it is more terrible than anything yet experienced.

On another level Eliot may have cast the cartomancy scene, albeit obliquely, in more personal terms. The whole death by water motif relies heavily for its source on Shakespeare's *The Tempest*. In the opening shipwreck scene, Gonzalo says of the boatswain: "I have great comfort from this fellow: methinks he hath no drowning-mark upon him; his complexion is perfect gallows. Stand fast, good Fate, to his hanging! make the rope of his destiny our cable, for our own doth little advantage! If he be not born to be hang'd, our case is miserable."

As Eliot probably knew from commentaries, the reference here is to a proverb current in Shakespeare's day, "He that is born to be hanged shall never be drowned." The proverb was recorded in William Camden's *Remains of a Greater Worke, Concerning Britaine* (1605) and somewhat later in George Herbert's *Jacula Prudentum*. It provides a valuable insight into the fortune-telling going on here.

Madame Sosostris does not find the Hanged Man card, indicating that her client—Eliot himself—was not born to be hanged, in which case he should fear death by drowning. Of course, in the hallucinatory mélange of the poem, nothing is quite clear. Although the drowned Phoenician Sailor is not Eliot, one cannot say to what degree he may have identified with him. It does seem certain that the cards drawn in this scene had personal associations for him, and we may never know them all. However, if the scene is of Bertrand Russell telling, or partially determining, the fortune of Eliot, then Belladonna, the beautiful lady of the deadly nightshade, may be none other than Vivien. In any case, the seed has been planted in the subconscious to set up a return to the subject of death by water in the next section of the poem.

I SEE CROWDS OF PEOPLE, WALKING ROUND IN A RING.

The game of fortune is over, the background of experience intrudes once more, reminding us that we are in the space of the mind and the time of eternal memory. We are on the brink of hell, either way you look at it—either the hell of spiritual death or the hell of the terrible ordeal that leads to awakening. It is the same scene that met the eyes of Dante as he first stepped into hell:

> Ed io, che riguardai, vidi una insegna,
>   che girando correva tanto ratta,
>   che d'ogni posa mi pareva indegna;

> e dietro la venia si lunga tratta
>   di gente, ch'io non avrei mai creduto,
>   che morte tanta n'avesse disfatta.

> [And I, who looked, saw an ensign,
>   which whirling ran so quickly
>   that it seemed to scorn all pause;

> and behind it came so long a train
>   of people, that I should never have believed
>   death had undone so many.][81]

Similarly, upon entering the underworld Aeneas beheld throngs of hapless souls moaning at their fate: "Continuò voces audite, et ingens vagitus, que animae infantum flentes in primo limine; quos exsortes dulcis vitae, et raptos ab ubere, atra dies abstulit, et mersit acerbo funere: juxta hos damnati mortis falso crimine." [Immediately voices are heard, and a great wailing, and the souls of infants weeping in the first entrance; whom deprived of sweet life, and snatched from the breast, black time bore away, and plunged in bitter death: near to these, those condemned to death for a false crime.][82] Or consider Marlow's vision of natives mindlessly devoted to the pursuit of ivory, obedient to their master, more living than dead but more dead than spiritually alive:

I went to work the next day, turning, so to speak, my back on that station. In that way only it seemed to me that I could keep my hold on the redeeming facts of life. Still, one must look about sometimes; and then I saw this station, these men strolling aimlessly about in the sunshine of the yard. I asked myself sometimes what it all meant. They wandered here and there with their absurd long staves in their hands, like a lot of faithless pilgrims bewitched inside a rotten fence. The word 'ivory' rang in the air, was whispered, was sighed. You would think they were praying to it. A taint of imbecile rapacity blew through it all, like a whiff from some corpse. By Jove! I've never seen anything so unreal in my life. And outside, the silent wilderness surrounding this cleared speck on the earth struck me as something

great and invincible, like evil or truth, waiting patiently for the
passing away of this fantastic invasion.[83]

Dante is the focus of this allusion, but Virgil and Conrad supply a richer
aura and more threads of connotation to be interlaced through the mesh
of the poem. Eliot knew both these sources intimately. The wailing of
the infants in the Virgilian underworld answers to the "Murmur of
maternal lamentation" in "What the Thunder Said," and the scene of
which Marlow says he has "never seen anything so unreal" in his life
forewarns of the "Unreal city" into which we are soon to be thrust. And,
lest it pass unnoticed, the natives "with their absurd long staves in their
hands" seem like phantasmagoric caricatures of "the man with three
staves."

THANK YOU. IF YOU SEE DEAR MRS. EQUITONE,
TELL HER I BRING THE HOROSCOPE MYSELF:
ONE MUST BE SO CAREFUL THESE DAYS.

It is usual to read Mrs. Equitone as Mrs. Equaltone, taking the name to
connote one who speaks without expression, in a monotone, as might
be expected from one of the living dead. However, the origins of
Madame Sosostris in *Crome Yellow* lead at once to a more satisfactory,
because more specific, interpretation. Abruptly switching from cartomancy to horoscopy and recalling that the framework of Huxley's novel
was fresh in Eliot's mind as he was writing this scene, the abrupt change
here from cartomancy to horoscopy considered in the context of the
novel turns attention from Mr. Scogan to Priscilla Wimbush, who spent
much of her afternoons casting horoscopes for football players and
horses to determine the bets she would later place on races and football
games.

   Thus, the true identity of Mrs. Equitone could stem from the Latin
root word, *equus* (horse), and more particularly, *equitare* (to ride), from
which comes *equitation*. The suffix, -*one*, still operative in the Romance languages (where it may be either -*one*, as in Italian, or -*on*, as in
French and Spanish), is sometimes an augmentative, serving only to
intensify the meaning of the root word. As of Greek origin, the suffix
denotes a female descendant. Applied to Mrs. Wimbush, the meaning
of Equitone becomes clear, for the mistress of *Crome Yellow* was one
who *rode* her bets on the horses. She was in that sense a rider.

   If this explains the personal origins of the name Equitone, fitting that
information into poetic context is relatively easy. Taking a cue from
Crome Yellow, purely as a catalytic force, Eliot began with cartomancy,
in which he reviewed certain persons whom he knew transformed into
tarot figures, then ended with the casting of horoscopes, making the
novel a point of structural reference. But more broadly, he simply

allowed one form of fortune-telling to merge phantasmagorically into another, a natural disjunctive shift within the integrative theme of attempting to read the design of fate or reality. I have already examined the psychological precedents for the particular form that the disjunctive shift took.

Here, at the end of the fortune-telling scene, Eliot has characterized the typical ambience surrounding all forms of augury, the mock seriousness that fools none but those who need to believe. He may even have been ridiculing slightly his own involvements with deciphering the riddle of destiny. He had, after all, just finished a scrutiny of certain phases of his life without coming to any real conclusion.

UNREAL CITY,
UNDER THE BROWN FOG OF A WINTER DAWN,

Leaving the quaint shop of the fortune-teller, one steps out into a city of specters, the city of Baudelaire's "Les Sept Vieillards" (The Seven Old Men), a poem from his *Les Fleurs du Mal* (The Flowers of Evil). This is the "Fourmillante cité, cité pleine de rêves, / Où le spectre en plein jour raccroche le passant!" ["Swarming city, city full of dreams, / Where the specter in broad daylight accosts the passer-by!"] and "Un brouillard sale et jaune inondait tout l'espace" ["A dirty yellow fog drenched the entire space"]. Here the poet meets seven old fearful men and runs home, half-mad, to lock himself in his room. "Ces sept monstres hideux avaient l'air éternel." ["These seven hideous monsters had the air of eternity."] Had there been an eighth, it would have been a "Dégoutant Phénix, fils et père de lui-même" ["Disgusting Phoenix, son and father of himself"], "Mais je tournai le dos au cortège infernal" ["But I turned my back upon the infernal procession"].[84]

In this same city lives the Empress Elizabeth. Her niece, in considering her aunt's fancies, said that she lived in an "unreal world," a world of dreams and artificialities.[85] Royalty meets the frenzied natives of an African village, as Larisch and Conrad blend allusively. Fog, brown or yellow, ubiquitous in Eliot's early poems as symbol of urbanity, hangs in the air like a miasma.

A CROWD FLOWED OVER LONDON BRIDGE, SO MANY,
I HAD NOT THOUGHT DEATH HAD UNDONE SO MANY.

Many times Eliot had seen the crowd of people going to work, walking from Southwark across London Bridge into King William Street, which leads to the Bank of England and Moorgate. He had been one of them, moving toward the bank through the business district, a swarming place spotted with churches that those people, bent on profit and

loss, probably rarely noticed. But Eliot noticed. At the angle formed by
the convergence of King William Street and Lombard Street stands the
Church of St. Mary Woolnoth, erected between 1716 and 1727 and
designed by Nicholas Hawksmoor, a pupil of Wren. It keeps the hour for
this busy district.

In parallel fashion, Dante entered the Gate of Hell whereon was
inscribed:

> Per me si va nella città dolente;
>   per me si val nell'eterno dolore;
>   per me si va tra la perduta gente.
>
> [Through me is the way into the doleful city;
>   through me is the way into the eternal pain;
>   through me is the way among the lost people.][86]

He sees a moving banner, and behind it, "si lunga tratta / di gente, ch'io
non avrei mai creduto, / che morte tanta n'avesse disfatta" ["so long a
train / of people, that I should never have believed, / that death had
undone so many"].[87]

And so the urban landscape of the waste land, already a nexus of real
and imaginary places, after flickering into a momentary glimpse of
London darkens once again to an infernal aspect. It becomes simultaneously the swarming city, the doleful city, the unreal city, an infernal
city precariously balanced halfway between reality and the inner mind.

It is possible that the infernalization of London may be connected
somehow with the Wagnerian strains heard intermittently at the beginning of "The Burial of the Dead." According to Igor Stravinsky, Eliot
had a profound interest in Wagner.[88] True, he never wrote of this
interest, even in his brief commentaries in the Criterion. But his use of
Wagnerian motifs throughout The Waste Land might indicate more than
a desire to implement a certain evocative atmosphere. Indeed, the
recurrence of these operatic allusions structurally mimics the Wagnerian use of the leitmotiv, a short figure, melody, or harmonic progression underscoring situations, personages, objects, or ideas as they
occur in a music drama.

Further, Herbert Knust argues that Wagner foreshadowed the mythic
method, the paralleling of historic with contemporary events or examples, in his operas, familiarity with which Eliot may have had. Wagner
even made the connection between the Grail legend and earlier religious myths, virtually the same drawn by Jessie Weston. In fact, as
Knust also points out, twenty-four years before the publication of From
Ritual to Romance Weston published Legends of the Wagner Drama.
She had, therefore, to have been aware of Wagner's ideas concerning the
genesis of the Grail mythology.[89]

It is difficult to say on what basis Eliot was drawn to the Wagnerian music dramas, but part of the attraction surely lay in the manner in which Wagner assimilated medieval myths to his purposes. Additionally, the aesthetic of the *Gesamtkunstwerk*, the synthesis of the arts, embraced by Wagner bears a resemblance to the allusive method of Eliot.

Against this background, then, "Wagner himself called London a modern counterpart of the underworld of the Nibelungen myth."[90] "London Bridge is falling down" thus would recall the fall of Valhalla.

SIGHS, SHORT AND INFREQUENT, WERE EXHALED,
AND EACH MAN FIXED HIS EYES BEFORE HIS FEET.

Entering the first circle of hell, Dante sees the heathens, those who had lived without baptism or Christianity. Their only torment is to live in constant but unfulfilled desire for God. Many had been men of merit, but their good works were insufficient to gain them grace to ascend to heaven.

> Quivi, secondo che per ascoltare,
>   non avea pianto, ma' che di sospiri,
>   che l'aura eterna facevan tremere:
>
> e ciò avvenia di duol senza martiri,
>   ch'avean le turbe, ch'eran molte e grandi,
>   d'infanti e di femmine e di viri.
>
> [Here, there was not to be heard,
>   plaints, but rather sighs,
>   which made the eternal air tremble:
>
> and this arose from sadness without torments,
>   of the crowds, which were many and great,
>   of children, of women, and of men.][91]

Like wooden soldiers the people march dumbly to work, then back home, alive and yet not fully conscious of their lack of commitment to life, a realization to befall them in hell.

FLOWED UP THE HILL AND DOWN KING WILLIAM STREET,
TO WHERE SAINT MARY WOOLNOTH KEPT THE HOURS
WITH A DEAD SOUND ON THE FINAL STROKE OF NINE.

St. Mary Woolnoth was the only church in the city to remain intact after the air raids of World War II. For Eliot, it was one of those lovely religious monuments that spoke in silent eloquence of the past, the great age of classicism in England. Forlorn in the business district, it may well have reminded him of the Perilous Chapel, where the quester for the Grail must undergo nightmarish visions, temptations, and other tests. Along this line, Robert A. Day has written perceptively:

> If St. Mary Woolnoth is a false or deserted chapel, desecrated and misunderstood, in a wilderness, the "deaf sound" on the stroke of nine becomes a cue for a parody of the Mass and the sacred event which it symbolizes. This bell cannot complete the ringing of the ninefold peal at the elevation of the Host, nor can it truly indicate the ninth hour, at which Christ cried out "I thirst" and was given the insulting hyssop, and afterwards exclaimed, "My God, why hast Thou forsaken me?" and gave up the ghost. We may even go so far as to see in the "dead sound" an echo of the wooden clapper which is substituted for bells at the Good Friday Mass of the Presanctified.[92]

On a more mundane level, nine o'clock was the hour when in London everyone went to work, "a phenomenon which I have often observed," Eliot says noncommittally in his notes. But it is the religious implications, not altogether Christian, that tie the substance of the poem together at this point. Frazer wrote: "On the twenty-fourth of Khoiak, after sunset, the effigy of Osiris in a coffin of mulberry wood was laid in the grave, and at the ninth hour of the night the effigy which had been made and deposited the year before was removed and placed upon the boughs of sycamore."[93]

The effigy was removed so that it could be determined whether or not the grain placed in it had sprouted, thus portending the fertility of the coming year. Naturally this recalls the passage from Corinthians at the heart of the rite for the Burial of the Dead, the passage in which the burying of the dead is likened to the planting of a seed, a simile dominating the rest of this scene.

THERE I SAW ONE I KNEW, AND STOPPED HIM, CRYING: "STETSON!
"YOU WHO WERE WITH ME IN THE SHIPS AT MYLAE!

In structure this owes something to Dante:

> Poscia ch'io v'ebbi alcun riconosciuto,
>   vidi e conobbi l'ombra di colui
>   che fece per viltate il gran rifiuto.

> [After I had recognized some amongst them,
>   I saw and knew the shadow of him
>   who from cowardice made the grand refusal.][94]

Rather irrelevantly here, the figure in question may have been Celestine V, who was elected pope in 1294 at the age of eighty and resigned five months later in favor of Boniface VIII. More generally this is a Dantean device, used throughout *The Divine Comedy* when the poet recognizes one whom he knows among the crowds of the tormented. It was a means of introducing into consideration figures familiar to Dante, real people with whom he wished to deal one way or another.

Eliot would have also encountered such a device in Dryden's *Annus Mirabilis*, a pertinent stanza of which he found quoted by Mark Van Doren in his biography of Dryden:

> Old expert Allen, loyal all along,
>   Famed for his action on the Smyrna fleet;
> And Holmes, whose name shall live in epic song
>   While music numbers, or while verse has feet.[95]

Eliot singled out one whom he calls Stetson, who has been identified by Valerie Eliot in a letter to the *London Times Literary Supplement* as a fellow bank employee. According to Mrs. Eliot, there was an employee named Stetson of whom she thought Eliot may well have heard. At any rate, she wrote that Eliot categorically denied that Stetson represented Ezra Pound (who in those days wore a big black Stetson hat), whom, Eliot said, he would be unlikely to encounter in the business district of London.[96]

Stetson, then, is one like Eliot himself, which makes him "mon semblable" (my double) and "mon frère" (my brother). By placing Stetson and himself "in the ships at Mylae," Eliot further links them in the common pursuit of business. The victory of the Romans over the Carthagenians at Mylae in 260 B.C. marked the beginning of Roman supremacy in naval power and in sea commerce.

"THAT CORPSE YOU PLANTED LAST YEAR IN YOUR GARDEN,
"HAS IT BEGUN TO SPROUT? WILL IT BLOOM THIS YEAR?
"OR HAS THE SUDDEN FROST DISTURBED ITS BED?

Fully elaborated here is the Pauline analogy between burying the corpse and planting a seed, the scriptural heart of the Burial of the Dead rite, itself undoubtedly derived from more ancient antecedents in the mysteries of the vegetative gods. Frazer describes, for example, how in the cult of Osiris an effigy of the god, made of corn bound with earth, is planted in the fall and dug up the following spring to see if the seeds have begun to sprout. Behind all such archetypes is the human longing for renewed life after the bleakness of winter, a longing unknown only in the tropics. This archetypical analogy also appears in Joyce's *Ulysses*, when at Dignam's funeral Bloom exclaims, "Plant him and have done with him,"[97] significant because fragments of this funereal episode found their way into *The Waste Land* at several points. Mixing with this echo may have been a passage from *Tarr* wherein Wyndham Lewis strikes a chord suitably contrapuntal to the Joycean strain:

> The new summer heat drew heavy pleasant ghosts out of the ground, like plants disappeared in winter; spectres of energy, bulking the hot air with vigorous dreams. Or they had entered into the trees, in imitation of pagan gods, and nodded their delicate distant intoxication to him [Tarr]. Visions were released in the sap, with scented explosion, the Spring one bustling and tremendous reminiscence.[98]

Not to be forgotten either were that terrible burial of Marie Vetsera that Countess Larisch had so poignantly described and the recent burial of Eliot's own father. And of course there was Jean Verdenal, who never was really buried.

Taken in their contexts, the source passages for these lines seem to support that they sustain a painful reminiscence, or a painful survey of the past. Memories appear to be concretized in the corpse. And *plant* carries the argotic connotations of burying or hiding.

That the corpse is buried in a garden recalls all that the garden image implies. In the garden, not only in *The Waste Land* but also elsewhere in Eliot's poetry and plays, are buried certain mysterious and painful memories pertaining to something that actually happened or to something merely fancied. Despite recent attempts to give these memories a narrowly homosexual character relating to Jean Verdenal, they remain essentially enigmatic because, as already noted, the roots of the garden image reach back into Eliot's childhood, long before his friendship with the ill-fated French youth. Moreover, the image as expanded in *Burnt Norton* retains explicit childhood associations, proving that it is not centered in Luxembourg Garden, where Eliot recalls spending a sentimental afternoon with his lost friend. Lacking more particular evidence, one must conclude this buried memories passage embodies longings, probably mixed and complex, nostalgically aimed at certain youthful fancies that never came to fruition but that assume haunting proportions when set against the emotionally devastating early years of Eliot's marriage.

"OH KEEP THE DOG FAR HENCE, THAT'S FRIEND TO MEN,
"OR WITH HIS NAILS HE'LL DIG IT UP AGAIN!

Well enough known is the primary source for these lines, "Call for the robin redbreast" from John Webster's play, *The White Devil:*

> Call for the robin redbreast and the wren,
> Since o'er shady groves they hover,
> And with leaves and flowers do cover
> The friendless bodies of unburied men.
> Call unto his funeral dole
> The ant, the field-mouse, and the mole,
> To rear him hillocks that shall keep him warm,
> And, when gay tombs are robbed, sustain no harm;
> But keep the wolf far hence, that's foe to man,
> For with his nails he'll dig them up again.[99]

Webster returned to the image of the wolf as gravedigger again in *The Duchess of Malfi*. Ferdinand, standing over the strangled body of his sister, says:

> Oh, I'll tell thee:
> The wolf shall find her grave, and scrape it up,
> Not to devour the corpse, but to discover
> The horrid murder.[100]

There has been much speculation about why Eliot transformed the wolf into a "Dog." It has been pointed out that both the dog and the wolf appear together on the moon card of the tarot pack, which may have helped to prompt the switch. More to the point, however, Eliot seemed to feel greater sympathy with the dog symbol. There is the fearful dog that intrudes upon the preadolescent seduction in "Dans le Restaurant," and in "Marina" one encounters "Those who sharpen the tooth of the dog, meaning / Death." "Preserve me from the enemy who has something to gain: and from the friend who has something to lose," he wrote in the fifth chorus from "The Rock," continuing some lines later, "Those who sit in a house of which the use is forgotten: are like snakes that lie on mouldering stairs, content in the sunlight. / And others run about like dogs, full of enterprise, sniffing and barking: they say, 'This house is a nest of serpents, let us destroy it.' " Eliot retains the scavenger image of the dog and impregnates it with overtones of disquietude and death.

To account of Eliot's capitalization of the word, the usual explanation plainly fits. "Dog" refers to Sirius, the Dog Star. This star heralded the festival of Sed, apparently intended, according to Frazer, "to procure for the king a new lease of life, a renovation of his divine energies, a rejuvenescence."[101] On the other hand, in the *Aeneid* Sirius burns the sterile fields and lays the land to waste. It therefore carries that implication of opposites that Eliot dearly loved in his imagery. He might have had considerably more difficulty achieving this ambivalence with the wolf.

What makes this symbol so troublesome to interpret is its sheer allusive complexity. However, if one bears in mind its substantive ambivalence, grounded in the portent of both new life and death, the allusive complexity becomes merely accretive to the central opposition. For instance, in the *Satyricon* Trimalchio gives instructions that his "bitch" (as he calls his wife) be placed at the foot of his effigy in his funereal monument; later, after an argument with his wife, he cries, "All right! I'll make you long yet to dig me up again with your fingernails." Eliot may have had this in the back of his mind when in "The Fire Sermon" he wrote of "The broken fingernails of dirty hands." This simply extends the import of the lines from Webster, adds a further dimension to them, but does not make the meaning fuzzy with irrelevancies.

One can deal with the scriptural linkages in like manner. Psalms 22:20 reads "Deliver my soul from the sword; my darling from the power of the dog," and Philippians 3:2 warns "Beware of dogs, beware of evil workers." Dogs in ancient times were scavenger beasts who instilled uneasiness in those who encountered them, especially because they were wild and often ran in packs. Eliot has caught this spirit of the image in "Dans le Restaurant," and the same connotations function here, where the animal threatens the quiet peace of the dead.

As disturber of the buried corpse, the dog is also the agent bringing unrest to the troubled mind, an identity difficult to formulate with psychological precision. Oppressive weight and a kind of persistent nagging are borne within the image, qualities felt also in a precedent passage in *Ulysses*: it depicts a man and a woman frolicking along a beach with their dog. The dog ambles along beside them, "a rag of wolf's tongue redpanting from his jaws," until he sniffs out a "dead dog's bedraggled fell."

Here the dog is "Looking for something lost in a past life,"[102] which identifies him with the "Dog" at least on one level. And can it really be coincidental that Joyce's dog has "a rag of wolf's tongue redpanting from his jaws"? Further, he stumbles on a carcass; he is a dog "vulturing the dead." He would make a suitable archetype for Eliot's purposes here.

To make the association seem even more ironclad, just three pages earlier there appear these absolutely telltale lines that Eliot could not have missed:

Five fathoms out there. Full fathom five thy father lies. At once he said. Found drowned. High water at Dublin bar. Driving before it a loose drift of rubble, fanshoals of fishes, silly shells. A corpse rising saltwhite from the undertow, bobbing landward, a pace a pace a porpoise. There he is. Hook it quick. Sunk though he be beneath the watery floor. We have him. Easy now.[103]

A paragraph further on includes the passage, "A seachange this, brown eyes saltblue." So many feelings shared by Joyce and Eliot at this juncture must have made this section of *Ulysses* accrue to the evocative mood that Eliot was attempting to construct. Further, another dog image from the novel crops up, albeit incidentally, at line 190 of the poem.

Returning to the image of the wolf in *The Duchess of Malfi*, recall that, in unearthing the corpse of the duchess, it would be discovering the guilt of the murderer. Tying that in with the Joycean dog who seeks to dig up the past, it would seem that in this exchange between Eliot, the poet in *The Waste Land*, and Stetson, his double, the former assures himself that guilt is part of the human condition, shared with the hypocrite reader, with all humans,.

The ambivalent value of the "Dog" acquires an additional dimension when it is designated "friend to men." This is play on "man's best friend," a typically Eliotian irony in light of how the beast is symbolically conceived. As disturber of the dead or "something lost in a past life," the dog can bring about a therapeutic catharsis or can disrupt the process of rejuvenation. It is a manikin of the mind upon which many virtues and sins may be displayed, in turn or simultaneously, as one chooses to perceive it.

"YOU! HYPOCRITE LECTEUR!—MON SEMBLABLE,—MON FRÈRE!"
["YOU! HYPOCRITE READER!—MY LIKENESS,—MY BROTHER!"]

Coming to the end of this first essay into introspective poetic rumination, the poet suddenly draws the reader in, proclaiming that these confusions and torments, incompleted ecstasies, cryptic insights, questing urges, all touch the common human soul, characterize the human condition. Ascending to heaven involves, as for Dante, descending into hell; the glory of the one entails the terror of the other.

"C'est le Diable qui tient les fils qui nous remuent!" exclaims Baudelaire in the preface "Au Lecteur" [To the Reader] to his *Les Fleurs du Mal*: [it is the Devil who holds the strings that move us]. "Chaque jour vers l'Enfer nous descendons d'un pas" [each day toward Hell we descend a step]. We are plagued by many vices, but among them there is one, "plus laid, plus méchant, plus immonde" [most ugly, most evil, most vile], which, "Quoiqu'il ne pousse ni grands gestes ni grands cris" [although it raises neither great gestures nor great cries], will one day level the earth and swallow it whole:

> C'est l'Ennui!—L'oeil chargé d'un pleur involontaire,
> Il rêve d'échafauds en fumant son houka.
> Tu le connais, lecteur, ce monstre délicat,
> —Hypocrite lecteur,—mon semblable,—mon frère!

[It is boredom!—Eye charged with an involuntary tear,
It dreams of gallows, while smoking its opium pipe.
You know it, reader, this delicate monster,
—Hypocrite reader,—my likeness,—my brother!][104]

After all, the "Unreal City" is Everywhere, and everyone dwells in it.
As Eliot wrote later in *Murder in the Cathedral*, "All things are unreal /
Unreal or disappointing."[105]

4

A Game of Chess

"A Game of Chess" is, aside from the much briefer "Death by Water," the least oblique section of *The Waste Land*. Although dimorphic, it is fixed around a single thematic center; both episodes illuminate that center. The mode of exposition is alternately purely descriptive or narrative. Allusion mainly adds depth to the meaning, which is apparent at the surface.

Conceptually this section seems to have grown out of the uncompleted poem "The Death of the Duchess," which appears in the facsimile edition of *The Waste Land* manuscript. The uncompleted poem was composed on the same typewriter used for parts 1 and 2 of *The Waste Land*, indicating that it belonged to the same inspiration from which the larger work evolved. Indeed, it revolves around the same concern that "A Game of Chess" does: alienation within the bond of marriage.

It seems safe enough to say that the duchess is some transformation of Vivien Eliot, for the situation described between her and her male partner is identical to that between Eliot and his first wife. The setting is Hampstead where "there is nothing new / And in the evening, through lace curtains, the aspidistra grieves," where "The inhabitants . . . are bound forever on the wheel." It is the urban scene of the wasteland, modified from Baudelaire. "In the evening people hang upon the bridge rail / Like onions under the eaves." They are imagined strange creatures with dog's eyes and heads like birds with "beaks and no words." Then comes the question, "What words have we?" Suddenly the predicament is clear: two people together but alone, solipsistically isolated from each other. It is caught in a Prufrockian manner: "I should like to be a crowd of beaks without words / But it is terrible to be alone with another person."

As in earlier poems, Eliot's male protagonist muses silently to himself while the duchess speaks. "My thoughts tonight have tails," he thinks to himself, "but no wings. / They hang in clusters on the chandelier / Or drop one by one upon the floor." He watches the duchess:

Under the brush her hair
Spread out in little fiery points of will
Glowed like words, then was suddenly still.
      into

'You have cause to love me, I did enter you in my heart
Before ever you vouchsafed to ask for the key.'

The allusive method recalls the world of John Webster, and the lady in
the poem becomes the duchess of Malfi. She is sitting in her bed-
chamber, brushing her hair and flirting with her surreptitious husband,
Antonio. Good-natured repartee passes between them, with Cariola, the
maidservant, joining in. At Antonio's behest, he and Cariola withdraw
to the adjoining room, as the duchess becomes so absorbed in combing
her hair that she will not notice them depart. Antonio wishes to anger
her slightly, in a teasing manner, for he says he loves to see her thus.
However, as she speaks, addressing her departed husband, her brother
Ferdinand enters unannounced to overhear her incriminating remarks:

Duchess. Doth not the colour of my hair 'gin to change?
    When I wax grey, I shall have all the court
    Powder their hair with arras, to be like me.
    You have cause to love me; I enter'd you into my heart
    Before you would vouchsafe to call for the keys.

At this point Ferdinand enters to hear the duchess muse upon the
sweet pleasure of love mixed with a sense of danger. As she says, "For
know, whether I am doom'd to live or die, / I can do both like a prince,"
he hands her a poniard, adding, "Die, then quickly!"[1] The duchess
protests her innocence, saying that she is lawfully married, but her
brother will hear none of it. Harboring what seems an incestuous
jealousy for his sister, he can see only that she has been defiled, and he
feels bloodthirsty for Antonio, whose identity he has yet to discover. He
warns the duchess that, if she expects her lover to survive, she had best
lock him away where he can speak only to dumb animals who can tell
no tales, and she were well to cut out her own tongue, lest it betray her.[2]
    The duchess protests but to no avail. Ferdinand leaves, vowing never
to see his sister again; he leaves to set into motion the plan to drive her
mad and then have both her and her husband killed.
    One can hardly guess in what way Eliot may have read this scene into
his own circumstances. It is not known how his courtship of Vivien
proceeded, except that it was apparently a rather hurried affair. It is
possible that Eliot fell into it more precipitously than he later found
wise, that Vivien, like the duchess, had entered him into her heart
before he would have vouchsafed to call for the keys.

In "The Death of the Duchess," the protagonist entertains two possibilities: he could tell the duchess he loves her, or he could tell her that he does not love her. Again in a Prufrockian tone of "Would it have been worthwhile," he concludes that either way would make no difference:

> We should say: This and this is what we need
> And if it rains, the closed carriage at four.
> We should play a game of chess
> The ivory men make company between us
> We should play a game of chess
> Pressing lidless eyes and waiting for a knock upon the door.
>
> 'When I grow old, I shall have all the court
> Powder their hair with arras, to be like me.
> But I know you love me, it must be that you love me.'
>
> I am steward of her revenue
> But I know, and I know she knew . . .

Thus, the poem ends with a distinct return to *The duchess of Malfi*, but there are some interesting changes from the Webster tragedy. "You have cause to love me . . ." is replaced by "But I know you love me, it must be that you love me," a much more uncertain and desperate plea, one that might better have suited the Vivien Eliot side of the character. Then, as if presuming the duchess dead, the protagonist becomes "steward of her revenue," hardly a remorseful role. The only hint of remorse is that "I know, and I know she knew," which could be construed in many biographical ways. For poetic purposes, it need not be specified; it simply suggests that neither really loved the other.

By projecting himself and Vivien into the roles of Antonio and the Duchess of Malfi, Eliot transforms the rather desperate idyll of the original into a solipsistic quandary to be escaped only through death, a common fantasy of one who feels trapped by circumstances that threaten to undermine the very soul. Miller believes that the secret Eliot and his wife shared was his supposed homosexual relationship with Jean Verdenal.[3] I believe, however, that the evidence for Miller's hypothesis is too thin and too open to alternative interpretations. Just as plausible would be that, in a disastrous marriage, impotence intervened to express silently what words refused to say.

At any rate, this feeling of alienation in marriage was carried over as the principal theme from "The Death of the Duchess" to "A Game of Chess," a section of *The Waste Land* originally to be called, apparently after the short story of the same title by Henry James, "In the Cage." An unnamed girl in the James story works in a telegraph office, where she delights in vicariously partaking of the lives of others. She dreams especially about the details of the amorous adventures of the wealthy. On occasion she even becomes involved in their escapades. But in the end she surrenders her life of vicarious enterprise to marry her fiancé.

The cage in this instance becomes, from the enclosure in which the girl works, a symbol of solipsistic isolation, from which others can be reached but only vicariously. In other words, communication between the one in the cage and those outside is more apparent than real. Then, too, the very expression *in the cage* connotes being on public display and being made simply an object of observation, like the sibyl of Cumae suspended before the crowd in her glass jar. Strangely, the girl in the cage at the telegraph office made others the objects of her wistful observations, introducing just the kind of ambiguous reversal that always attracted Eliot.

But he decided to change the title of this section of his poem to "A Game of Chess," which can be related either to Thomas Middleton's *A Game at Chesse* or to the game of chess in the second scene of the second act of his *Women Beware Women*, or to both. In *A Game at Chesse*, Middleton portrayed the rivalry of England with Spain and the projected marriage between the two royal houses unsuccessfully negotiated in 1623. The English were designated as the white chessmen and the Spanish as the black. By implication life was reduced to a game, analogous no doubt in Eliot's mind to the actual chess games that he and Vivien played together to wile away hours of lonely boredom.

The game of chess in *Women Beware Women* is fraught with more subtle complications. It concerns the seduction of Bianca, a character based on Bianca Capello, mistress of Francesco de' Medici. She is married to a merchant's clerk, Leantio. One day, espying her at her window, the duke is smitten with her and sets about to seduce her. The seduction occurs while the mother of Bianca has her attention diverted in a chess game. For the sake of a doubtfully conceived honour, the duke has Leantio murdered so that he may wed Bianca. So involved does this manoeuver become that it leads in the end to a wholesale slaughter of the characters.

The meaning of the chess game transported from the play into the poem is rather tenuous. Certainly the notion of deception carries over, but that makes for a rather vague allusion. It perhaps would be more sensible to take the game of chess in its most obvious symbolic implication, that the marriage depicted in the poem is like a complex game; and look further for the meaning of the specific linkage to Middleton.

Eliot has given us the necessary clues in his essay on Middleton. There he remarks that, unlike Shakespeare or Jonson, "[h]is greatness is not that of a peculiar personality": "He remains merely a name, a voice, the author of certain plays, which are all of them great plays. He has no point of view, is neither sentimental nor cynical; he is neither resigned nor disillusioned, nor romantic, he has no message. He is merely the name which associates six or seven great plays."[4] In other words, Middleton simply reflects the situations without coloring them with his own values. Eliot seems to have been reaching toward the same emotionless objectivity in "A Game of Chess" possibly because it was the only way he could deal with the underlying personal experience of the episodes without breaching decorum. And there is a further dimension of the style of Middleton that Eliot may have had a mind to explore in that section. Arthur Symons put his finger on it in describing *A Game at Chesse*:

> Banter turns into a quite serious and clear and bitter satire; burlesque becomes a severe and elegant thing; the verse, beginning formally and always kept well within bounds, is fitted with supreme technical skill to this new, outlandish matter; there are straight confessions of sins and symbolic feasts of vices, in which a manner acquired by the city chronologer for numbering the feasts and feastings of the city is adapted by him to finer use.[5]

Much of the description would apply with equal justice to "A Game of Chess," in which banter turns into biting satire; burlesque, in the pub scene for instance, is carried off with classical detachment, sins are confessed, and all is retold with almost journalistic starkness, noncommittal reportage.

Finally, if his titular allusion was meant to infuse Bianca into the unnamed person in the opening scene of "A Game of Chess," that too would be well within the spirit of the section. "Bianca," Eliot asserts in his essay on Middleton, "is a type of the woman who is purely moved by vanity."[6] He also says she is "a real woman," and not a dramatic stereotype. Thereby she is linked, in her vanity and humanness, with the Empress Elizabeth and probably also with Vivien Eliot.

Like every other aspect of *The Waste Land*, the names of the sections do not devolve to a single meaning. Evocative symbolism was deliberately exploited. It would be foolish to attempt to state the significance of the section titles in any simple formula. The evocations in the title "A Game of Chess" can hardly be further reduced. They belong to the living semantic tissue of the poem.

However, to restate without amplification, "A Game of Chess" connotes most superficially the feeling that life is kind of game, and that meaning is limited within the confines of the rules of the game, whatever they might be. More pointedly, the game is that of love, one of the most poignant efforts to escape solipsism. But solipsism has the closure of a game; there is no real escape from it, except symbolically or transcendentally.

Specific coloration, or a kind of feeling tone, is lent to this game concept through allusion to Bianca, Empress Elizabeth, Vivien Eliot, and the other figures introduced referentially. And it is played out on two different social levels. It has some of the complexity of the real game of life, which for Eliot most personally was the game he and Vivien played in the evening hours, a game that brought them together and yet, symbolizing boredom, entered as a wedge to keep them emotionally apart.

Synopsis: "A Game of Chess"

A woman, unvisaged, sits in a room almost rococo in elaborate detail, described with a richness reminiscent of the opening of Baudelaire's "Une Martyre." She is never more than a spirit figure whose presence haunts the room. At first she has the character of Cleopatra, a regality that seems to thin and evaporate as the scene unfolds. With the close of the descriptive passage, she transforms into the duchess of Malfi; then, as she speaks, while retaining Websterian traits of expression, she becomes quite definitely Vivien Eliot.

As she complains and nags at the protagonist—Eliot himself, if one reads the section autobiographically—he entertains thoughts of death, finally growing so distracted that a nonsense song breaks through what she is saying, almost as if to parody her monologue as the same old song gone berserk. The two are caught in a listless boredom that they fill with a slow mutual destruction, with the woman the initiator and the man passive, there only to be her foil. The final line, "Pressing lidless eyes and waiting for a knock upon the door," indicates the interminable extent of the unilateral exchange.

Next we are in a pub, listening in on the retelling of the domestic calamities of Lil and Albert, a couple quite obviously from the lower class of society. It is near the end of day, and the proprietor wishes to close the pub. The tale is a familiar one, simple and direct, ungarnished with any allusive overlays. In it marriage looms as a pointless trap, an inevitable wreck of incompatibilities. There is no nobility in this tragedy. It is lowly, and in its obvious crudity is displayed the same ugliness that is also present in the first scene but less evident because it is embedded in a milieu of luxury. In a way, then, the pub scene completes the opening episode by extrapolating the underlying tones and placing them into sharper relief.

Consonant with the overall structure of the poem, the section closes as the pub scene melts away dreamlike, the tipsy imbibers departing, the woman who was speaking suddenly transforming into the mad Ophelia, sister of Hamlet. With this final transformation, striking a chord of insanity, the infernal aspect of the waste land is reaffirmed.

THE CHAIR SHE SAT IN, LIKE A BURNISHED THRONE,
GLOWED ON THE MARBLE,

It is widely known that these lines transform from Shakespeare's description of Cleopatra in her royal barge:

> The barge she sat in, like a burnished throne,
> Burned on the water; the poop was beaten gold;
> Purple the sails, and so perfumed that
> The winds were love-sick with them; the oars were silver,
> Which to the tune of flutes kept stroke, and made
> The water which they beat to follow faster,
> As amorous of their strokes. For her own person,
> It beggar'd all description; she did lie
> In her pavilion—cloth-of-gold of tissue—
> O'er-picturing that Venus where we see
> The fancy outward nature: on each side her
> Stood pretty dimpled boys, like smiling Cupids,
> With divers-colour'd fans, whose wind did seem
> To glow the delicate cheeks which they did cool,
> And what they undid did.
>   (O, rare for Anthony!)
> Her gentlewomen, like the Nereides,
> So many mermaids, tended her i' the eyes,
> And made their bends adorning: at the helm
> A seeming mermaid steers: the silken tackle
> Swell with the touches of those flower-soft hands,
> That rarely frame the office. From the barge
> A strange invisible perfume hits the sense
> Of the adjacent wharfs. The city cast
> Her people out upon her; and Anthony
> Enthron'd i' the market-place, did sit alone,
> Whistling to the air: which, but for vacancy,
> Had gone to gaze on Cleopatra too
> And made a gap in nature . . .[7]

Aside from the initial image, Eliot seems to have followed also the brocaded style of that passage with its Titianesque vocabulary and complex sentence structure. The change from "barge" to "Chair," natural enough in the boudoir setting of the poem, probably owed something unconsciously to a doggerel couplet that Edward Fitzgerald wrote for his friend Thackeray. It is from "To Will Thackeray," and Eliot would have come across it in Benson's biography of Fitzgerald, lines from which found their way into *Gerontion*.

> The chair that Will sat in I sit in the best,
> The tobacco is sweetest which Willy has blest.[8]

Eliot's lady has no specific identity, though she is closest to the duchess of Malfi and Vivien Eliot, as was the case in her appearance as female protagonist in "The Death of the Duchess." Fleetingly she takes on some of the beauty and mystery of Cleopatra. Her surroundings are regal, recalling Belinda's dressing table in *The Rape of the Lock*, the boudoir of Imogen in *Cymbeline*, and the fancied luxury of Marie Larisch and the Empress Elizabeth. More morbidly they have the same aura that surrounds the bedroom of the lust-murdered decapitated woman in Baudelaire's "Une Martyre":

> Au milieu des flacons, des étoffes lamées
>   Et des meubles voluptueux,
> Des marbres, des tableaux, des robes parfumées
>   Qui trainent à plis somptueux,
>
> Dans une chambre tiède où, comme en une serre,
>   L'air est dangereux et fatal,
> Où des bouquets mourants dans leurs cercueils de verre
>   Exhalent leur soupir final . . .

> [Amidst flasks, rich brocades
>   And voluptuous furnishing,
> Marble statues, paintings, perfumed dresses
>   Which trail in sumptuous folds,
>
> In a tepid room where, as in a hothouse,
>   The air is dangerous and fatal,
> Where bouquets dying in their glass coffins
>   Exhale their final breath . . .][9]

WHERE THE GLASS
HELD UP BY STANDARDS WROUGHT WITH FRUITED VINES
FROM WHICH A GOLDEN CUPIDON PEEPED OUT
(ANOTHER HID HIS EYES BEHIND HIS WING)

Critics have tended to look to French sources for the "Cupidon," despite the plain fact that in his recorded version of the poem Eliot gives the word an English pronunciation.[10] There is precedent for using it as an English word in the twelfth canto of the fifteenth book of Byron's *Don Juan*, a description of the peerless lover:

> His manner was perhaps the more seductive,
> Because he ne'er seem'd anxious to seduce;
> Nothing affected, studied, or constructive
> Of coxcombry or conquest: no abuse
> Of his attractions marr'd the fair perspective,
> To indicate a Cupidon broke loose,
> And seem to say, "Resist us if you can"—
> Which makes a dandy while it spoils a man.

Eliot uses the word not so much in the oblique sense of a lady-killer, one who dandifies himself for amorous exploits, as in the direct denotation of a Cupid, yet the former connotation may not be entirely out of place in these lines.

The Cupidons have a rich heritage in which numerous strands of allusion intersect. In Imogen's boudoir, described in act 2, scene 4 of Shakespeare's *Cymbeline*, hangs a picture of the meeting of Anthony and Cleopatra, which ties in with the opening two lines of this section. Further:

> The roof o' th' chamber
> With golden cherubins is fretted. Her andirons—
> I had forgot them—were two winking Cupids
> Of silver, each on one foot standing, nicely
> Depending on their brands.

This recalls Cleopatra in her barge, and "on each side her / Stood pretty dimpled boys, like smiling Cupids." And this web is completed within the context of the source of the following line.

DOUBLED THE FLAMES OF SEVENBRANCHED CANDELABRA

In Exodus 25:31–32, God ordains that a sevenbranched candelabra, actually a lamp holder, be made for his tabernacle:

> And thou shalt make a candlestick of pure gold; of beaten work shall the candlestick be made: his shaft, and his branches, his bowls, his knobs, and his flowers shall be of the same.
> And six branches shall come out of the sides of it; three branches of the candlestick out of the one side of it, and three branches of the candlestick out of the other side.

Later, at 37 : 7–9, there is a significant description of the finished tabernacle:

> And he made two cherubim of gold, beaten out of one piece made
> he them, on the two ends of the mercy seat. . . .
> And the cherubim spread out their wings on high, and covered
> with their wings over the mercy seat, with their faces one to another.

Thus the cherubim are transformed into Cupids, and the Cupids, in
the instance of the *Cymbeline* passage, pass from silver into gold. In
this rather complicated interchange, the room of the mysterious lady
assumes for a moment an air of sanctity, as if the mind perceiving it
flickered from the oppressive hothouse boudoir of marital frustration to
an imagined atmosphere in which the relationship about to be contemplated might offer some hope of salvation.

REFLECTING LIGHT UPON THE TABLE AS
THE GLITTER OF HER JEWELS ROSE TO MEET IT,
FROM SATIN CASES POURED IN RICH PROFUSION;
IN VIALS OF IVORY AND COLOURED GLASS
UNSTOPPERED, LURKED HER STRANGE SYNTHETIC PERFUMES,
UNGUENT, POWDERED, OR LIQUID—TROUBLED, CONFUSED
AND DROWNED THE SENSE IN ODOURS; STIRRED BY THE AIR
THAT FRESHENED FROM THE WINDOW, THESE ASCENDED
IN FATTENING THE PROLONGED CANDLE-FLAMES,

There is much of French syntax here, recalling the perfume flasks, the
flower-scented air of Baudelaire's martyred woman, and simultaneously
echoing the "strange invisible perfume" wafting from Cleopatra's barge.
In fact, the "robes parfumées / Qui trainent à plis sumptueux" [per-
fumed dresses / Which trail in sumptuous folds] correlate perfectly
with the purple sails of Cleopatra's barge "so perfumed that / The winds
were love-sick with them." As the perfume from the barge "hit the
sense," so the strange synthetic perfumes of the mysterious lady "troubled, confused / And drowned the sense."

All that stirs in the room is a slight breath of air "freshened from the
window." But it is not really sufficient to dispel the impression of an
atmosphere made stifling by an excess of synthetic fragrances.

FLUNG THEIR SMOKE INTO THE LAQUEARIA

Eliot refers readers to *The Aeneid*, to part of a description of a feast
given by Dido in honor of Aeneas and his Trojan compatriots. There
"dependent lychni laquearibus aureis incensi, et noctem flammis

funalia vincunt" [the lighted lamps hang down from the golden ceiling, and the night with flaming torches is vanquished].[11] To this feast Venus sends her son Cupid, disguised as Ascanius, son of Aeneas, and when Dido embraces the boy, he smites her with love for Aeneas. Later, however, when Aeneas leaves Carthage, Dido kills herself in grief. Even in this noblest of all epics, which Eliot took to be the epitome of civilized expression, love fails those who give themselves over to it.

STIRRING THE PATTERN ON THE COFFERED CEILING.
HUGE SEA-WOOD FED WITH COPPER
BURNED GREEN AND ORANGE, FRAMED BY THE COLOURED STONE,
IN WHICH SAD LIGHT A CARVÈD DOLPHIN SWAM.

In this dolphin lies one of the unresolved enigmas of the poem. Classical literature contains many references to the dolphin, including the famous story told by Pliny of the dolphin who carried a boy on its back across a lake to school every morning. But none of these refer to a "carvèd dolphin." Thucydides mentions a weight of iron or lead, apparently shaped like a dolphin, hung at the yardarm, that was sometimes let down suddenly on an enemy ship, but this hardly fits the context here. Not much closer is the association with the Delphic oracle of Apollo. Δελφίς is the Greek for *dolphin*, the creature having been tied somehow into the Apollo mythology. While this would fit in with the prophetic theme of the poem, it would not really elucidate the image.

According to the lore of the sea, the appearance of a dolphin is a favorable omen, since the creature is considered friend to man. As such an omen the dolphin passes briefly through an episode described by Dante, but again the reference is no more than peripheral to what Eliot is doing here. From sea lore, the emblem of the dolphin passed into early Christian symbolism, invoking charity and friendship, in which guise it would make sense here: the symbol of love and charity being consumed by "green and orange" flames suggesting the lust about to be enunciated in the Philomel legend.

Perhaps the actual imagery Eliot spun around the dolphin owed something reminiscently to John Donne's *The Progresse of the Soule*, in which the fate of the soul of the apple eaten by Eve is traced from creature to creature, allowing Donne to comment satirically on the relativity of good and evil. By the thirty-second stanza, the soul has entered "Into an ambrion fish," from whence it emerges a whale, and:

> Swimme in him swallow'd Dolphins, without feare,
> And feels no sides, as if his vast wombe were
> Some inland sea, and ever as hee went

> Hee spouted rivers up, as if he ment
> To joyne our seas, with seas above the firmament.

When Donne wrote this poem in 1601 he "still had an emotional attachment to Catholicism, but his animus against the queen and the world in general was more than religious," as Douglas Bush writes:

> A serious text, the entire relativity of good and evil, is plainly stated in the abrupt conclusion, though it has not been worked out. The poem is obviously another product of Jack Donne's conventional libertine naturalism. One impression left is of nature red in tooth and claw, but that is submerged in a kind of brutal sexuality; the young man who in a few months was to marry for love dwells with mingled gloating and loathing upon a succession of animal couplings.[12]

Eliot, with similar animus—he called it a "grouse"—against the world, contemplated with more loathing than gloating the animal couplings of man, a parallel in spirit possibly strong enough for him to recall, at least unconsciously, the work of Donne, extracting from it "swimme" and "Dolphins" to transmute them into his own poetic coinage.

ABOVE THE ANTIQUE MANTEL WAS DISPLAYED
AS THOUGH A WINDOW GAVE UPON THE SYLVAN SCENE
THE CHANGE OF PHILOMEL, BY THE BARBAROUS KING
SO RUDELY FORCED;

In the Ur-text Eliot had originally written:

> Above the antique mantel was displayed
> In pigment, but so lively, you had thought
> A window gave upon the sylvan scene,
> The change of Philomel, by the barbarous king
> So rudely forced

Above the mantel hangs a painting depicting one of the most lurid tales in all of classical mythology. Philomel was the daughter of Pandion, king of Athens. Her sister Procne, pining to see her after a long separation, prevailed upon her husband, Tereus, king of Thrace, to obtain permission from Pandion to bring her to Thrace. This Tereus did, but on the way from Athens he raped Philomel and, after cutting out her tongue, left her in a lonely place to die. According to the version of the story in Ovid's *Metamorphoses*, he even raped her a second time, after removing her tongue so that she could not relate his crime to anyone. However, Philomel wove her terrible fate into a tapestry, which she then had conveyed to her sister. To avenge the deed, Procne murdered her son and served him up for dinner to his father. Upon learning of his wife's treachery, Tereus drew his sword upon her and her returned sister, but as he did he was turned into a hoopoe, Philomel into a nightingale, and Procne into a swallow.

This painting is so unusual because it seems a window giving upon "the sylvan scene," which is how Milton described the Garden of Eden before the Fall, as seen by Satan. It is as if the rape of Philomel represents the satanic vision of innocent love, or that, at the extreme, love degenerates into empty lust and violence, just another manifestation of the imperfection of man.

An interesting parallel use of the word *force* appears in a discussion of the *Elucidation* in Jessie Weston's *From Ritual to Romance*. The *Elucidation* is a Grail text often prefixed to the poem of Chretien de Troyes, *Perceval*.

> It opens with the passage quoted above in which Master Blihis utters his solemn warning against revealing the secret of the Grail. It goes on to tell how aforetime there were maidens dwelling in the hills who brought forth to the passing traveller food and drink. But King Amangons outraged one of these maidens, and took away from her her golden Cup:
>
> > *One of the maidens he took by force*
> > *And from her seized her golden cup.*
>
> His knights, when they saw their lord act thus, followed his evil example, forced the fairest of the maidens, and robbed them of their cups of gold. As a result the springs dried up, the land became waste, and the court of the Rich Fisher, which had filled the land with plenty, could no longer be found.[13]

Not only the Fisher King but also the waste land itself is mentioned, to make the passage stand out in Eliot's mind. Then there is the rather obvious correspondence between this story and that of the three Rhine Maidens who appear symbolically in "The Fire Sermon." Undoubtedly any influence that the Weston passage may have had on these lines was largely unconscious.

> YET THERE THE NIGHTINGALE
> FILLED ALL THE DESERT WITH INVIOLABLE VOICE
> AND STILL SHE CRIED, AND STILL THE WORLD PURSUES,
> "JUG JUG" TO DIRTY EARS.

In his description of the centers of worship of the vegetation gods in Asia Minor, Frazer noted one that was approached through ravines walled by steep precipices of red and grey rock, beyond which was the valley where the actual place of worship was, "with its cool bracing air, its mass of verdure, its magnificent stream of pure ice-cold water—so grateful in the burning heat of summer—and its wide stretch of fertile land, the valley may well have been the residence of an ancient prince or high priest." He went on to say that "the place is a paradise of birds" where "the thrush and the nightingale sing full-throated."[14] Outside, surrounding this holy place, were vast stretches of desert. Certainly Eliot's waste land is in some mysterious way a place haunted by birds, where birds seem almost out of place and therefore phantasmagorical. Here, as if Philomel had been carried to the valley of life, far off and unseen, the nightingale is heard across the silent sands of the desert waste land, its voice pure and beyond violation.

Still the world pursues it, feigning worship, ready to violate it if it should be found. Eliot originally had the nightingale cry into the dirty ears of "death," then of "lust," and finally the present truncation was adopted. Perhaps simply "dirty ears" connotes successfully what may lie between death and lust or what may encompass both. Pure songs cannot be heard as pure by impure ears.

The song the nightingale sings is an onomatopoeia much used by the Elizabethans. For instance, the model for its employment may be in these two couplets from John Lyly's *Alexander and Campaspe*, an Elizabethan prose comedy about the temporary infatuation of Alexander the Great for his Theban captive Campaspe:

> What bird so sings, yet so does wail?
> Oh, 'tis the ravished nightingale,
> Jug, jug, jug, jug, tereu, she cries,
> And still her woes at midnight rise.[15]

Some prompting to this allusion may have come from the couplet:

> Cupid and my Campaspe play'd
> At cards for kisses; Cupid paid.[16]

It refers both to Cupid and to a card game, the latter looking back to the cartomancy scene with Madame Sosostris and more directly to an analogy with the chess game.

David Ward has called attention to an alternate interpretation of the legend of Philomel suggested by Plato in the *Phaedo*: that the three birds—nightingale, swallow, and hoopoe—are "figures for prophetic philosophy."[17]

> But men, because of their fear of death, misrepresent the swans and say they sing for sorrow, in mourning for their own death. They do not consider that no bird sings when it is hungry or cold or has any other

trouble; no, not even the nightingale or the swallow or the hoopoe, which are said to sing in lamentation. I do not believe they sing for grief, nor do the swans; but since they are Apollo's birds, I believe they have prophetic vision, and because they have foreknowledge of the blessings in the other world they sing and rejoice on that day more than ever before.[18]

Thus again Eliot eats his cake and has it too, by expressing opposite ideas and feelings through allusive methods. A long tradition exists for regarding the songs of birds as prophetic; many a wise man in folklore has been credited with the power to understand the birds. Eliot could hardly have been unaware of this, nor could he have missed reading the *Phaedo*.

But what analysis reveals is not necessarily a part of conscious intent. Writers work by feelings, impressions, and the impetus of the moment. One should not suppose that every line Eliot ever read was at all times at his conscious command. Rather, what he read helped to build the complex of feelings to which his poetry gave expression. What he must have been aware of while writing his poetry was mainly the total feeling, the conscious state, not all the precedent experiences that gave rise to it.

Nevertheless, the prophetic motif of *The Waste Land* was sufficiently paramount that the Platonic reference would well have accreted to it, making a perfect synthesis with the more superficial description of innocence violated. What is not understood in the message of the seer is in that sense violated and falls upon deaf ears; perhaps the ultimate "dirty ears" belong to the seer himself who, as Eliot said, at least must pretend to understand something.

AND OTHER WITHERED STUMPS OF TIME
WERE TOLD UPON THE WALLS;

Pound and Eliot boiled this first line down from "And other tales, from the old stumps and bloody ends of time," a somewhat clumsy original that does, however, lend a measure of clarity to the revision. Inspiration may well have come from that bloodiest of all plays ascribed, incorrectly or not, to Shakespeare, *Titus Andronicus*. There is much to compel this conclusion.

In the play Lavinia, daughter of Titus, a Roman general, suffers the same fate as Philomel; she has her tongue cut out after having been raped. With her father, she achieves revenge as she holds a basin "tween her stumps"—for her hands too have been cut off, that she may not weave her tale into a tapestry, as Philomel had done—to catch the blood of her violators as Titus slits their throats. There is a key association when Titus vows, "For worse than Philomel you us'd my daughter / And worse than Procne I will be revenged."[19] Thus, the "withered stumps of time" growing from "the old stumps and bloody ends of time" are the remnants of innocence after it has been subjected to the ravages of lust, and the "other withered stumps of time" are those remnants from multiplied instances of the same crime. They appear like magic writing on the wall, phantasmagorical images to haunt the mind.[20]

STARING FORMS

LEANED OUT, LEANING, HUSHING THE ROOM ENCLOSED.

Here again, the line was first conceived with less subtle meaning: "where staring forms / Leaned out, and hushed the room and closed it in." Eliot was plainly aiming to conjure the claustrophobic feelings that such visions would bring the protagonist or anyone who shared his consciousness. Something of this kind of feeling can, along with the key words "lean out," be perceived in these source lines from Tennyson's "The Mermaid":

> All things that are forked, and horned, and soft
> Would lean out from the hollow sphere of the sea,
> All looking down for the love of me.[21]

And from Rossetti comes a touch of Pre-Raphaelitism, recalling the lady gone to heaven and yearning for contact with her beloved left on earth: the opening stanza of "The Blessed Damozel":

> The blessed damozel leaned out
>   From the gold bar of heaven;
> Her eyes were deeper than the depth
>   Of waters stilled at even;
> She had three lilies in her hand,
>   And the stars in her hair were seven.[22]

The underlying feelings behind the passages of Tennyson and Rossetti suggest similarity by which they might have been brought together in the unconscious strivings of poetic inspiration. Both evoke feelings of loneliness, desperate isolation from that which is felt to be real, in atmospheres of unreality. Within the Eliotian context, they add to the tone of futile expectancy, from which only the disturbing images of dream can emerge.

FOOTSTEPS SHUFFLED ON THE STAIR.

The room is hushed only to have the passing silence opened slightly, like a slightly opened door, for the quiet trespass of a footstep upon the stair. After the observation in "The Death of the Duchess" that "it is terrible to be alone with another person," there was a kind of wishful negation of this unnerving situation:

> We should have marble floors
> And firelight on your hair
> There will be no footsteps up and down the stair.[23]

Eliot has left ample testament to the ambivalence that he felt toward this image. Feeling impending disaster, in *Murder in the Cathedral* the chorus voices its inner turmoil:

> Numb the hand and dry the eyelid,
> Still the horror, but more horror
> Than when tearing in the belly.
>
> Still the horror, but more horror
> Than when twisting in the fingers,
> Than when splitting in the skull.
>
> More than footfall in the passage,
> More than shadow in the doorway,
> More than fury in the hall.[24]

These represent vague, free-floating anxieties, feelings that disappear into depths into which one cannot peer, all the more disturbing for remaining undefined and indefinable. Yet there is another side to the image, displayed in *Burnt Norton:*

> What might have been is an abstraction
> Remaining a perpetual possibility
> Only in a world of speculation.
> What might have been and what has been
> Point to one end, which is always present.
> Footfalls echo in the memory
> Down the passage we did not take
> Towards the door we never opened
> Into the rose-garden.[25]

Here the footfalls would lead to that moment of ecstasy in the garden, perhaps only imagined, but, if so, for that, all the more keenly felt. It is a peculiarly Eliotian image, yet it does not appear in his earlier poetry, which supports the possibility that it may have developed in part from the repetitive motif, "her footsteps on the stair," found in "The Silver Music," a poem from *On Heaven and Poems Written on Active Service* by Ford Madox Hueffer. A review of the book by Eliot appeared in the *Egoist,* May 1918. Though not significant in itself, the poem contains suggestive phrases worth noting for the light they may throw on the genesis of this potent image. It describes a soldier plodding "along the road / That leads to Germany," while reminiscing about his beloved left behind at a castle in Chepstow. He recalls a sunny day, the air heavy with the perfume of cat's valerian. As his beloved approached, the flowers all around heard "[h]er footsteps on the stair." Then he imagines that, while he is gone, another will take his place and hear "the silver music / Of her footstep on the stair."[26]

Eliot may have responded to this more sympathetically than he normally might have because of its origins in the war, something that seemed to be preying on his mind during those years as, indeed, upon many thoughtful people who were living at the very periphery of potential collapse. Be that as it may, the footstep on the stair motif had sufficient emotional aura to be purified to Eliot's austere purposes.

As this line moves into the passage borrowed from "The Death of the Duchess," it is apparent that the footstep also relates to the stealthy approach of Ferdinand as he intrudes upon the duchess at her evening toilet. By extension, the footsteps are of death, for that is what Ferdinand brings, madness and death.

UNDER THE FIRELIGHT, UNDER THE BRUSH, HER HAIR
SPREAD OUT IN FIERY POINTS
GLOWED INTO WORDS, THEN WOULD BE SAVAGELY STILL.

Originally from "The Death of the Duchess," these lines plainly go back to the moment in *The Duchess of Malfi* when the duchess is left by her teasing husband only to be discovered by Ferdinand as she continues her affectionate banter with the surreptitiously departed mate. It is the moment of her doom, when she gives Ferdinand the wanted proof of her marriage, and Eliot captured it succinctly in this scene, the original version of which I have previously described. Transposed into the Ur-text of *The Waste Land*, "Spread out in little fiery points of will" was retained and truncated only in the final revision. In speaking of the lady's hair spreading out into fiery points of will to "glow into words," Eliot must have had in mind those damned souls in hell who, as described by Dante, could speak only by willing a voice through the flickering tip of the flame that enveloped them. For, in a real sense, the duchess of Malfi was damned in the judgement of her brothers and she served out her damnation on earth.

For the "hair / Spread out in little fiery points," he probably turned to many sources, recalling from Shelley's "Ode to the West Wind":

> Thou on whose stream, mid the steep sky's commotion,
> Loose clouds like earth's decaying leaves are shed,
> Shook from the tangled boughs of Heaven and Ocean,

> Angels of rain and lightning: there are spread
> On the blue surface of thine airy surge,
> Like the bright hair uplifted from the head
>
> Of some fierce Maenad, even from the dim verge
> Of the horizon to the zenith's height,
> The locks of the approaching storm . . .[27]

mixed with the admonition of the ghost of Hamlet's father:

> To tell the secrets of my prison-house,
> I could a tale unfold whose lightest word
> Would harrow up thy soul; freeze thy young blood;
> Make thy two eyes, like stars, start from their spheres;
> Thy knotted and combined hairs to part,
> And each particular hair to stand on end,
> Like quills upon the fretful porcupine.[28]

Hair standing out from the head is an archetypical image of fear or rage, sometimes even connoting ecstasy, as in the "sacerdos effusa crines" [priestess with disheveled hair (or, more literally, whose hair spreads out)] and the sculptural representation of Maenads, the frenzied female followers of Dionysus. Again in The Aeneid, as she made her pronouncements the color of the sibyl's face changed and "comae non mansere comtae" [her hair did not remain smoothed][29] as with the priestess.

Full use has been made of this archetypical image. Fear is imminent in the approaching footsteps. Transformed into Vivien Eliot, the lady assumes a fearsome aspect. She is about to speak, and what she has to say will be tormenting; her mien must be likewise. The whole situation, the repetitive experience of being alone with his wife evening after evening, was a terrible ordeal for Eliot.[30]

> "MY NERVES ARE BAD TO-NIGHT. YES, BAD. STAY WITH ME.
> "SPEAK TO ME. WHY DO YOU NEVER SPEAK. SPEAK.
> "WHAT ARE YOU THINKING OF? WHAT THINKING? WHAT?
> "I NEVER KNOW WHAT YOU ARE THINKING. THINK."

So she begins her inquisition, picking, nagging, tormenting, worrying, rendered so faithfully that Pound marked this passage off with the comment, "photography." Eliot was all too familiar with this pattern of fretting; it had a very personal significance for him, but it also had a broader meaning. In that volume of Hesse's Blick ins Chaos [A Glimpse into Chaos], which Eliot so admired that he quoted it in his notes to lines 366–76, there is a peculiar discussion of the syndrome that Vivien displayed: " 'having bad nerves' is the popular expression for hysteria and neurasthenia, for moral insanity, for all those evils that one can evaluate in various terms but, taken together, are precisely synonymous with Karamazovianism," which is "the Asiatic, chaotic, wild, dangerous, amoral element" in the nature of twentieth-century man. But he says that it "can be evaluated positively as well as negatively," just as Alyosha, in *The Brothers Karamazov*, turns more vicious as Dimitri becomes more saintly, reversals of each character's initial temperament.[31] So again that ambivalence of value that Eliot coveted points toward a Bradleyan synthesis, a discovery of the Absolute through the fusion of opposites.

The lady implores the male protagonist to speak, but he never does—he only muses to himself, if one abides by the quotation marks—which recalls the protagonist in the hyacinth garden, who also could not speak. In the kind of situation in which the lady places her mate, solipsism is complete, and speech is to no avail.

If he will not speak, she will attempt to pry into the most personal boundaries of his mind. She cannot succeed, of course, though she can guess what he is thinking; yet the artifice reinstates the Websterian setting. When the duchess of Malfi is surrounded by the madmen her brother has sent to torment her, her maid asks, "What think you of, madam?" to which she replies, "Of nothing; / When I muse thus, I sleep." In a peculiar way, Eliot has placed himself in the role of the duchess—another example of his doubling—and the lady, who assumes her identity outwardly, becomes the tormentor. Complete failure of mutual understanding, complete solipsism, comes with the confession, "I never know what you are thinking."

I THINK WE ARE IN RATS' ALLEY
WHERE THE DEAD MEN LOST THEIR BONES.

More telling was the first of these lines as set down in the Ur-text: "I think we first met in rats' alley." If this whole scene, the snatches of speech, fundamentally reflects the typical interchange between Eliot and his first wife, then he was evidently trying to say that they met in the valley of death. Perhaps they met under the shadow of the recently dead Jean Verdenal, and Eliot clutched Vivien out of despair; certainly they did meet and marry, rather suddenly, just after the death of Eliot's young friend. However that may be, the marriage was disaster from the start; and Eliot may have changed "first met" to "are" because he felt it more to the point that they continued to exist in a state of mutual death.

Behind the image would seem to be an allusion to the "valley of bones" shown to Ezekiel by God, who says "these bones are the whole house of Israel" and promises to breath new life into them. This Ezekial witnesses in a land described as "waste and desolate."[32] Further color of a morbid and barren tone is lent the image through remembrance of the rat in the graveyard scene in *Ulysses*, more fully explained in the commentary for line 187, "A rat crept softly through the vegetation." Suffice it to say here that the rat carries the usual rather unpleasant connotations.[33]

"WHAT IS THAT NOISE?"
          THE WIND UNDER THE DOOR.
"WHAT IS THAT NOISE NOW? WHAT IS THE WIND DOING?"
          NOTHING AGAIN NOTHING.

Eliot continues his dual exposition of personal experience transformed through a dream-warp of *The Duchess of Malfi*. Act 4, scene 2 of that play haunts these lines. It is the aftermath of the exposure of the duchess's marriage; Ferdinand is about to begin his plan of revenge. He sends madmen to plague his sister. "How now! what noise is that?" she asks, as she hears them outside. Ferdinand's servant explains, "I am come to tell you / Your brother hath intended you some sport."

For "The wind under the door," Eliot in his notes refers to Webster's *The Devil's Law Case*, or rather to a line from it that he does not identify except to give Webster as the author. At any rate, in the play a man is stabbed, but instead of dying from the wound he recovers, because it allows some noxious matter, from which he had been dying, to escape from his body. A physician discovers the supposed corpse still to be breathing and queries, "Is the wind in that door still?" Characteristically, Eliot has made the line more oblique, less precise. It is at once a feeble assertion that he, the corpse, lives, though just barely; and it has a more vague, more disquieting effect, much like the shuffle of the foot upon the stair. It helps to maintain the free-floating anxiety of the scene.

Not content that only a feeble ember of life has been left glowing, the lady must know what it is doing, she must expose the last detail of spiritual death. "Nothing again nothing," muses the protagonist, looking ahead to the helpless realization, "I can connect / Nothing with nothing." On the other hand, *nothing*, in the tradition of Eastern thought that Eliot had been considering also in the composition of *The Waste Land*, is conceived as the fullest of concepts since it is the foundation from which all existence must spring. Thus, to do *nothing* can be construed as gaining enlightenment, with all its implications of detachment. From this perspective, the male protagonist may be drawing away from the lady and her world of appearance to approach, perhaps through the dark night of the soul, the void of the Absolute, reality.

A later transmutation of this wind image appears in *Murder in the Cathedral* near the end of part one, just before the interlude. In an interchange between priests, tempters, and chorus, the tempters ask, "Is it rain that taps at the window, is it wind that pokes at the door?" After a series of such queries of anxiety, the chorus pronounces that "Death has a hundred hands and walks by a thousand ways".[34] From this it would seem that Eliot associated the actions of the wind at the door with death, which here would be a natural extension of the running distortive reflection of *The Duchess of Malfi*. This assumption is further substantiated in the Ur-text. To the question, "What is the wind doing?" Eliot originally had written "Carrying / Away the little light dead people," referring, so Valerie Eliot explains, to Paolo and Francesca. Dante encounters them in the second circle of hell and is immediately attracted to them. "Volontieri / parlerei a que' duo, che insieme vanno, / e paion s' al vento esser leggieri" [Willingly would I speak to those two, who go together, and seem to be light upon the wind].[35]

This Dantean allusion might well have been retained, for the two lines are of the utmost economy and they carry overtones singularly illuminating to the moment at which they originally occurred. Recounting her story to Dante, Franscesca observes that "Nessun maggior dolore, / che ricordarsi del tempo felice / nella miseria" [(there is) no greater pain than to recall a happy time in wretchedness][36] All of the recollections of the male protagonist are gathered from the vantage point of hell into which his relationship with the lady has cast him.

                                    "DO
"YOU KNOW NOTHING? DO YOU SEE NOTHING? DO YOU REMEMBER
"NOTHING?"

While the lady continues her neurotic inquisition, the play on the double-edged implication of *nothing* is drawn further on. There is the pejorative sense in which the lady intends it, and the more pregnant import that it carried in the scene in the hyacinth garden where, at the critical moment, the protagonist declared, "I was neither / Living nor dead, and I knew nothing." He was looking into "the silence," just as here the male protagonist confronts the silence and boredom that exists between him and his mate, a silence interrupted only by the lady's nagging.

Ecclesiastes 9:5 provided Eliot with the allusive foundation of his imagery: "For the living know that they shall die; but the dead know not anything; neither have they anymore a reward; for the memory of them is forgotten." Spiritual death for the male protagonist is once more suggested. And there is an air of unreality to the whole situation, as for Marlow when looking back on the almost chimerical figure of Kurtz: "I did not see the man in the name any more than you do. Do you see him? Do you see the story? Do you see anything? It seems to me I am trying to tell you a dream. . . ."[37]

I REMEMBER
THOSE ARE PEARLS THAT WERE HIS EYES.

The original lines were, "I remember / The hyacinth garden. Those are pearls that were his eyes, yes!" Here the words of Francesca de Rimini would contribute strongly to the allusive fabric of the poem, for, in the midst of wretchedness, a happy time is momentarily recalled. But Eliot did not allow himself even that short respite. Instead, he chose to dwell exclusively on a death motif that had vast personal significance to him, relating to the deaths of his father and Jean Verdenal and reaching out to entangle the less personal demise of the mad king Ludwig.

"ARE YOU ALIVE, OR NOT? IS THERE NOTHING IN YOUR HEAD?"

This line was marked "photo." by Pound, again probably because it seemed an acutely faithful reproduction of the speech pattern of Vivien. Also it carries back once more to the hyacinth garden, where the protagonist was "neither / Living nor dead." In this context, the questions reflect a blank numbness on the part of the male protagonist.

On another level, the thread of *The Duchess of Malfi* winds through this whole scene; this line recalls a room in the house of the duchess. It is the first scene of act four. Ferdinand brings the duchess the hand of a dead man, purportedly the hand of Antonio, then lights are lit to reveal behind a traverse the artificial figures of Antonio and his children made to look as if they were dead. Coming just after "Those are pearls that were his eyes," it would be singularly appropriate to ascribe the questions, "Are you alive, or not? Is there nothing in your head?" to the duchess grown perhaps a bit incredulous in this distortive dream sequence. This is made the more likely if one compares the words of Francesca to those of the duchess after her discovery of the supposedly dead Antonio:

> That's the greatest torture souls feel in hell,
> In hell, that they must live, and cannot die.

Each expresses essentially the same sentiment of living or feeling out of infernal condemnation, though in two distinctly different images.

BUT

O O O O THAT SHAKESPEHERIAN RAG—
IT'S SO ELEGANT
SO INTELLIGENT

Almost with the effect of a comic relief, the tension of the scene causes a momentary collapse of the rational faculties, as a bit of nonsense patter breaks in upon the brooding of the male protagonist. Likewise the taut extensity of *The Duchess of Malfi* is at once mitigated and yet, by contrast, heightened in the second scene of act four by the introduction of the madmen with their illogical gibberings. Here the patter seems also to parody grotesquely the madness of the inquisition being conducted by the lady; it is a letting lose of tension, a berserk mimicry.

"That Shakespearian Rag" was a minor hit song of 1912, with music by Dave Stamper and lyrics by Gene Buck and Herman Ruby. In fact, it was included in the Ziegfield's Follies of that year. The lyrics are about on the level of "Mairzy Doats."

> That Shakespearian rag,—
> Most intelligent, very elegant,
> That old classical drag,
> Has the proper stuff, the line "Lay on Macduff,"
> Desdemona was the colored pet,
> Romeo loved his Juliet—
> And they were some lovers, you can bet, and yet,
> I know if they were here today,
> They'd Grizzly Bear in a diff'rent way,
> And you'd hear old Hamlet say,
> 'To be or not to be,'
> That Shakespearian Rag.[38]

Eliot has doctored the song to suit his own purposes. He has altered "Shakespearian" to the more syncopated "Shakespeherian," which is given an added swing rhythm by the four *Os*, which themselves echo the quadruple "Oh" groans of Othello when he hears from Iago that his beloved Desdemona has apparently been unfaithful to him. It was, of course, the handkerchief that Othello had given to her that brought her unjustly to her death; the same here is designated pejoratively as "that Shakespeherian Rag." Failure of love lurks in this secondary allusion, fitting into the series of failed loves chronicled throughout *The Waste Land.*

"WHAT SHALL I DO NOW? WHAT SHALL I DO?"
"I SHALL RUSH OUT AS I AM, AND WALK THE STREET

"WITH MY HAIR DOWN, SO. WHAT SHALL WE DO TO-MORROW?
"WHAT SHALL WE EVER DO?"

A crescendo closing the inquisition, this last fretful barrage of rhetorical and half-real questions brings the situation to a culmination, as the ennui is finally met squarely. The duchess, the lady now plainly appears mad—prepared to "rush" out and walk the street with her hair down, dishevelled like a Maenad. She and her companion are at stalemate.

THE HOT WATER AT TEN.
AND IF IT RAINS, A CLOSED CAR AT FOUR.
AND WE SHALL PLAY A GAME OF CHESS,
PRESSING LIDLESS EYES AND WAITING FOR A KNOCK UPON THE DOOR.

At first, Eliot had thought, "The hot water bottle at ten," or had considered it early as a possibility, as he wrote "bottle" in pencil above the typed line. The "closed car" was originally "the closed carriage"; he went to "car" because, as he wrote to Pound, he felt he could not use "taxi" more than once, though perhaps "taxi" was what he had in mind. Pound felt that "closed carriage" gave the passage an 1880 flavor that violated the 1922 period of the scene.

Then there was a deletion made at the behest of Vivien. Preceding "Pressing lidless eyes . . .," Eliot had initially written "The ivory men make company between us." His wife apparently felt that this was too cruel an exposure of the state into which their relationship had degenerated, and she prevailed upon him to suppress the line. In a note to the facsimile edition of the poem, Valerie Eliot points out that Eliot restored the line from memory when he made a fair copy of the poem for a sale to assist the London library in June 1960. Obviously he felt it after all an integral part of his intent. It does complete the meaning of the line preceding it and lends fuller canvas to the line following it.

The symbolism here is self-sustaining, in need of no allusive support. The meaning of the chess game, as considered in discussing the title of the section, applies quite well here. The game becomes both a paradigm of life and a diversion by which the thoughts of men are made to bypass the essence of the situation. Both functions are two sides of the same coin since, by Bradleyan metaphysics, human life, human consciousness, comprehends not reality but appearance, mere deception. Grover Smith points out that the chess game as a symbol of life has its roots in Elizabethan literature.[39] He also traces the motif of walking in the street with hair in disarray to several literary sources, but they are a bit too tenuous to satisfy.[40] Upon seeing the ships of Aeneas leave

Carthage, Dido tears her hair but does not walk the streets. Tearing of hair at distress is a common gesture, especially in classical literature. Closer come these lines, also cited by Smith, from Beaumont and Fletcher's *Philaster*, act 3, scene 2:

> Thou hast overthrown me once;
> Yet, if I had another Troy to lose,
> Thou, or another villain with thy looks,
> Might talk me out of it, and send me naked,
> My hair dishevelled, through the fiery streets.[41]

Whatever literary allusions may or may not be transported into this segment of the duchess scene, it seems reasonable to suppose, upon the basis of evidence already presented, that the assimilation and transformation of thematic material from *The Duchess of Malfi* should continue through this denouement. To see this most clearly, consider the opening of the second scene of act four, which is after the duchess has beheld the seeming corpses of her husband and children, and just before the entrance of the madmen:

> *Duchess.* What hideous noise was that?
> *Cariola.* 'Tis the wild consort
> Of madmen, lady, which your tryant brother
> Hath plac'd about your lodging: this tyranny,
> I think, was never practis'd till this hour.
> *Duchess.* Indeed, I thank him: nothing but noise and folly
> Can keep me in my right wits; whereas reason
> And silence make me stark mad. Sit down;
> Discourse to me some dismal tragedy.

Cariola protests that it would only increase the duchess's melancholy, to which the duchess replies that, she being in a prison, to hear of greater griefs would only lessen hers. Cariola opines that the duchess will live to overcome this hardship. Not so, counters the duchess, the "robin-redbreast and the nightingale / Never live long in cages."

> *Cariola.* Pray, dry your eyes.
> What think you of, madam?
> *Duchess.* Of nothing; when I muse thus,
> I sleep.

Miraculously, though the heavens overhead be of molten brass and the earth of burning sulphur, the duchess says that, much to her sorrow, she is not yet mad. Cariola tries to comfort her mistress, but it is a hopeless task. The duchess is distracted by the din of madmen outside. "How now! what noise is that?"[42]

The careful reader will note many details that have flaked from this short segment of a scene into "A Game of Chess." First of all, the pattern of nervous questioning resembles that of the poem's lady. Then there is the pervading atmosphere of madness and death, which is attenuated but nonetheless ubiquitous in this section of The Waste Land. "The robin-redbreast and the nightingale / Never live long in cages" vibrates with association, like a pebble tossed into the waters of the poem. It recalls "Oh keep the Dog far hence, that's friend to men, / Or with his nails he'll dig it up again!" which alluded to "Call for the robin redbreast." Of course, the nightingale has already figured prominently in this scene. Just prior to these lines the Ariel song was quoted, and that links back to "Call for the robin redbreast," by way of Lamb's comparison of the two. And that these wondrous birds cannot long endure in cages reminds one of a central theme of the section embodied in the original title, "In the Cage."

Finally, in her longest speech from the quoted segment, the duchess of Malfi delineates her state of mind in words that would have done equal justice to the plight of Eliot and Vivien. Eliot felt himself driven to the extremity of apprehension, though not quite yet mad. He was, like the duchess of Malfi, absorbed in contemplation of death. Certainly these similarities would go a long way toward explaining why he was so attracted to the play that he attempted to compose a poem built around it, then salvaged the abortive effort by transferring elements of it into "A Game of Chess."

At any rate, this influence clarifies the macabre and mystifying image of "Pressing lidless eyes." When Cariola asks her mistress, "What think you of, madam?" and the duchess of Malfi replies, "Of nothing; when I muse thus, / I sleep," the maidservant then remarks quizzically, "Like a madman, with your eyes open?" Through the imagination of Eliot, this state of sleeping with eyes open has been converted into a blank stare somewhere between sleep and mindless wakefulness, even with overtones of death. Cariola and the duchess, unknowingly waiting for the knock upon the door that will bring their executioner, in "A Game of Chess" assume the guise of Vivien and Eliot, pretending absorption in their game, waiting for the knock upon the door that will save them, at least temporarily, from themselves.

THE PUB SCENE

Least opaque of any part of The Waste Land, devoid of allusions except in the final line, this scene requires little or no exegesis. It is a secondhand story that Eliot acquired from a servant woman named Ellen Kellond who did housework for him and Vivien. As Robert

Sencourt tells it, shortly after Eliot and Vivien married, Eliot, at the insistence of his family, returned to Gloucester, Massachusetts, for a visit. That was in the late summer of 1915, then:

> Some months after his return from America, and when he and Vivienne had ceased to be the guests of Bertrand Russell, Mary Culpin [a friend whom Eliot had met in a Soho restaurant] helped them to move into 18 Crawford Mansions, a little flat in Crawford Street off Edgware Road—a vulgar quarter where their rough, crude charwoman talked boldly of abortions, and so went down into literary history as Lou in The Waste Land.[43]

Sencourt does not say how he knows that Ellen Kellond became Lou rather than May; he may be suspected of speculation. Notwithstanding, his recounting adds the color of particularity to the genesis of the pub scene.

As a recollection from the earliest days of Eliot's marriage, the tale of Lil and Albert emerges naturally from the domestic intimacy of the duchess scene. It also serves as a foil to enhance the theme of solipsism heightened by failed love. It is a transliteration of the mundane tragedy of the Eliots into a cockney counterpart in which most of the subtleties of mental anguish are absent. Reflecting an oft-quoted observation of Eliot, Lil and Albert, as well as Bill, Lou, and May, are too dimly aware of their own experience to suffer much from it. That is perhaps the key difference between them and the duchess and her lover; the contrast between the two scenes pivots around that difference.

Eliot seems to have had little problem with this scene. Mainly he modified a few words and expressions. Vivien gave him some assistance with the cockney. Pound extricated him from the difficulties of the original first line, "When Lil's husband was coming back out of the Transport Corps." Eliot had also considered, "Discharge out of the army?" None of this was sufficiently economical. Unerringly attuned to the intricacies and vagaries of his tongue, Pound suggested "demobbed," a colloquial shortening of demobilized then recently come into use—Partridge assigns it a first appearance date of 1919 in his Dictionary of Slang and Unconventional English.

Before "Others can pick and choose if you can't," Eliot struck out "No ma'am, you needn't look old fashioned at me" as a rejoinder to "Then I'll know who to thank, she said, and gave me a straight look." "Them pills" Lil took "to bring it off" began as "medicine" and fell to an indecisive "stuff" before acquiring their final apothecary form. And "What you get married for if you don't want to have children" started out as "You want to keep him home, I suppose." None of these alterations made a difference to the ultimate significance of the lines. They simply sharpened the speech, made it more to the point.

Throughout the story of Lil and Albert in a pub, overheard right at closing time, the proprietor has been giving the traditional call, "HURRY UP PLEASE ITS TIME." Finally, the story ended or, more likely, cut short, the drinkers depart and tipsiness gives way to madness. Blurry-eyed and with speech slurred to a "Goonight," Bill, Lou, and May stagger out into a phantasmagoric night in which they melt into the smog and rematerialize at the royal court in *Hamlet*.

> Good night, ladies, we're going to leave you now.
> Merrily we roll along, over the dark blue sea.

This old college song turns immediately to melancholy. Ophelia, driven mad by the aspersions of Hamlet, wandered in before the king and queen and, as she left, spoke dementedly: "And so I thank you for your good counsel. Come, my coach! Good night, ladies; good night, sweet ladies; good night, good night."[44] Then Ophelia goes off to meet her death by drowning. And so the pub scene, and with it "A Game of Chess," concludes with one final stroke of madness pointing inexorably toward death.

5

The Fire Sermon

INDECISION marked the composition of "The Fire Sermon." Apparently the last half, after the seduction of the typist, was written at a separate sitting. Eliot had sketched out four lines, commencing "This music crept by me upon the waters," which appeared at the end of the seduction scene, but they were vastly revised and enlarged for the final version. Specifically, that portion introduced by "O City city" was worked out on another sheet and then joined to "And along the Strand, up Queen Victoria Street." Another segment that Eliot labored over was the apostrophe to London, which, along with the Fresca episode with which the section originally began, was ultimately removed. Finally, leaving aside all the minor revisions, the seduction scene was, at the insistence of Pound, shortened and toned down.

Actually, the section was realized in several stages. One thing does seem clear: the thematic core of inspiration from which it grew was lust. Fresca and the typist with her seducer dominate the section in the Ur-text. Moreover, even for Eliot the sexual details were unusually explicit, and not simply to enhance the positive aspects of concupiscence. Quite pointedly Eliot was displaying a flagrant misogamy, disgusted perhaps by the demands of his wife or by her infidelities—assuming there was some substance behind the rumors of her infidelities. Yet even homosexuality did not escape his poetic purview. Contrary to the thesis that Eliot himself may have entertained a homosexual attachment to Jean Verdenal, homosexuality here fares no better than heterosexuality; Mr. Eugenides comes off as an unwanted nuisance. Also, it seems rather questionable that Eliot, with his passion for privacy, would have made public an episode, based on an actual experience as he himself testified, that might threaten to expose something in his nature that he would have wanted kept secret.

Rather, he seems to have fallen much under the influence of the Pauline doctrine of antisexuality. Nominally his source was St. Augustine; in fact, he was embracing an attitude simply congruent with his own. As he confessed to Paul Elmer More, he felt a void in life and "I am one whom this sense of void tends to drive towards asceticism or sensuality."[1] Little wonder that he chose St. Augustine to provide a kind of spiritual framework for "The Fire Sermon," for in the latter's *Confessions* were told the transformations of a youthful sinner into a saintly ascetic. Augustine had struggled against the powerful desires of the flesh and had won, if we are to believe his account; Eliot was waging a similar battle against himself.

Ostensibly Eliot was attempting a synthesis between East and West in bringing into collocation the Augustinian outcry of subdued flesh and the admonitions of the Buddhistic Fire Sermon, but the result is closer to a sacrifice of the impartiality of Buddhistic asceticism to the erotophobia of the Pauline doctrines. Whatever diversions from sexuality occur in this section—and there are several—they do not come near to balancing out the more central sexual revulsion.

The "burning" in Buddha's Fire Sermon was not, like that in Augustine's *Confessions*, situated in the loins but in the mind and soul. It was the flame kindled by involvement with appearance, the chimerical reality of the senses—sensuous, not sensual. This encompasses the delights of the voluptuary but does not pertain to them exclusively or even centrally. Yet Eliot departs from sensual burning only once to hint vaguely at commerce, involvement with goods, and even then he turns the episode, that of Mr. Eugenides, into a potential sexual exploit. When he lingers over "The pleasant whining of a mandoline" or the "Inexplicable splendor of Ionian white and gold" in Magnus Martyr, it is almost impossible to perceive this as unwanted involvement.

At the very beginning of the section is a passing reportage on the lack of social conscience marking the decadence of Europe with which Eliot so much concerned himself—not only in *The Waste Land* but also in his other poems, in certain of his essays, and in his commentaries written for the *Criterion*. He was witnessing the first moments of the ecological nightmare that has come to engulf us all. But this was something personal to Eliot, this awakening to the Karamazovian element, which he felt that he shared with Hermann Hesse. If he saw it in terms of the Buddha's Fire Sermon, that was certainly a personal construction that he placed upon it.

"Fire Sermon" is in fact a misnomer if applied to the section with any strict Buddhistic reference. Such fire as pervades it is Pauline and stems not from the illusions of the egoistic perceiver, the finite center, but from the loins. One cannot help but feel that the vagaries of sexuality that Eliot portrays here are reflections of personal disappointment and anguish, rather than projections of a religio-philosophic doctrine. Of course, it is part of his method to universalize personal experience by mounting it in a larger frame in which it becomes embedded in some deep perspective of historical tradition. For once, however, the larger frame seems off center. Not that all overtones of Buddhistic asceticism are missing. On Margate Sands, he must have had occasion to contemplate such things. He considered becoming a Buddhist monk. But "The Fire Sermon," as it now exists, contains few remnants of these contemplations.

The Buddhistic overtones were eliminated in the arduous process of revision. Most particularly, the London apostrophe was excised. "London, your people is bound upon the wheel!" was the pivotal concept from which the Buddhistic overtones were to be generated.[2] Throughout the section the karmatic wheel was to turn, moving toward the still point, when it would cease to turn, not here on earth but in another world, either the state of nirvana or the Civitas Dei.

This germinal center was removed; Eliot had not pursued karmatic involvements except for those of the flesh, so the plan was imperfectly realized. There should be little need for reflection on the ultimate poetic validity of the section itself. It is a mere matter of mismatch between the title and the content, between the apparent initial intention and the subsequent realization. If the title "The Fire Sermon" could be pruned of its Buddhistic associations and assume more Pauline implications, it would then more neatly align with the section's content. Perhaps that is how one must in the final evaluation construe it. After all, the section evolved from great indecision, so perhaps one should not attempt further to force it to greater decisiveness than its rather precarious structure can sustain.

Synopsis: "The Fire Sermon"

Lust is contemplated from many vantage points, as if the invisible protagonist were walking through London on a voyeuristic pilgrimage to some chapel that he never finds. In contrast with "A Game of Chess," where sexual disappointments are viewed more introspectively, here they are seen more from the outside. London is transformed into a kind of Fellinian tenement in which on each floor the beetle-like couplings of humans are enacted at a different social level. Though not entirely absent, the possibility of redemption in each case has waned extremely faint—most often it has been obliterated within the cast of revulsion thrown over the whole panorama like a net of damning implication.

Throughout his voyeuristic wandering, Eliot stops here and there to enjoy, possibly for the last time, a few of the sights and sounds of the city toward which he must have had a certain ambivalent feeling. He was keenly aware of the impermanence of some of these sights. War had brought many of them to ruin. Urban renewal threatened many lovely churches, landmarks that Eliot often visited on his lunch hour from the bank. In the *Criterion* he inveighed against the unnecessary destruction of such irreplaceable monuments of architectural tradition. Trying to save them became one of his pet projects. It is worth noting that in the Ur-text he mentions not only Magnus Martyr but also Michael Paternoster Royal, a Wren church located on Upper Thames Street, where Valerie Eliot says her husband used to go when he was working in the city.

In his peregrinations the invisible protagonist, the disembodied spirit of the poet himself concretized only transitorily in the figure of Tiresias, witnesses the slow disintegration of the city, the outward manifestations of spiritual decay that seemed to overtake all of Europe following the devastation of World War I. Readers can now view the wreckage as the ultimate consequence of technological affluence joined to the weaknesses of human nature, a destructiveness that waxes and wanes with the progressions and retrogressions of civilization. Doubtlessly Eliot's estimation of the situation was tainted by his own personal disillusionment, what he later called his "grouse against life."

Once or twice Eliot pauses to vent a personal sorrow, the fate that brought him to Margate to try to reassemble the pieces of his life. These occasions are quite in keeping with the intensely personal nature of the section. There is a despairing and shadowy remembrance of Jean Verdenal, a brief lingering over death, undoubtedly also that of his father. But most of all there is an obsessive preoccupation with whoredom, seduction, and the perversion of the sexual impulse to forms of exchange in which the possibility for ennoblement is nonexistent.

THE RIVER'S TENT IS BROKEN: THE LAST FINGERS OF LEAF
CLUTCH AND SINK INTO THE WET BANK. THE WIND
CROSSES THE BROWN LAND, UNHEARD.

Heart of Darkness lurks in the spirit of these lines, not so much in any verbatim transcription of images as in the aura of the diction. For a moment, the sepia tones of the Ganges as it flowed darkly through that narrative flicker into awareness only to die away and then revive several lines later. Sad anguish of a summer gone is felt in "the last fingers of leaf" that "Clutch and sink into the wet bank." "Clutch and sink" captures the essential form of the convulsion of death, the last gasp of life. After that is sterility and desolation: "The wind / Crosses the brown land, unheard."

THE NYMPHS ARE DEPARTED.
SWEET THAMES, RUN SOFTLY, TILL I END MY SONG.

Contrasted with this bleak autumn is the almost fairy spring of a bygone English countryside painted by Spenser in one of the most euphonious poems in the language, "Prothalamion."

> Calme was the day, and through the trembling ayre
> Sweete breathing Zephyrus did softly play,
> A gentle spirit, that lightly did delay
> Hot Titans beames, which then did glyster fayre:
> When I, whom sullein care,
> Through discontent of my long fruitlesse stay
> In princes court, and expectation vayne
> Of idle hopes, which still doe fly away,
> Like empty shaddowes, did afflict my brayne,
> Walkt forth to ease my payne
> Along the shoare of silver streaming Themmes;
> Whose rutty bancke, the which his river hemmes,
> Was paynted all with variable flowers,
> And all the meades adornd with daintie gemmes,
> Fit to decke maydens bowres,
> And crowne their paramours
> Against the brydale day, which is not long:
> Sweete Themmes, runne softly, till I end my song.[3]

A prothalamion is a song to be sung before a wedding. This one has all the melodious qualities of a song. Spenser wrote it in 1596 to celebrate the double wedding of the two daughters of the earl of Worcester. In the poem, the ladies appear as two white swans; it tells how they journeyed up the Thames in a ceremonial visit to Essex House, formerly the residence of Spenser's patron, the earl of Leicester, where they are greeted by their future husbands. One is reminded that this same earl of Leicester will soon be on a barge with his beloved Queen Elizabeth.

> There, in a meadow, by the rivers side,
> A flocke of nymphes I chaunced to espy,
> All lovely daughters of the flood thereby,
> With goodly greenish locks all loose untyde,
> As each had bene a bryde:
> And each one had a little wicker basket,
> Made of fine twigs entrayled curiously,
> In which they gathered flowers to fill their flasket;
> And with fine fingers cropt full feateously
> The tender stalkes on hye.[4]

This recalls, as it did for Eliot, one of Laforgue's "Dimanches" [Sundays]:

> Le fleuve a son repos dominical;
> Pas un chaland, en amont, en aval.
>
> Les Vêpres carillonnent sur la ville.
> Les berges sont desertes, sans idylles.
>
> [The river has its dominical repose;
> Not a barge, upstream or down.
>
> Vespers carillon over the town.
> The shores are deserted, without idylls.][5]

It is raining, and a group of students pass by. Suddenly, a poor girl among them, a girl with "neither muff nor furs," breaks rank and dashes to the river, where she throws herself in—another death by drowning.

This rather melodramatic little piece is explained by the following epigraph in English at its head:

> Hamlet. Have you a daughter?
> Polonius. I have, my lord.
> Hamlet. Let her not walk in the sun:
>   conception is a blessing; but not
>   as your daughter may conceive.

Considering the allusion to Hamlet, and specifically to Ophelia, with which the preceding section closed, it would not be surprising that this poem of Laforgue may have passed across Eliot's mind as he was writing these lines; it certainly fits the mood and detail of what is to follow.

"The nymphs are departed" carries two levels of meaning. Relative to the Spenserian source, it announces that nymphs are no more. Within the present moment, it rues their passing while stating that their modern counterparts, the lady picnickers "And their friends," as we are soon told, have at late season vacated the premises.

THE RIVER BEARS NO EMPTY BOTTLES, SANDWICH PAPERS,
SILK HANDKERCHIEFS, CARDBOARD BOXES, CIGARETTE ENDS
OR OTHER TESTIMONY OF SUMMER NIGHTS.

Here that strange and pregnant image, "The river's tent is broken," assumes its full meaning. Tents are symbols of camping. The camping and picnicking season is over. Beyond that, the tent as a tabernacle or place of worship has been destroyed. As Eliot wrote in "The Dry Sal-

vages," "I think that the river / Is a strong brown god." Polluted and
surrounded by the death of a dying season, the river itself has been
demythologized. There is no longer any worship along its banks. Further, as Eliot also wrote in "The Dry Salvages," "The river is within us."
Nothing noble has been left within humankind or so one might for a
second feel.

THE NYMPHS ARE DEPARTED.
AND THEIR FRIENDS, THE LOITERING HEIRS OF CITY DIRECTORS;
DEPARTED, HAVE LEFT NO ADDRESSES.

No need to look for allusions: this speaks clearly enough out of
firsthand experience. At the bank, and undoubtedly elsewhere, Eliot
must have met more than enough of these people to last a lifetime.
During the summer, such people may be seen mindlessly scattering
their debris over the river banks after having just as mindlessly failed to
perceive the awesomeness of the scene before them, surrounding them
with sights which in earlier times inspired men to reverence. To call the
ladies involved "nymphs" strikes an unmistakable note of irony.

BY THE WATERS OF LEMAN I SAT DOWN AND WEPT . . .
SWEET THAMES, RUN SOFTLY TILL I END MY SONG,
SWEET THAMES, RUN SOFTLY, FOR I SPEAK NOT LOUD OR LONG.

In keeping with the cantatory nature of the "Prothalamion," Eliot
bases his line on Psalm 127:

> By the rivers of Babylon, there we sat down, yea, we wept, when we
> remembered Zion. We hanged our harps upon the willows the midst
> thereof. For they that carried us away captive required of us a song;
> and they that wasted us required of us mirth, saying, Sing us one of
> the songs of Zion. How shall we sing the Lord's song in a strange
> land? If I forget thee, O Jerusalem, let my right hand forget her
> cunning.

Lake Leman is the old name of Lake Geneva. Eliot wrote part of The
Waste Land beside it. By equating Leman with Babylon, Eliot seems to
imply that modern Europe is like a place of captivity, where the soul
cannot sing but of sorrow. It is a place also where we are strangers,
where we have been "wasted." Significantly, it was by the waters of
Leman that Francois Bonivard (1493–c. 1570) was incarcerated by
Charles III, duke of Savoy. Bonivard, prior of a small monastery outside
Geneva, joined the patriots who were trying to make Geneva a republic,
free from the control of Charles III. He was imprisoned in the castle of
Chillon from 1530 until 1536, when Chillon was captured by the

Bernese. He was released and made a member of the Council of Geneva. Byron retold his story in "The Prisoner of Chillon," using the old name of Leman. This allusion brings to the fore once more the solipsistic notion of being each imprisoned in one's own mind.

Of course, in the autobiography of Marie Larisch many of the love affairs take place around lakes, principally the Starnbergersee. Eliot may have been aware that the word *leman*, of Middle English origin, means a sweetheart or mistress. Thus it would have been symbolically within the bonds of his marriage—with possible overtones of his wife's infidelity (if it occurred)—that he sat down and wept. As usual the mixed allusions lend multiple dimensions to the meaning of the lines. While he is weeping, he is singing a prothalamion to a bridal day "which was not long," another oblique reference to the shortness of his marital happiness.

BUT AT MY BACK IN A COLD BLAST I HEAR
THE RATTLE OF THE BONES, AND CHUCKLE SPREAD FROM EAR TO EAR.

A false beginning, one that will be repeated at line 196, is an interesting device that Eliot uses several times throughout the poem. It is a disjunctive turn much in keeping with the dreamlike structure. Here a line from Andrew Marvell transforms into digressive thought connecting with a recurring preoccupation. Since Marvell's poem "To His Coy Mistress," is so well known, Eliot obviously was striving to pervert the familiar, thereby turning expectation into an unanticipated corridor of experience. Compare the established lines with the dream aberration of them:

> Had we but world enough, and time,
> This coyness, lady, were no crime.
> . . . .
> But at my back I always hear
> Time's wingèd chariot hurrying near;
> And yonder all before us lie
> Deserts of vast eternity.
> Thy beauty shall no more be found,
> Nor in thy marble vault shall sound
> My echoing song; then worms shall try
> That long preserved virginity,
> And your quaint honour turn to dust,
> And into ashes all my lust.[6]

This is an interesting and complex transformation. "Time's winged chariot" brings death, which is objectified differently as "The rattle of the bones." These are the bones, we are soon to learn, "cast in a little low dry garret, / Rattled by the rat's foot only, year to year." Also they recall "I think we are in rats' alley / Where the dead men lost their bones." Inspirationally all these allusions go back to the graveyard scene in *Ulysses*, where a rat is witnessed crawling about in the freshly dug grave. This rat personifies all that death connotes, or rather all that it connotes within the context of a graveyard.

On the way to Paddy Dignam's funeral: "The carriage climbed more slowly the hill of Rutland square. Rattle his bones. Over the stones. Only a pauper. Nobody owns." A songlike quality must have arrested Eliot's attention on these lines. They do in fact come from "The Pauper's Drive," with words by Thomas Noel and music by J. J. Hutchinson. Elsewhere Eliot has attuned his ear to snatches of songs, a kind of allusion no doubt related to his love of opera and the music halls. The refrain of "The Pauper's Drive" is "Rattle his bones over the stones: / He's only a pauper whom nobody owns!"[7]

Interestingly, just before this trip to the graveyard in *Ulysses*, there occurs a near-death by drowning. Reuben J. and his son are "piking it down the quay" toward the Isle of Man when suddenly the "young chiseller" tumbles over the wall into the river. Mr. Dedalus asks nervously, "Is he dead?" Not really, Martin Cunningham assures him. A passing boatman fished him from the Liffey and landed him back upon the quay, "[m]ore dead than alive." In his dolorous mood, Eliot must have found this all quite in sympathy with his sentiments. One cannot fail to hear a faint ring of similarity, quite in passing, between "the Isle of Man" and "the Isle of Dog." "Is he dead?" also echoes "Are you alive, or not?" and "I was neither / Living nor dead," and the latter perhaps catches something from "More dead than alive."[8]

A similar complicated interlocking occurs with "To His Coy Mistress." First there is the suggestion of the waste land in "And yonder all before us lie / Deserts of vast eternity." Then "your quaint honour turn to dust" certainly evokes an emotional kinship with "fear in a handful of dust." Finally, "Nor in thy marble vault shall sound / My echoing song" has the semantic tint of "Sweet Thames, run softly till I end my song . . . for I speak not loud or long."

None of this is to suggest that all these interrelations were consciously planned. But such associations assuredly operate subconsciously to draw remembered material forth into new combination and creative synthesis. Similarities, however, disjunctively arrived at, act like magnets to coalesce mental data into meaningful originality via lines set down in the task, in this case, of composing a specific poem.

A RAT CREPT SOFTLY THROUGH THE VEGETATION
DRAGGING ITS SLIMY BELLY ON THE BANK

Finally arrived at the graveyard, Paddy Dignam's funeral concludes. An "obese grey rat toddled along the side of the crypt, moving the pebbles." At this point, a nerve may have been touched. "The grey alive crushed itself in under the plinth" strikes a chord with that earlier line of Eliot, "Come in under this grey rock," a line from "The Death of St. Narcissus," tickling something hardly remarked in the back of his mind, helping to make him take notice. Then, as the scene with the rat continues, he would have found more to point focus his attention. "One of those chaps would make short work of a fellow. Pick the bones clean no matter who it was."[9] This last sentence almost certainly influenced Eliot in his translation of "Un courant de sousmer l'emporta tres loin" [A current under sea carried him away very far] from "Dans le Restaurant" into "A current under sea / Picked his bones in whispers" in "Death by Water."

This much of a tie with *Ulysses* suggests the unconscious source for the remainder of the image or, at any rate, for a major impetus for the formation of it:

> You were going to do wonders, what? Missionary to Europe after fiery Columbanus. Fiacre and Scotus on their creepystools in heaven split from their pinpots, loudatinlaughing: *Euge! Euge!* Pretending to speak broken English as you dragged your valise, porter threepence, across the slimy pier at Newhaven.[10]

Emotional and dictional tone may have helped transpose "dragged your valise . . . across the slimy pier" into "A rat crept softly . . . / Dragging its slimy belly on the bank." Other elements also established the relationship. "*Euge! Euge!*" has linguistic ties with "Mr. Eugenides" who speaks "demotic French" while the porter speaks "broken English." This latter parallel was perhaps even closer, since in the Ur-text the Smyrna merchant spoke "abominable French." As Eliot plucked these details from Joyce, he plainly transformed them into something bound in only the most tenuous manner to the context of their source. This is a most fortuitous circumstance, an unconscious association of terms almost totally shorn of their original meanings. Further magnetism to draw these images into Eliot's poetic matrix was supplied by the remainder of the vignette:

> *Comment?* Rich booty you brought back; *Le tutu,* five tattered numbers of *Pantalon Blanc et Culotte Rouge,* a blue French telegram, curiosity to show:
> —Mother dying come home father.[11]

Such a telegram Eliot had received with "mother" and "father" reversed. In itself this might have been sufficient to plant in Eliot's mind certain words appearing in the passage.

WHILE I WAS FISHING IN THE DULL CANAL
ON A WINTER EVENING ROUND BEHIND THE GASHOUSE
MUSING UPON THE KING MY BROTHER'S WRECK
AND ON THE KING MY FATHER'S DEATH BEFORE HIM.

Still intent somehow on *Ulysses*, Eliot begins to depart into other strands of meaning as the scene fragments like an exploding diamond, sending flashes of memory out in many directions. Of course, the first line reinstates the Fisher King motif, with Eliot himself partly in that role. And he continues to dwell on the funeral scene in *Ulysses*, casting this entire episode within the framework of a graveyard, hollow with the echoes of those who have gone beyond. Mr. Bloom passes the "gas works" on his way to the funeral of Paddy Dignam. The carriage stops. Mr. Bloom leans out of the carriage window and sees the "grand canal." He also sees an old dog "[c]anvassing for death."[12] It may be significant that two pages later, still riding in the carriage to the funeral, Mr. Bloom thoughtfully muses on his fingernails. Whether before or after the fact, this near juxtaposition of the dog with Bloom's contemplation of his nails may have triggered something bearing upon "Oh keep the Dog far hence, that's friend to men, / Or with his nails he'll dig it up again!" or even upon "The broken fingernails of dirty hands," with, in this latter case, the dog reference forgotten or suppressed.

Both the "gas works" and the "grand canal" have been borrowed from Joyce for their funereal connotations; they have been changed ever so slightly to the "gashouse" and the "dull canal," so that they may acquire further laminations of meaning. Specifically, in *The Tempest*, just before Ariel sings his song containing the line, "Those were pearls that were his eyes," Ferdinand hears the spirit in the air:

> Where should this music be? i' the air or the earth?
> It sounds no more; and, sure, it waits upon
> Some god o' the island. Sitting on a bank,
> Weeping again the king my father's wreck,
> This music crept by me on the waters,
> Allaying both their fury and my passion
> With its sweet air: thence I have followed it,
> Or it hath drawn me rather. But 'tis gone.
> No, it begins again.[13]

Then follows the song of Ariel. On hearing it, Ferdinand remarks that "The ditty does remember my drown'd father." Thus the protagonist in

"The Fire Sermon" partakes of both the Fisher King and Ferdinand who sits upon the bank of the waters and weeps over his father whom he believes erroneously to be dead. Soon the music will creep by upon the waters, haunting a figure whose face cannot clearly be drawn, for it is but a protean mask that shapes to the identity of others as they revolve, as on the carrousel of a magic lantern.

As one pursues this mask, the features fade. Otto (1848–1916), king of Bavaria, came to the throne upon the drowning death of his brother, the mad king Ludwig II, who in turn had ascended the throne upon the death of his father, Maximilian II. Hence, "the king my brother's wreck" and "the king my father's death before him" take on historical reality when seen from the vantage point of King Otto; all the associations are suggested through the Larisch narrative. That this odd perspective should be projected into this episode seems sensible only insofar as it accords with the theme of contemplating death, these historical figures having been absorbed into the weave of the poem. They are part of the human tragedy.

This paradigm of familial demise also occurs in certain versions of the Grail legend. In Wolfram von Eschenbach's *Parzival*, for example, Trevrezent the hermit is the brother of the Fisher King, Anfortas. He tells Parzival that he weeps evermore for Anfortas. Their father, Frimutel, is already dead. So again the father and the brother are no more.

Such a reticulum of allusions surely was spun out from a center of personal experience. Eliot still must have been feeling the death of his father, and it is reasonable to suppose that the "brother" was Jean Verdenal. The shadows of both men stretched across the canvas of the earlier portions of the poem; one would therefore expect to find them here, too. Moreover, the presence of Verdenal in memory grows even more pronounced in the following lines.

WHITE BODIES NAKED ON THE LOW DAMP GROUND
AND BONES CAST IN A LITTLE LOW DRY GARRET,
RATTLED BY THE RAT'S FOOT ONLY, YEAR TO YEAR.

Just as he seemed to envisage the loss of his young French friend most squarely, Eliot virtually buries the painful thought under an avalanche of allusions. Verdenal died on the battlefield, that Eliot knew, there or in the waters. If on the battlefield, he would have been one of the "White bodies naked on the low damp ground." Eliot speculated that his friend had died in the "mud of Gallipoli,"[14] cognate with "the low damp ground." Everything else is said through the implications of allusion.

"White naked bodies on the low damp ground" echoes in cadence and in sound "We're Tenting Tonight," a Civil War song by Walter Kittredge. Also known as "Tenting on the Old Camp Ground," the song was composed by Kittredge, a professional singer, early in 1863, just as he was about to be drafted into the Union army. Actually he was rejected on medical grounds and never had to serve. Nevertheless, in the song, which became immensely popular after it was introduced by the famous Hutchinson family in the year of its composition, Kittredge described the feelings of a soldier during a lull in battle. It was meet that Eliot should have recalled this refrain just here, for he had already lingered on the "Prothalamion" of Spenser—repeating the refrain—and Ariel's ditty, and he would soon be iterating the bawdy ballad of Mrs. Porter. The Kittredge song was also, with its battlefield setting, the perfect allusive vehicle for Eliot's nostalgic pain over the death of Jean Verdenal. He amalgamated the refrain from this song with that of another written during the same period, Stephen Foster's "Massa's in de Cold, Cold Ground." That song was published in 1852 and first sung by the Christy Minstrels—the leader of the group, E. P. Christy, paid Foster ten dollars for the privilege. The allusion to this, one of the most popular of Foster's Negro ballads, adds to the battlefield setting introduced via Kittredge.

The "low dry garret" into which the bones are cast brings in a complicated allusion to *Crime and Punishment,* a work to which Eliot may have been prompted to turn because of the attention that Hesse gave to Dostoyevsky in his *Blick ins Chaos* [Glimpse into Chaos]. Regardless, the association with *Crime and Punishment* is a rich one.

The novel deals with the unsuccessful attempt of the young Russian student Rodion Raskolnikov to commit the perfect crime, in this case the ax murder of an old widowed pawnbroker and her stepsister. More pertinent to *The Waste Land* is Svidrigailov, a wealthy gentleman who had once employed Dounia, Raskolnikov's sister, as a governess. While she was in his employment, he had mistreated her; later, when his wife died, he came to St. Petersburg to atone for his sins against her by settling a large amount of money on her. Through fortuitous circumstances, he overhears Raskolnikov confess his crime to a prostitute; he discloses this knowledge to Dounia, to attempts to force her to marry him. When she tries to shoot him with a pistol, he relents and releases her. Leaving all this behind, he "crossed the bridge to the mainland," and holed up at a hotel, "a long, blackened wooden building" that "was so conspicuous in that God-forsaken place that he could not fail to see it even in the dark":

> He went in and asked a ragged fellow who met him in the corridor for a room. The latter, scanning Svidrigailov, pulled himself together and led him at once to a close and tiny room in the distance, at the

end of the corridor, under the stairs. There was no other, all were occupied.

Svidrigailov accepts the room, lights a candle, and examines it more carefully. It is tiny; the bed and chair nearly fill it. The walls seem made from ordinary plank, coverd with dirty paper. One wall is steeply sloped beneath the stairs; and overall the ceiling is so low, he cannot stand erect. Dostoyevsky emphasizes that "the room was not an attic, but just under the stairs."[15]

Already a web of interconnections has begun to form. Plank wall with shabby and dusty paper, the design almost faded away, recalls "withered stumps of time" that "Were told upon the walls" in a "room enclosed" from which "Footsteps shuffled on the stair." Svidrigailov's room was located "just under the stairs," so that he would have heard many footsteps shuffling on the stairs above.

In this room Svidrigailov is overcome by a "feverish shiver" and dozes off, only to be awakened by a "mouse" that runs over his arm and leg to disappear into the bedclothes, from which he has to shake the creature out. Mouse-become-rat is not a great transformation. He has to bundle up because it is windy out and "there was a damp draft from the window," comparable to "The wind under the door" and "What is the wind doing?"

As he lay in bed, "one image rose after another, incoherent scraps of thought without beginning or end passed through his mind," a description of disjointed reminiscence that might aptly be applied to The Waste Land itself, and one not unlike similar accounts of recollection found in Heart of Darkness and Bubu of Montparnasse. Feverish nightmare visions rise in his mind, visions that explain why Eliot was subconsciously drawn to revive the image of the "little low dry garret." He dreams of a English country cottage with flowers growing everywhere. There are fragrant narcissus in the windows and when he enters the house, he finds everything decorated with flowers. He moves up the stairs into a drawing room, where the floor is covered with freshly cut hay. In the middle of the room is a coffin wreathed with flowers and among "the flowers lay a girl in a white muslin dress, with arms crossed and pressed on her bosom, as though carved out of marble. But her loose fair hair was wet; there was a wreath of roses on her head. The stern and already rigid profile of her face looked as though chiselled of marble too, and the smile on her pale lips was full of an immense unchildlike misery and sorrowful appeal." Svidrigailov recognizes the girl as one who "had drowned herself." He doesn't say what had happened to the girl; only that she was a mere fourteen and that she had suffered "unmerited disgrace" which tore from her "a last scream of despair, unheeded and brutally disregarded, on a dark night in the cold and wet while the wind howled."[16]

Dostoyevsky said that Svidrigailov represents desperation. This is borne out in the dream. The dead girl symbolizes all that has slipped away from him, his dead wife and Dounia. Cruelty on his part has left him bereft of anyone to love. Wrongs committed by him are projected onto the girl. It is he who has caused her "last scream of despair"; her despair is now his despair. For Eliot, in similar fashion, the girl would have represented not what he had destroyed but something he had never been able to realize, the purity of the rose, the hyacinth girl, the innocent Beatrice figure who might have lifted him from a life that he found disgusting. Certainly she must have been identified in his mind with the hyacinth girl: she is surrounded by flowers, and her hair is wet. Violated, she has the aspect of Philomel. Having died by drowning, she is the female counterpart to Phlebas. In short, she belongs comfortably to the personae of *The Waste Land*, even though she appears only by peripheral implication.

"Bones cast in a little low dry garret," therefore, are the skeletons of the dead met regularly in the place of nightmares, where they are "Rattled by the rat's foot only, year to year." The origins of this image rest in the funeral scene from *Ulysses* and from "The Pauper's Drive" (also known as "The Pauper's Funeral"). The rat, identified as well with the mouse in Svidrigailov's garret, carries with it the connotations of death. Here it is death in memory that rattles the bones, reminiscences of lost ones, year to year. In this respect, the "little low dry garret" has much in common with "rats' alley / Where the dead men lost their bones": both are objective correlatives for closely allied, if not identical, complexes of memories and emotions.

It should be noted in passing that the role of the prostitute in *Crime and Punishment* may have had something to do with the lead-in to Mrs. Porter and her daughter in the following lines.

BUT AT MY BACK FROM TIME TO TIME I HEAR
THE SOUND OF HORNS AND MOTORS, WHICH SHALL BRING
SWEENEY TO MRS. PORTER IN THE SPRING.
O THE MOON SHONE BRIGHT ON MRS. PORTER
AND ON HER DAUGHTER
THEY WASH THEIR FEET IN SODA WATER.

A partial repetition of line 185, "But at my back in a cold blast I hear," transmutes the line of Andrew Marvell from "To His Coy Mistress" into a line from John Day's The Parliament of Bees and thence twists ironically into a bawdy ballad. "Time's wingèd chariot" vanishes as the object to be heard, replaced naturally enough by "A noise of horns and hunting," modified into something more modern. Again, the context in The Parliament of Bees is important to consider, if we are to understand the use of the allusive method in this instance.

Remember that in this allegorical play or masque, Day represents various character types in the forms of bees. Thraso, or Polypragmus, the Plush Bee, is told by his servant of a newly built hive of what he calls "Poor bees! potguns, illegitimate scum, / And bastard flies, taking adulterate shape / From reeking dunghills." He asks how it is built; his servant tells him it is made from straw quaintly dyed, with rows of Indian bent intersticed. Polypragmus scoffs at such a modest domicile. He declares that his will be like Pompey's theater, with gilt ceiling decorated with pearls.

> My great hall I'll have paved with clouds; which done,
> By wondrous skill, an artificial sun
> Shall roll about, reflecting golden beams,
> Like Phoebus dancing on the wanton streams.
> And when 'tis night, just as the sun goes down,
> I'll have the stars draw up a silver moon
> In her full height of glory. Overhead
> A roof of woods and forests I'll have spread,
> Trees growing downwards, full of fallow-deer;
> When of the sudden, listening, you shall hear
> A noise of horns and hunting, which shall bring
> Actaeon to Diana in the spring,
> Where all shall see her naked skin; and there
> Actaeon's hounds shall their own master tear,
> An emblem of his folly that will keep
> Hounds to devour and eat him up asleep.
> All this I'll do that men with praise may crown
> My fame for turning the world upside-down.[17]

The palace of Polypragmus recalls one of the winter palaces of King Ludwig II described by Marie Larisch: "The King had a wonderful winter garden at Munich, which was built on the roof of the Residenz. There was also an artificial lake with a painted panoramic background of the Himalaya Mountains, and when the King sat in the garden a 'property' moon shed its gaseous light above the snow-capped peaks."[18] On the ceiling the upside-down scene depicting Actaeon discovering Diana at her bath foreshadows the topsy-turvy scene of inverted towers in "What the Thunder Said." It also serves as a thematic segue into the bordello scene with Mrs. Porter and her daughter.

In Greek mythology Actaeon, son of Aristaeus, god of various kinds of husbandry, came upon Artemis (identified by the Romans with Diana) bathing in the stream and was punished for the indiscretion by being turned into a stag, whereupon he was attacked and devoured by his own dogs. Actaeon here turns into Sweeney, the pugilistic figure from Eliot's earlier poetry, and Diana becomes Mrs. Porter, a madame. Sweeney, symbol of the common man at his crudest, is once more among the nightingales.

Hunting horns become automobile horns and to this noise is added that of the automobile engines themselves, converting a pastoral into a modern urban setting. Into this is brought a distorted fragment of an Australian soldiers' song:

> O the moon shines bright on Mrs. Porter
> And her daughter,
> For she's a snorter.
> O they wash their feet in soapy water,
> And so they oughta,
> To keep them clean.

It has a second version or chorus quite scabrous:

> The moon shines bright on Mrs. Porter
> And on her daughter;
> She washes out her cunt in soda water,
> And so she oughta,
> To keep it clean.[19]

Eliot plainly wanted to convert this scene from classical mythology into the crudest terms compatible with the poetic diction he had established. "They wash their feet in soda water" implies a double shuffle of words, in which "soda water" may be seen as replacing "soapy water," "feet" as replacing "cunt," or both simultaneously. At any rate, the motif of washing feet, with its biblical connotations, leads logically, through disjunction, into the final line of the episode.

ET O CES VOIX D'ENFANTS, CHANTANT DANS LA COUPOLE!

[AND O THOSE CHILDREN'S VOICES, SINGING IN THE CHAPEL!]

Parsifal has mastered the temptations of lust, and cured the king of his wound; now he adores the Holy Grail, while a choir of children sing from within the chapel. It is to the sonnet, "Parsifal," by Paul Verlaine that attention is turned. "Parsifal a vaincu les Filles" [Parsifal has conquered girls]; "et sa pente / Vers le Chair de garçons vierge" [and his bent / Toward virgin boys' Flesh]. "Il a vaincu la Femme belle, au coeur subtil" [He has conquered the beautiful Woman, with the subtle heart]; "Il a vaincu l'Enfer" [He has conquered Hell]. "Avec la lance qui perça le

Flanc supreme! / Il a guéri le roi, le voici roi lui-meme" [With the lance that pierced the supreme Side, / He has cured the king, has become king himself]. Possessing the grail itself, he prepares to worship, as the voices of children are heard singing in the chapel.[20]

With a dreamlike turn of the mind, the brothel scene has faded into a sacred ritual, symbolic consummation of the latent potentiality existing in even the basest moment. Miller sees this oblique reference to the homosexual temptation of Parsifal as again reflective of Eliot's attachment to Jean Verdenal. Certainly Eliot included a suspicious number of such allusions in *The Waste Land*, but there is much latitude in which to interpret them. Without corroborative biographical evidence, I can only say that homosexuality was apparently on Eliot's mind at the time, and that the most likely person with whom such feelings might have been associated would have been Verdenal. However, I still do not know the extent of the feelings, nor—and Miller totally neglects this possibility—whether they may have been those of Verdenal toward Eliot and not the other way around. It might have involved an episode, a clumsy gesture, something possibly to disrupt a friendship rather than to cement it. That would explain quite logically Eliot's affirmation of deep affection in his Dantean allusion in the dedication of his first book of poems to Verdenal.

TWIT TWIT TWIT
JUG JUG JUG JUG JUG JUG
SO RUDELY FORC'D.
TEREU

After the long opening section devoted to contemplation of lust and death comes a repetition of the Philomel motif with its aviary symbolism. Lust and death coincide in that myth, so that it acts as a kind of summing up of all that has come before it. Interestingly, the onomatopoeic "Tereu" linguistically suggests Tereus, ravisher of Philomel.

UNREAL CITY
UNDER THE BROWN FOG OF A WINTER NOON
MR. EUGENIDES, THE SMYRNA MERCHANT
UNSHAVEN, WITH A POCKET FULL OF CURRANTS
C.I.F. LONDON: DOCUMENTS AT SIGHT,
ASKED ME IN DEMOTIC FRENCH
TO LUNCHEON AT THE CANNON STREET HOTEL
FOLLOWED BY A WEEKEND AT THE METROPOLE.

Still in London, through a reiteration of lines 60–61, Eliot reaffirms the Baudelairean decadence of the place, the time having advanced from "dawn" to "noon." In this setting, he relates an actual experience he had as an employee at the bank, changing the actual Syrian client to one from Smyrna. He was, however, a wholesaler of dried currants, and he did invite Eliot for a weekend at the posh Metropole at Brighton Beach, the Coney Island of England. Eliot had not known that it was a gathering place for gay people.

"Eugenides" is of Greek origin, a name that Eliot probably put together himself for the occasion. Ironically, it means *well bred*, something Mr. Eugenides definitely wasn't. At first Eliot had him speaking "abominable French," then "vile French," and finally "demotic French," a term normally applied to the simplified script of ancient Egypt. Thus the merchant becomes identified more positively with his counterpart in ancient commerce. Singled out as "Unshaven," he is made to appear as uncouth as the quality of his language might suggest. This is further underscored with his inviting Eliot to luncheon at the Cannon Street Hotel, a singularly common lodging place in London.

Aside from its classical overtones, that Eliot made the Syrian wholesaler a "Smyrna merchant" probably had something to do with the Smyrna issue then in the news. After World War I, Izmir (the modern name of Smyrna) was claimed by both Greece and Italy. When the Greeks were authorized to occupy the area, they moved in on 15 May 1919 and promptly began committing atrocities against the Turkish population. Constant strife between the Greeks and the Turks ensued. The Greco-Turkish War, 1921–22, ended with the Turks victorious on 9 September 1922; by the treaty of Lausanne on 24 July 1923 the Turks were given full sovereignty over the territory. For Eliot these events belonged to the decline of Europe, the ascendency of the Karamazovian element of chaos; the political turmoil in Smyrna was tangible evidence of the further waning of the classical order to which that city had in ancient times contributed. Certainly the spokesman for the new order— or perhaps I should say, the new disorder—Mr. Eugenides, had little vestige of the legendary men of the Heroic Age who had inspired poets for more than two thousand years.

This vignette acquires a touch of authenticity from the otherwise inconsequential "C.i.f. London: documents at sight," which Eliot adequately glossed in his notes: "The currants were quoted at a price 'carriage and insurance free to London'; and the Bill of Lading etc. were to be handed to the buyer upon payment of the sight draft." This is standard procedure in international trade.

In the Ur-text the episode with Mr. Eugenides was followed by a repetition with variations on the Philomel motif:

Twit twit twit
Jug jug jug jug jug jug
Tereu
O swallow swallow
Ter[21]

"O swallow swallow," with its complex plethora of allusive connotations, was transplanted to the end of "What the Thunder Said." The
rest was justifiably struck out as redundant.

Then came the apostrophe to London, whose people are bound upon
the wheel of life, the endless round of birth, death, and rebirth, whose
people are like "pavement toys," dead puppets moving jerkily through
routines of an unrehearsed farce, all nonetheless according to formula.
Eliot had a sound poetic idea going here, but the writing was too
uneven to be saved. Still, it is helpful to know that he intended to
articulate quite starkly the London in which this whole section is
geographically and spiritually framed.

AT THE VIOLET HOUR, WHEN THE EYES AND BACK
TURN UPWARD FROM THE DESK, WHEN THE HUMAN ENGINE WAITS
LIKE A TAXI THROBBING WAITING

Personal experience is the point of departure. Working underground
in a veritable cell at Lloyd's Bank in the foreign exchange department,
after a full day of work, many times Eliot must have turned eyes and
back upward from his desk, nearly at twilight, to brook the journey
home to meet the anxieties of a personal hell, always a replay of the
same basic scene. How easily he must have projected himself into the
figure of Tiresias, waiting but knowing in advance what the next moment will bring.

I TIRESIAS, THOUGH BLIND, THROBBING BETWEEN TWO LIVES,
OLD MAN WITH WRINKLED FEMALE BREASTS, CAN SEE
AT THE VIOLET HOUR, THE EVENING HOUR THAT STRIVES
HOMEWARD, AND BRINGS THE SAILOR HOME FROM SEA,
THE TYPIST HOME AT TEATIME, CLEARS HER BREAKFAST, LIGHTS
HER STOVE, AND LAYS OUT FOOD IN TINS.

Syntactically this opening sentence, beginning "At the violet hour,"
is a labyrinth of disjunctive twists in which the subject of attention
gradually shifts, like the perspective at landings descending a spiral
stairway. It is as if Eliot, rising from his desk, turns into Tiresias who is
then the omniscient observer of a daily event, the proceedings of dusk,
which brings the sailor back from sea, the typist home at noon. Pre-

cisely here the most radical shift occurs, for the phrase "The typist home at teatime" is the direct object completing "the evening hour . . . that brings," while simultaneously it functions as the subject for the predicate, "clears her breakfast." So, not only does the time change from "the violet hour" to "teatime," but the whole perceptual vantage point is suddenly transformed, just as in a dream, when you are going toward someone or something, than all at once you are in a different situation doing another thing.

In his notes, Eliot quotes the passage from Ovid's *Metamorphoses* that relates how Tiresias, with a blow of his staff, once struck two mating serpents and was turned into a woman. After seven years, he chanced upon the serpents again, struck them again, and was changed back into a man. Because he knew the experience of both man and woman, Tiresias was asked to arbitrate in an argument between Jove and Juno as to whether the man or the woman derived more pleasure from sex. Jove felt that women derive the greater pleasure, and Tiresias agreed. This so angered Juno that she blinded Tiresias, and in recompense Jove bestowed upon him the power to know the future. In telling the tale, Ovid provides no embellishments; nothing in the Latin text bears upon *The Waste Land*, nothing but the barest account of the story itself. When Eliot wrote that the "whole passage from Ovid is of great anthropological interest," he was certainly baiting the critics for, however true it may be, the fact has little to do with his poem.

Actually, Eliot turned not to Ovid but rather to Swinburne for the form of his line about the ancient prophet. In Swinburne's "Tiresias," one reads:

> I, Tiresias the prophet, seeing in Thebes
>   Much evil, and the misery of men's hands
>   Who sow with fruitless wheat the stones and sands,
> With fruitful thorns the fallows and warm glebes,
>   Bade their hands hold lest worse hap come to pass;
>   But which of you had heed of Tiresias?
>
> I am as Time's self in mine own wearied mind,
>   Whom the strong heavy-footed years have led
>   From night to night and dead men unto dead,
> And from the blind hope to the memory blind;
>   For each man's life is woven, as Time's life is,
>   Of blind young hopes and old blind memories.
>
> I am a soul outside of death and birth.
>   I see before me and afterward I see,
>   O child, O corpse, the live dead face of thee,
> Whose life and death are one thing upon earth

Where day kills night and night again kills day
And dies; but where is that Harmonia?[22]

"I, Tiresias the prophet, seeing in Thebes / Much evil" not only gave
Eliot part of his syntax, it also presaged an idea of urban degeneracy, an
idea restated again at the end of "The Fire Sermon" in the allusion to St.
Augustine, "to Carthage then I came, where a cauldron of unholy loves
sang all about mine ears." A land where humans "sow with fruitless
wheat the stones and sand" is a waste land; it is the more so as the child
and the corpse unite in a single creature possessing a "live dead face."
Tiresias, as Swinburne portrays him, is the perfect uniting figure for
Eliot, since his timeless perspective reduces everything to an endless
round of birth and death, and the cycles are played out against a
background of sterility. Also Tiresias, being "outside of death and
birth," can be conceived as the finite center in which all experience is
enigmatically focused. In that sense, he is the sudden personification of
the murky consciousness in which the rest of the poem is suspended,
that is, the implied consciousness in which everything in the poem
takes place. Only in such terms can I find justification for Eliot's statement in the notes that "Tiresias, although a mere spectator and not
indeed a 'character,' is yet the most important personage in the poem,
uniting all the rest."

Utilizing the form, "I Tiresias," Eliot may also have had in mind
Revelation 22:8–9: "I John am he who heard and saw these things. And
when I heard and saw them I fell down to worship at the feet of the
angel who showed them to me; but he said to me, 'You must not do that!
I am a fellow servant with you and your brethren the prophets, and with
those who keep the words of this book. Worship God.'" What Tiresias
sees is not the glory of the Final Judgement but something much less
momentous, until one realizes that, paradoxically, each event, being an
affirmation of the human spirit, contains within it all events, as history
exists at a single timeless point.

As an example of the rather light deception sometimes found in the
notes, Eliot relates "the sailor home from sea" to the famous poem by
Sappho:

> Hesperus, you bring home all things
> That the shining morning scattered;
> You bring the sheep,
> You bring the goat,
> You bring the child to the mother.[23]

Byron paraphrased this in stanza 107, book 3 of Don Juan:

Oh, Hesperus! thou bringest all good things—
   Home to the weary, to the hungry cheer,
To the young bird the parent's brooding wings,
   The welcome stall to the o'erlabor'd steer;
Whate'er of peace about our hearthstone clings,
   Whate'er our household gods protect of dear,
Are gather'd round us by thy look of rest;
   Thou bring'st the child, too, to the mother's breast.[24]

Hesperus, of course, is the evening star, Venus, thought by the ancients to lead in the other stars of night. Significantly perhaps, the Romans called that planet Lucifer—literally the bringer of light—an interesting association since, as I shall show, the "young man carbuncular" is partially identified with Lucifer, the Devil.

While Eliot obviously had in mind the poem of Sappho, it was not from that poem that he derived the wording of his line but from Robert Louis Stevenson's "Requiem":

Under the wide and starry sky,
Dig the grave and let me lie.
Glad did I live and gladly die,
And I laid me down with a will.

This be the verse thou grave for me:
Here he lies where he longed to be;
Home is the sailor, home from sea,
And the hunter home from the hill.[25]

So Eliot continued to brood on death, reinforcing the feeling that what the typist and the "young man carbuncular" are about to do is a mechanical act endlessly repeated by the living dead who, even in the most intimate moment, remain insular.

In this syntactically subtle opening to the seduction scene, by transforming himself into Tiresias Eliot makes himself the passive witness to an act of emotional sterility that could easily be taken as a counterpart, an objective correlative, to the typical evening with Vivien to which he was condemned "At the violet hour, when eyes and back / Turn upward from the desk" and he headed home from the bank.

As for Eliot's appeal to Tiresias to supply a kind of unity to the poem, such unity can be deemed only metaphorical. As characterized by Eliot, Tiresias is simply too insubstantial to carry a heavier burden. Even if he is lent a greater substance than he possesses, viewing the poem as a continuous vision of Tiresias adds no illumination to the whole. Yet Tiresias is a product of the earliest stage of the composition of the poem, so he is hardly to be discounted. Plucked from antiquity, he does become a timeless seer to whom the human actions set before him are as old as humankind. He is blind. His vision is an inner sight that reveals not the appearance of things but their spiritual significance. And what he sees is by and large no different from the actions of the dead that he witnessed in the underworld, as related in *The Odyssey*. In short, he sums the curse of Athene as conceived by Tennyson in his dramatic monologue on the subject: "Henceforth be blind, for thou hast seen too much, / And speak the truth that no man may believe." Within that truth, for Eliot, was the realization of the tragic isolation of the individual.

In a sense Tiresias can be perceived as a literary device rather than as a character. But he represents a device not to bring unity to the poem, as Eliot alleged; his presence as witness serves merely to intensify the solipsistic quandary around which the poem revolves. His is the timeless consciousness within which all history settles to a still and eternal point.

OUT OF THE WINDOW PERILOUSLY SPREAD
HER DRYING COMBINATIONS TOUCHED BY THE SUN'S LAST RAYS,
ON THE DIVAN ARE PILED (AT NIGHT HER BED)
STOCKINGS, SLIPPERS, CAMISOLES, AND STAYS.

This is one of the most ironical allusive twists in the poem, one in which expectation of the wondrous is dashed upon mundanity; Eliot must have wanted this to hit home, for the reference to Keats's "Ode to a Nightingale" would be missed by few lovers of poetry. It needed no gloss, being from one of the most magic passages in all of English poetry:

> Thou wast not born for death, immortal bird!
> No hungry generation tread thee down;
> The voice I hear this passing night was heard
> In ancient days by emperor and clown:
> Perhaps the self-same song that found a path
> Through the sad heart of Ruth, when, sick for home,
> She stood in tears amid the alien corn;
> The same that oft-times hath
> Charm'd magic casements, opening on the foam
> Of perilous seas, in faery lands forlorn.[26]

Eliot wished to yoke this with something violently contrasting. Originally the camisoles were "dirty", and at the very commencement of the scene the typist "begins to clear away her broken breakfast" and "lays out squalid food in tins." To all of this Pound remarked that "verse not interesting enough as verse to warrant so much of it."

I TIRESIAS, OLD MAN WITH WRINKLED DUGS
PERCEIVED THE SCENE, AND FORETOLD THE REST—
I TOO AWAITED THE EXPECTED GUEST

Perhaps the best commentary on these lines is the clause omitted
from the final version: "I Tiresias . . . foretold the rest, / Knowing the
manner of these crawling bugs." Pound struck this line as "too easy,"
but it certainly leaves no doubt how Eliot as Tiresias felt about the
whole proceedings.

HE, THE YOUNG MAN CARBUNCULAR, ARRIVES,
A SMALL HOUSE AGENT'S CLERK, WITH ONE BOLD STARE,
ONE OF THE LOW ON WHOM ASSURANCE SITS
AS A SILK HAT ON A BRADFORD MILLIONAIRE.

A concise and incisive portrait, this was distilled from one that was
more elaborate, more explicit, and yet admittedly awkward and loose.[27]
A youth of twenty-one, this is an ordinary fellow one might see almost
anywhere, a loiterer, perhaps "a cheap house agent's clerk," with greasy
hair and brash manners. He is a fellow who "knows his way with
women," as he tilts back on his chair and flicks his cigarette ashes
impertinently on the floor. This smug upstart displays his self-as-
surance in the most questionable taste, as the nouveau riche of Bradford, a textile center in Yorkshire, make ostentatious and gawdy show of
their wealth. Genesius Jones has called attention to a possible parallel
between this "cheap house agent's clerk" and the Devil as described by
Milton in *Paradise Lost,* 9:499–500, in serpent form, about to tempt
Eve, "his head / Crested aloft, and Carbuncle his eyes."[28] This might be
coincidental, solely on the basis of the pivotal word, "Carbuncle"—and
that is all Jones offers—but further search brings out another rather
telling bit of evidence. Consider this narration of the entrance of Lucifer
into the Garden of Eden:

> The Sun was sunk, and after him the Star
> Of Hesperus, whose Office is to bring
> Twilight upon the Earth, short Arbiter
> Twixt Day and Night, and now from end to end
> Night's Hemisphere had veiled the Horizon round:
> When Satan who late fled before the threats
> Of Gabriel out of Eden, now improv'd
> In meditated fraud and malice, bent
> On man's destruction, maugre what might hap
> Of heavier on himself, fearless return'd. (48–57)[29]

Hesperus might have been the catalyst to coax the carbuncular image into consciousness, if it was not already there. Both Satan and the clerk move at dusk, the "violet hour," the time of Hesperus, to have their wills. And in a symbolic sense, we can see the young man playing the Devil, albeit to a less-than-innocent Eve. Certainly he, too, has come "In meditated fraud and malice," but without consciousness of all that his plotting may represent, consciousness that Satan definitely had.

THE TIME IS NOW PROPITIOUS, AS HE GUESSES,
THE MEAL IS ENDED, SHE IS BORED AND TIRED,
ENDEAVOURS TO ENGAGE HER IN CARESSES
WHICH STILL ARE UNREPROVED, IF UNDESIRED.
FLUSHED AND DECIDED, HE ASSAULTS AT ONCE;
EXPLORING HANDS ENCOUNTER NO DEFENCE;
HIS VANITY REQUIRES NO RESPONSE,
AND MAKES A WELCOME OF INDIFFERENCE.

No revision was needed here. Eliot was certain about the scene. It is terse, spare, uncomplicated as the actions he might have assigned to the insects with which he originally thought to compare the typist and her seducer. As he derived the name Madame Sosostris from *Crome Yellow*, one cannot help wondering whether he owed a certain tone, too, in this scene to a brief exchange between Anne and Gombauld in that same novel by Huxley. While Anne and Gombauld are chattering back and forth, at one point, Gombauld asks, "Why do you tell me you'd like me to paint your portrait?" Anne explains that she simply likes Gombauld and considers him a good painter. Gombauld will have none of that, insisting that what Anne really wants is to have him make love to her.

> Anne threw back her head and laughed. 'So you think it amuses me to have to evade your advances. So like a man! If only you knew how gross and awful and boring men are when they try to make love and you don't want them to make love! If you could only see yourselves through our eyes!'[30]

Personal experience was enough to give Eliot the basis for his feelings about loveless sex, but that bit from *Crome Yellow*, which he was reading at the same time he was working on *The Waste Land*, may have helped him to crystallize those feelings into a suitable form. If nothing more, it must have lent a certain conviction to his intent.

(AND I TIRESIAS HAVE FORESUFFERED ALL
ENACTED ON THIS SAME DIVAN OR BED;

I WHO HAVE SAT BY THEBES BELOW THE WALL
AND WALKED AMONG THE LOWEST OF THE DEAD.)

Tiresias lived in Thebes, and in book 11 of *The Odyssey* he is encountered as an inhabitant of Hades; but that he has "walked among the lowest of the dead" also links him with Dante. He thus confirms, through his personification of the finite center of *The Waste Land*, the poem as a journey through a personal hell.

BESTOWS ONE FINAL PATRONISING KISS,
AND GROPES HIS WAY, FINDING THE STAIRS UNLIT . . .

Eliot origanlly had him stop near the stable "to urinate, and spit," but Pound rightly called this "over the mark." In the final version, the clerk's exit is sparsely theatrical, reading much like a stage direction and thereby underscoring the mechanical aspect of the whole act. With "the stairs unlit," the clerk descends, symbolically as Satan, back into the dark pit of hell.

SHE TURNS AND LOOKS A MOMENT IN THE GLASS,
HARDLY AWARE OF HER DEPARTED LOVER;
HER BRAIN ALLOWS ONE HALF-FORMED THOUGHT TO PASS:
"WELL NOW THAT'S DONE: AND I'M GLAD IT'S OVER."

As through blurred vision, one momentarily sees another figure standing there. Marie Larisch has just conducted Marie Vetsera to the secret meeting with Rudolph. As they had approached the crown prince's apartment, they went up many flights of stairs, down a passageway, and into a gunroom adjoining the anteroom, where a pet raven swooped at the countess. She waited for Baroness Vetsera, who of course would not return, for she had been spirited off to meet her fate: "I went to the mirror and smoothed my hair, which had been disarranged by the raven's sudden swoop, and as I did so I heard the sound of military music. It was the hour for changing of the guard."[36] Likewise the typist "smoothes her hair with automatic hand" while looking in the mirror, puts a record on the gramophone, and then, as her identity transforms, "This music crept by me upon the waters." Identification with Countess Larisch, at the moment when she has delivered her young friend into lust and death, lends an echo of magnitude to the proceedings that the nonchalance of the typist would otherwise totally belie.

WHEN LOVELY WOMAN STOOPS TO FOLLY AND
PACES ABOUT HER ROOM AGAIN, ALONE,

SHE SMOOTHES HER HAIR WITH AUTOMATIC HAND,
AND PUTS A RECORD ON THE GRAMOPHONE.

A favorite device of Eliot was to allow a fragment of some well-known masterpiece or otherwise popular work to float to the surface like a scrap of ribbon then plunge back into the stream of surface events, to hint at a familiar tune that then dissolves into the former harmonies of the piece. So Eliot reaches into chapter twenty-four of Oliver Gold-smith's *The Vicar of Wakefield* to tease the strings of memory into sympathetic response. One of the kindly vicar's daughters, Olivia, has been seduced by an unprincipled nobleman after a mock marriage (which later proves to have been legal). Later, the family breakfasts "together at the honeysuckle bank, where, while we sate, my youngest daughter, at my request, joined her voice to the concert on the trees about us. It was here my poor Olivia first met her seducer, and every object served to recall her sadness." This is the song that she sang:

> When lovely woman stoops to folly,
>   And finds too late that men betray,
> What charm can sooth her melancholy,
>   What art can wash her guilt away?
>
> The only art her guilt to cover,
>   To hide her shame from every eye,
> To give repentance to her lover,
>   And wring his bosom—is to die.[32]

Since she met her seducer on the honeysuckle bank, she becomes allied with the "nymphs" along the Thames at the beginning of "The Fire Sermon." And her guilt identifies her with the typist, though the latter either does not recognize her guilt or suppresses it. In any case, the deliberate allusion to Olivia's song reinforces the earlier reference to the guilt of Countess Larisch and the tragedy of the seduction she aided, reinforces it as an unconscious fortification of the present mechanical seduction of the typist.

"THIS MUSIC CREPT BY ME UPON THE WATERS"
AND ALONG THE STRAND, UP QUEEN VICTORIA STREET.

Another transformation: the record on the gramophone leads to the music of Ariel's song as it reaches the ears of Ferdinand, who sits musing on the death by water of his father. Then the song drifts along the Strand, great commercial thoroughfare of London, and "up Queen Victoria Street," both running generally parallel with the Thames. Eliot has again materialized, however nameless, to continue his wandering through the city.

O CITY CITY, I CAN SOMETIMES HEAR
BESIDE A PUBLIC BAR IN LOWER THAMES STREET,
THE PLEASANT WHINING OF A MANDOLINE
AND A CLATTER AND A CHATTER FROM WITHIN
WHERE FISHMEN LOUNGE AT NOON: WHERE THE WALLS
OF MAGNUS MARTYR HOLD
INEXPLICABLE SPLENDOUR OF IONIAN WHITE AND GOLD.

Recurring apostrophe to London, this one finds Eliot in spirit on Lower Thames Street, a narrow and congested fisherman district, reeking of fish from end to end. Down from the bank, not far from the river, it is a place he knew well. With his lifetime love of boating, he must have found this a congenial spot, despite the smell. St. Magnus the Martyr, visible even from London Bridge, caters to many of the fishmen round about. The original church of that name stood on old London Bridge until the bridge burned in the Great Fire of 1666 of which Dryden wrote in *Annus Mirabilis*. Ten years later it was rebuilt by Christopher Wren. The interior is decorated in white and gold with columns of the Ionian order. Curiously, Eliot had originally called them Corinthian. White and gold, incidentally, are traditional ecclesiastical colors of Easter.

THE RIVER SWEATS
OIL AND TAR

To appreciate the poignancy of this passage, recall Eliot writing of the river as a great brown god that is somehow within it. The fate of the river is in a real sense our fate. As it becomes polluted and sterile, so do we. Eliot derives his imagery from *Heart of Darkness* (I italicize the key words):

> The idleness of a passenger, my isolation amongst all these men with whom I had no point of contact, *the oily and languid sea*, the uniform somberness of the coast, seemed to keep me away from the truth of things, within the toil of a mournful and senseless delusion.

Little wonder that these words might linger in Eliot's mind; not only had he begun this section, "The Fire Sermon," under Conrad's notion that "Nothing is easier . . . than to evoke the great spirit of the past upon the lower reaches of the Thames," but he must have felt himself too "within the toil of a mournful and senseless delusion." Within this same portion of the Conrad story he might have found and retained these further promptings:

> Once, I remember, we came upon a man-of-war anchored off the coast. There wasn't even a shed there, and she was shelling the bush. It appears the French had one of their wars going on thereabouts. Her ensign dropped limp like a rag; the muzzles of the long six-inch guns stuck out all over the low hull; *the greasy, slimy swell* swung her up lazily and let her down, swaying her thin masts.

And:

> We called on some more places with farcical names, where the merry dance of death and trade goes on in a still and earthy atmosphere as of an overheated catacomb; all along the formless coast bordered by dangerous surf, as if Nature herself had tried to ward off intruders; in and out of rivers, *streams of death in life, whose banks were rotting into mud, whose waters, thickened into slime,* invaded the contorted mangroves, that seemed to writhe at us in the extremity of an impotent despair.[33]

All this is perfectly *The Waste Land*. Scattered far and wide throughout the story, these images might not have remained with Eliot so clearly, but appearing within the space of a few pages they could only have had a cumulative effect. He could hardly have dismissed in his existing state of mind such inwardly reflecting candor as was expressed in "impotent despair," especially since Conrad described this part of the journey as "like a weary pilgrimage amongst hints for nightmares."

THE BARGES DRIFT
WITH THE TURNING TIDE
RED SAILS
WIDE
TO LEEWARD, SWING ON THE HEAVY SPAR.

Still within the style of Conrad, this description tallies with one given within the same immediate context as that containing the reference to evocation of the past along the Thames; in it, he tells how "the tanned sails of the barges drifting up with the tide seemed to stand still in red clusters of canvas."[34] Considering the significance of *Heart of Darkness* for *The Waste Land*, Eliot might have wished to conjure from it a recurring atmospheric aura throughout this poem, for in Conrad the atmosphere is always pregnant with the sense of the story. It is almost an objective correlative of the emotional tone of the story, just as it is in *The Waste Land*.

THE BARGES WASH
DRIFTING LOGS
DOWN GREENWICH REACH
PAST THE ISLE OF DOGS.

Greenwich is a borough of London, about five miles south of London Bridge, separated into a southern and a northern district by Greenwich Reach. Humphrey, duke of Gloucester, had a palace built there in 1433, and it became a favorite residence of the Tudor sovereigns. Today it is a part of a great hospital complex, still the most notable feature of the borough.

Opposite Greenwich is a peninsula, the Isle of Dogs, commonly supposed to have derived its name from the royal kennels located there. These belonged to Greenwich Palace. The Isle of Dogs is a blunt peninsula formed by a loop in the Thames. On its southern tip is the railway station of North Greenwich, from whence Greenwich Tunnel, a foot passageway for pedestrians, passes under the Thames to Greenwich.

Described here is an implied movement down the Thames: "The barges wash, / Like drifting logs," Eliot had originally written. By suppressing "Like," he gained an almost ideographic quality in the simile while the sense of movement remained. It recalls the procession of barges celebrating the marriage of Henry VIII and Anne Boleyn. Some of the barges, according to a contemporary historian, carried "trumpets, shawns, and other divers instruments all the way playing and making great melody."[35] Later their daughter Queen Elizabeth with her paramour Robert Dudley, earl of Leicester, enjoyed numerous trysts during outings on the lower Thames. And in 1717, down the Thames floated a grand marine pageant, featuring barges of musicians to perform for George I the famous *Water Music* composed for the occasion by George Frederick Handel.

Aside from the musical processions spun out imaginatively from the gramophone of the typist, lighting centuries along the way, this literary excursion takes a disjunctive turn at Greenwich. It was there that Henry VIII was born, and also his two daughters, Mary and Elizabeth. Elizabeth entertained the earl of Leicester at Greenwich Palace. That historical thread leads easily into the next episode, after the cries of the Rhine Maidens. Whatever vague relations may be stirred between the Isle of Dogs and the Dog in "The Burial of the Dead" give rise to only a momentary uneasiness which quickly passes. All along the Thames, after all, lurk the spirits of the past, shades that the mysterious Dog, seeker of the buried, ever threatens to dig up or expose.

WEIALALA LEIA
WALLALA LEIALALA

These are imitations of the playful cries of joy of the Rhine Maidens before the sacred gold that they guard is stolen from them, before they are symbolically violated. A ring forged from the gold would give its wearer rule over the world. Alberich, the ugly dwarf whose overtures the maidens spurn, eventually steals the gold, and this violation ultimately brings about the twilight of the gods. Again, there is a tragic implication to lust, whether for power (the surface motive here) or sex (the symbolic undertone), that is not realized until it is too late; in this instance, when the Rhine Maidens each in turn tell their tales.

In his notes, Eliot refers to *Götterdämmerung* 3.1 for the song of the Rhine Maidens. There they sing to Siegfried and warn him that he shall be killed. But, as Herbert Knust indicates, the actual song that Eliot quotes appears nowhere in the Ring cycle but comes closest to the one sung in the first act of *Das Rheingold*.[36] Eliot modified Wagner's onomatopoeia to suit his own needs. More interestingly, though, he says that the song of the Rhine Maidens, whom he identifies as Thames-daughters, begins at line 266, "The river sweats." Thus, a song of joy mourns first the death of the river, then the sterile lust of Elizabeth and Leicester, and finally the downfall of each of the Thames-daughters or Rhine Maidens. By associating the Thames with the Rhine, he makes it an archetypical river, truly symbolizing the river as the brown god. He turns the Thames-daughter Rhine Maidens into English women, each representing a different social class. And finally he identifies himself with the third maiden. All this he accomplishes by a thread of disjunctive association that must be carefully followed.

ELIZABETH AND LEICESTER
BEATING OARS
THE STERN WAS FORMED
A GILDED SHELL
RED AND GOLD
THE BRISK SWELL
RIPPLED BOTH SHORES

Rather notorious was the longstanding affair between Elizabeth and Leicester. Bishop de Quadra, ambassador of Philip of Spain, reported the affair to the Spanish court in a series of letters, portions of which are quoted in James Anthony Froude's *Elizabeth*, to which Eliot alludes in his notes. In the letter quoted by Eliot, de Quadra described an escapade on the Thames: "In the afternoon we were in a barge, watching the games on the river. (The queen) was alone with Lord Robert and myself on the poop, when they began to talk nonsense, and went so far that Lord Robert at last said, as I was on the spot there was no reason why they should not be married if the queen pleased."[37]

That they were "on the poop," and "The stern was formed / A gilded shell / Red and gold," recalls the barge of Cleopatra:

> The barge she sat in, like a burnish'd throne,
> Burn'd on the water: the poop was beaten gold;
> Purple the sails, and so perfumed that
> The winds were love-sick with them . . .[38]

In fact, Eliot originally wrote "The barge was formed," then crossed out "barge" and replaced it with "stern." His diction here remains Elizabethan, though none of the images is found in Shakespeare. Cleopatra's barge has in a sense devolved into that of Elizabeth, which in turn is reduced to the canoe of the first Thames-daughter by virtue of a partial identification of her with Elizabeth through geographical allusions.

SOUTHWEST WIND

South wind is a biblical phrase, appearing five times in the Bible, usually with favorable connotations. Commentators, however, have linked Eliot's "Southwest wind" (which was never a plain south wind even in the first draft) with Luke 12:55, "And when ye see the south wind blow, ye say, There will be heat; and it cometh to pass," which is the single biblical use of the phrase with negative connotations. While one cannot rule out such an association—which has the interesting implication of bringing heat rather than rain to the sterile waste land—I feel that a more likely source would be Acts 27:12–13, for two reasons. First, this is the most detailed account of a sea voyage and shipwreck in ancient literatures, which alone would make it important for Eliot. And second, it is the only passage in the Bible wherein *south wind* is mentioned in a context with *southwest* (which itself occurs in the Bible only here). The passage concerns Paul's missionary trip to Rome, where he is incarcerated and his ultimate fate sealed to history:

> And because the haven was not commodious to winter in, the more part advised to depart thence also, if by any means they might attain to Phenice, and there to winter; which is an haven of Crete, and lieth toward the south west and north west.

> And when the south wind blew softly, supposing that they had obtained their purpose, loosing thence, they sailed close by Crete.

But they were blown off course by a tempest and landed on the island of Melita, from whence they finally completed their voyage to Rome on an Alexandrian ship moored in the isle.

Beyond this biblical allusion, a southwest wind would most directly
carry ships down the Thames from below the Tower of London along
the east side of the Greenwich peninsula, where many a royal barge
glided in bygone centuries.

CARRIED DOWN STREAM
THE PEAL OF BELLS
WHITE TOWERS

Downstream may be heard the bells from the Tower of London, really
a building complex with several towers. The oldest, located centrally on
a slight rise, is the White Tower. It was begun about 1078 on a site
previously occupied by two bastions built by King Alfred in 885.
Supposedly it got its present name from the fact that it was white-
washed in 1240. Though originally a fort, the Tower of London has
down through the centuries been most frequently used as a prison.
Notice that Eliot pluralizes *tower* so that it refers to the entire building
complex. Of all the notable persons incarcerated there, one should
single out Elizabeth, who spent two months there in 1554 under the
reign of her sister, Mary, and Robert Dudley, earl of Leicester, who was
imprisoned in the previous year because of his father's part in the
conspiracy to place Lady Jane Grey on the throne.

There may be in the "White Towers," as so many commentators have
pointed out, the outline of the Perilous Chapel, although the association
seems forced and remote. It adds little more than atmosphere to the
scene.

WEIALALA LEIA
WALLALA LEIALALA

Mixed with the pealing of the bells is heard the song of the Thames-
daughters, descendents of the Rhine Maidens, reminding one that the
river is archetypical, the scene fairylike, hovering between myth and
reality. Also, one may suddenly become aware just how musical the
whole structure of the poem is, a music of ideas, as I. A. Richards called
it; leitmotifs weaving in and out of the text, snatches of opera and song
touching the ear, sometimes quite faintly, then dying away in the contrapuntal orchestration of the whole. But such musical appearances are
never without provocation or purpose. Here the song heralds the brief
tales of the three Thames-daughters, told in succession.

"TRAMS AND DUSTY TREES.
HIGHBURY BORE ME. RICHMOND AND KEW

UNDID ME. BY RICHMOND I RAISED MY KNEES
SUPINE ON THE FLOOR OF A NAROW CANOE."

Brief, indeed, and quintessential is this song. It is little more than a paradigm. A bit of landscape, indication of a social background, and the familiar fall through lust are all that is conveyed, on the surface. In the Ur-text the speaker is from a humble and conservative background, neither rich nor working-class. Her father has a small business that provides a comfortable home and an annual three-week vacation at Shanklin or Bognor, bourgeois resort areas.

Eliot has projected the life of Elizabeth into that of a modern middle-class English woman. Highbury is a distinctly middle-class residential district in the new section of London, near Hampstead Heath. It is quite ordinary, as Eliot's description suggests. Shanklin and Bognor are both pleasant but unpretentious seaside resorts, just the sort of places where a person of medium means might vacation. But this is background.

"Richmond and Kew / Undid me," marks the crucial turning point in the narrative, where background gives way to action. Also at this point Eliot chose to employ a Dantean mode of expression, enlisting a most peculiar allusion:

> ricorditi di me, che son la Pia;
> Siena me fe', disfecemi Maremma:
> salsi colui che innanellata, pria
> disposando, m'avea con la sua gemma.
>
> [remember me, who am La Pia;
> Siena made me, Maremma undid me:
> it is known to him who, first
> plighting troth, had me with his gem.][39]

Neither the identity nor the sin of La Pia are known, so she makes a perfect template after which to fashion the identity of the unnamed woman from Highbury.

Richmond and Kew were favorite spots of Elizabeth. She often stayed at the palace in Richmond, entertaining many guests, including Leicester. "At Kew we had tea" would be more in keeping with the queen than with the woman from Highbury, albeit she too could have lunched there after visiting the famous botanical gardens. That acts as a kind of bridge between the two women. But then the sexual escapade of the Highbury woman, "Supine on the floor of a narrow canoe," is definitely a parody of the similar adventures of the queen on her barge. That it was originally a "perilous canoe," hinting some vague connection with the Perilous Chapel, and that the woman in question is a

Thames-daughter, somehow allied with the spirit or god of the river, make the seduction both a physical and a spiritual desecration.

This is one of the clearest *moral episodes* in the poems, and it is well to remember here Eliot's position on such things. The possibility of damnation was important to him. He once criticized Paul Elmer More for his failure to acknowledge God as the creator of hell as well as of heaven. Prospects of paradise occupied him hardly at all, except in the nebulous sense in which they entered the work of St. John of the Cross, namely, as an ineffable experience hiding behind all attempts to seize it. It can never truly be experienced because it transcends all categories of knowing; it involves the self-contradictory task of expressing the infinite in finite terms. It seems that for Eliot life was something from which to be saved, a not-uncommon premise from which a broad spectrum of idealistic thought has been launched.

Spiritual turmoil, central to his own experience, formed much of the grist for Eliot's poetic mill. "It is in fact in moments of moral and spiritual struggle depending upon spiritual sanctions, rather than in those 'bewildering minutes' in which we are all very much alike, that men and women come nearest to being real."[40] One must, to be most human, not act out of mechanistic necessity, for that would preclude the struggle for significance. "So far as we are human, what we do must be either evil or good; so far as we do evil or good, we are human; and it is better, in a paradoxical way, to do evil than to do nothing; at least, we exist."[41] To Eliot humans cannot be defined simply as rational beings— after all, computers can reason—they are moral beings, capable of moral decision. If not that, they have no special significance and the search for meaning in life is useless. Though the woman in this passage behaved in a way Eliot would not have regarded as moral, she at least is aware of her transgression and therefore has the possibility of salvation, unlike the woman who submitted to the "young man carbuncular."

"MY FEET ARE AT MOORGATE, AND MY HEART
UNDER MY FEET. AFTER THE EVENT
HE WEPT. HE PROMISED 'A NEW START.'
I MADE NO COMMENT. WHAT SHOULD I RESENT?"

Moorgate is a slum district in London, above London Bridge and beyond the Bank of England. The second Thames-daughter represents the lower class, but she too has no simple identity. Contrasting with her station, she may be identified with the transformational Madonna in Revelation 12:1: "And there appeared a great wonder in heaven; a woman clothed with the sun, and the moon under her feet, and upon her head a crown of twelve stars." It is said that "she brought forth a

man child, who was to rule all nations with a rod of iron," which makes
her the Blessed Mother of the millennium.

> "ON MARGATE SANDS.
> I CAN CONNECT
> NOTHING WITH NOTHING.
> THE BROKEN FINGERNAILS OF DIRTY HANDS.
> MY PEOPLE HUMBLE PEOPLE WHO EXPECT
> NOTHING."

It was of course at Margate, a popular resort on the Thames, that Eliot
spent a month, from 11 October 1921, recuperating after his nervous
breakdown. There he wrote the first drafts of parts of The Waste Land.
When he wrote the Thames-daughters section of "The Fire Sermon," he
probably intended from the beginning to ally himself through them
with the spirit of the river. After all, a bond of involvement—perhaps
even with a core of lust, natural lust—between him and Vivien had
brought him to the banks of the great river Thames to seek succor from
the environment, strength from the river god. Transition from the second Thames-daughter to his own situation may have been facilitated
through the Madonna of Revelation, who, according to 12:14, was
"given two wings of a great eagle, that she might fly into the wilderness,
into her place, where she is nourished for a time, and times, and half a
time, from the face of the serpent." The sixteenth verse states that "the
earth helped the woman." Such a description, though strange in its
symbolism, could surely have been construed by Eliot to have
dovetailed with his own situation, to serve as an objective correlative of
it.

Eliot's identification with the third Thames-daughter is fairly obvious
in the opening reference to Margate and in "I can connect / Nothing
with nothing," but it was even more explicit in the first draft. There he
wrote that he "was to be grateful," for at Margate he found "many
others" apparently in the same state as he. Then, as if slipping back into
the female disguise, he recalled enigmatically "the pressure of dirty
hand," which he later changed to cite merely the image of broken
fingernails of dirty hands.

Eliot was trying to fit back together the pieces of his life, but at that
juncture he could "connect / Nothing with nothing." Nevertheless, he
"was to be grateful" to be at rest, away from Vivien, and apparently
among "many others" like him. A further dimension of his state of mind
is brought out, perhaps, when he again uses "nothing with nothing" in
part two of Murder in the Cathedral, where the chorus speaks of:

The horror of the effortless journey, to the empty land
Which is no land, only emptiness, absence, the Void,
Where those who were men can no longer turn the mind
To distraction, delusion, escape into dream, pretence,
Where the soul is no longer deceived, for there are no objects, no tones,
No colours, no forms to distract, to divert the soul
From seeing itself, foully united forever, nothing with nothing.[42]

In that passage are mingled the horror of judgement and the indescribable torment of the dark night of the soul, but the roots of those feelings must be sought in some prior psychological anxiety. Eliot's religious sentiment after his conversion certainly had its origins in the experiences that led him to Margate, and in the innate temperament that shaped his response to his experiences.

Grover Smith contends that "The broken fingernails of dirty hands" identifies the speaker with the typist from the seduction scene, but that reading seems off target in light of the original version of the line, "I still feel the pressure of dirty hand."[43] If the speaker is Eliot himself, then the "dirty hand" may be related to his marital experience, though this is pure speculation. Sticking closely to the text, in both the original and the final versions, one can say that the image is associated with a felt violation, whether of body or soul or both. From this angle, *dirty* may have only a symbolic denotation. Purely as a verbal image, it could have found promptings from *Satyricon*, where the wife is wishfully imagined by her husband, Trimalchio, to desire him so much after he would have died that she would dig him up with her fingernails. That would explain the shift from "dirty hand" to "broken fingernails of dirty hands." Eliot might also have had a fleeting fantasy about his wife like the one Trimalchio had about his.

Finally, the images behind the images include from *Heart of Darkness*, "They are simple people—and I want nothing, you know," said by the Russian about the natives, as an unconscious source for "My people humble people who expect / Nothing," and "Heaven fashioned us of nothing, and we strive / To bring ourselves to nothing," from *The Duchess of Malfi*, as possibly bearing upon "I can connect / Nothing with nothing."[44]

LA LA

The song of the Thames-daughters dies away, leaving only the last syllable.

TO CARTHAGE THEN I CAME

With the first words of the opening sentence in the third chapter, or book, of St. Augustine's *Confessions*, "To Carthage then I came, where a cauldron of unholy loves sang all about mine ears," Eliot begins the brief coda of "The Fire Sermon." Augustine goes on to describe how, before his conversion, in Carthage he pursued a life of sensual pleasure, unchecked by any religious sentiments. As pointed out earlier, Eliot avowed that one of his purposes in *The Waste Land* was to attempt a kind of synthesis of different religious traditions, explaining his "collocation" of fragments from St. Augustine and Buddha.

If there is a continuity of the poem, at this point a connection can be seen between the confessional third Thames-daughter episode and the quotation from Augustine: both represent confessions and, on a deeper level, Eliot saw the foundation of his problematic situation as one of involvement with things earthly, possibly even as a matter of concupiscence (almost always a factor in any youthful marriage).

BURNING BURNING BURNING BURNING

From the actual *Fire Sermon* of Buddha, this line is a verbal mirror of the manner in which all things are conceived by Buddhists to be consuming themselves with a symbolic fire, much as individuals, insofar as they involve themselves with material things, are consumed with emotions of attachment, greed, possessiveness, and other attitudes that bind them to appearances (which they take as reality). Actually, whether the objects of attention consume themselves, or individuals consume themselves with them, makes no real difference, as both are merely ways of conceiving and stating the relation between humans and their illusions (called *maya* by Buddhists), the relation that keeps them in the karmatic cycle of endless rebirth until they free themselves from it all by practices of detachment.

From the Christian side, of course, *burning* carries connotations of lust, which are reinforced by the immediately preceding line in which Augustine begins to confess his preconversion lechery. Furthermore, the obsessive repetition of the word suggests an untoward preoccupation with the problem that is, at the very least, fervent.

It is worth observing that Aeneas, too, to Carthage came there to burn with love for Dido, and she with love for him. In *The Heroides*, she says, "Uror, ut inducto ceratae sulpure taedae, / ut pia fumosis addita tura focis" [I am burning, like pine torches tipped with sulphured wax, / like pious incense placed on smoking altar-fires].[45] When Aeneas departed, she literally burned, throwing herself upon a lighted pyre.

Finally, this concept of burning extends to an incident so strange that, once acquainted with it, a person would not be apt totally to forget it.

Marie Larisch tells in her autobiography how her aunt Elizabeth described an apparition of King Ludwig, which appeared to her the first night that she slept in Bavaria after the king's death. Elizabeth is relating the incident to her niece:

> We gazed at each other in silence, and then the King said slowly and sadly:
> 'Cissi, are you frightened of me?
> 'No, Ludwig, I am not frightened.'
> 'Ah me!' he sighed. 'Death has not brought me peace. Cissi, she burns in torment. The flames encircle her, the smoke suffocates her. She burns and I am powerless to save her.'
> '*Who* burns, dear cousin?' I asked.
> 'I do not know because her face is hidden,' he answered. 'but I know that it is a woman who loved me, and until her destiny is fulfilled I shall not be free. But afterwards you will join us and we three shall be happy in Paradise together.'[46]

The identity of the burning woman is never revealed. But Eliot might have assimilated the episode to his own situation, especially the statement, "I know that it is a woman who loved me, and until her destiny is fulfilled I shall not be free." Until Vivien died, Eliot was haunted by her. He refused to speak with her when she approached him after a public talk he gave, some years after they separated. That is not the action of a man free from the influence of a woman he once married.

So, the repeated "Burning burning burning burning" must be taken, all things considered, as a kind of incantation, embodying in the widest sense the plight of humans to struggle endlessly with reality, more narrowly with the consuming passion of lust. On a personal level the words convey painful emotions of Eliot's entanglement with a woman who seemed to consume his soul with the burning of a relationship relentless and terrible in its consequences.

O LORD THOU PLUCKEST ME OUT
O LORD THOU PLUCKEST

BURNING

An expression of faith in the saving grace of God, this returns to the end of the *Confessions* of St. Augustine, where he discusses how humans are led astray by the appeal to the eye of earthly things, the Christian counterpart to the deception of *maya* as conceived in Buddhism: "And I, though I speak and see this [i.e., the truth of God], entangle my steps with these outward beauties [i.e., earthly things]; but

Thou pluckest me out, O Lord, Thou pluckest me out; *because thy loving-kindness is before my eyes.*"[47] Augustine echoes *Psalms 25 : 5– 7:*

> Lead me in thy truth, and teach me: for thou art the God of my salvation; on thee do I wait all the day.
> Remember, O Lord, thy tender mercies and thy loving kindnesses; for they have been ever of old.
> Remember not the sins of my youth, nor my transgressions: according to thy mercy remember thou me for thy goodness' sake, O Lord.

And Augustine writes: "These seductions of the eyes I resist, lest my feet wherewith I walk upon Thy way be ensnared; and I lift up mine invisible eyes to Thee that Thou wouldest *pluck my feet out of the snare.*"[48] This echoes again Psalms 25 : 15: "Mine eyes are ever toward the Lord; for he shall pluck my feet out of the snare." Behind this half-assertion, half-plea was still felt the burning, the inextricable involvement in which was summed a depth of anxiety, torment, confusion, and frustration into which it was impossible to peer, to discern at bottom any ultimate peace. That is the last word of "The Fire Sermon."

6

Death by Water

Of all the sections of *The Waste Land*, "Death by Water" grew and survived in the strangest manner, finally presenting a kind of anachronism that Eliot himself thought to reject. It is now the tailpiece of "Dans le Restaurant" snipped away, translated, and reworked to be grafted on as a coda to the shipwreck episode originally forming the major portion of "Death by Water." Pound edited out the shipwreck scene, leaving behind the coda. Eliot then asked if he should not discard the Phlebas bit also, but Pound advised keeping it, since Phlebas had appeared earlier, in the cartomancy episode, as "the drowned Phoenician Sailor." Eliot acquiesced, and the twice-coda fragment remained as the total substance of the section.

Because of this singular evolution, the section bears in relation to the poem as a whole the extremity of the organizing principle, a continuity of thematic concerns, which is stretched to the breaking point. Pound indicated the most concrete connection between the section and the rest of the poem. Then there is the more general thematic link of death by water, meaningful to Eliot personally and belonging also to the folkloric and mythological considerations, deriving mainly from Frazer, that helped to give Eliot an archetypical framework. Beyond that, the section is insulary, sharing no allusive connections with the rest of the poem. To press for such connections runs counter to the fact that the Phlebas fragment materialized at quite another time and in a different context. It is only the concern with death by drowning—and the Phoenician commonality—that draws it successfully into *The Waste Land*.

While Eliot incorporated many fragments from earlier poems into *The Waste Land*, in all other cases he infused them with allusive connotations that wove them into the overall pattern of their contexts. If they did not already suggest an allusive source used in the poem, Eliot insinuated source material into them or built some further allusive passages around them. But with the Phlebas episode he did little or none of this. It relates to the other sections only through participation in

193

a continuity of concern, specifically with an alien and transformative kind of death.

To know that "Death by Water" is a translation and slight reworking of the final section of "Dans le Restaurant" is of only slight help, since even there the meaning of it was far from forthright. Most authorities feel that it recalls the death of Jean Verdenal. Though that is a reasonable assumption, it entails some difficulties, not the least of which is that Verdenal did not die by drowning and Eliot likely knew that he didn't. Also, no one has really explained why Eliot should wish to have recalled the death of his friend on the heels of an old waiter recounting a youthful sexual experience that strikes the listener in the poem as rather distasteful. Nevertheless, to get a handle on this episode one must start with the poem from which it was taken. With the French text readily available, I provide not a literary but rather a literal translation:

> The sickly garçon who has nothing better to do
> Than tap his fingers and lean over my shoulder:
>> "In my country the weather will be rainy;
>> Windy, brightly sunny, and then again rainy;
>> That's what we call the beggars' wash day."
> (Chatterbox, slobbery, with rounded hips,
> I beg of you, at least do not slobber in the soup.)
>> "Dripping willow, and new buds on the brambles—
>> It's there, in a downpour, that we took cover.
> I was seven, she was even younger.
>> She was thoroughly drenched, I gave her primroses."
> The stains on his vest ran to the number of thirty-eight.
>> "I tickled her to make her laugh.
>> I experienced an instant of power and delirium."
>
>> But then, old lecher, at that age . . .
> "Sir, the fact is hard.
>> A huge dog came along and pawed at us;
>> I got scared, I left her at midway.
>> It's too bad."
>> But then, you have your vulture!
>
>> Go polish the wrinkles off your face;
> Wait, my fork, scour your skull.
> By what right do you pay for experiences like I have?
> Wait, here's ten sous for the bathroom.
>
>> Phlebas, the Phoenician, fifteen days ago drowned,
> Forgot the cries of gulls and swell of the Cornwall sea,
> And the profits and the losses, and the cargo of tin:
> A current under sea carried him far away,
> Passing him through the stages of his former life.

Consider, then, he was a trying fellow;
Nonetheless, he was formerly a handsome man, of tall stature.

The first thing to notice is that the waiter's experience is a debasement
of the experience in the Hyacinth garden: "You gave me hyacinths"
becomes "I gave her primroses." The "hyacinth girl" had wet hair,
paralleling the drenched condition of the little girl under the willows.
Curiously, too, a dog intervenes to disrupt the erotic escapade, and a
dog also figures in "The Burial of the Dead" as a disturbing agent. All
this makes clear the line, "But then, you have your vulture!" The
vulture is a transmutation of the eagle that daily pecked the liver of
Prometheus as he lay helpless, bound to a rock. Gide made the eagle a
symbol of all that torments certain artists to create, in *Le Prométhée mal
enchaîné*, to which Eliot referred in *The Use of Poetry and the Use of
Criticism*:

> Wordsworth . . . wrote his *Preface* . . . while in the plenitude of his
> poetic powers and while his reputation was still only sustained by
> readers of discernment. And he was of an opposite poetic type to
> Coleridge. Whether the bulk of his genuine poetic achievement is so
> much greater than Coleridge's as it appears, is uncertain. Whether his
> power and inspiration remained with him to the end is, alas, not even
> doubtful. But Wordsworth had no ghostly shadows at his back, no
> Eumenides to pursue him; or if he did, he gave no sign and took no
> notice; and he went droning on the still sad music of infirmity to the
> verge of the grave. His inspiration never having been of that sudden,
> fitful and terrifying kind that visited Coleridge, he was never, appar-
> ently, troubled by the consciousness of having lost it. As Andre Gide's
> Prometheus said, in the lecture which he gave before a large audience
> in Paris: *"Il faut avoir un aigle."* [One must have an eagle.] Coleridge
> remained in contact with his eagle.[1]

Thus the waiter, like the narrator, has something in his past that haunts
him and that, if he were an artist, would probably precipitate acts of
exorcistic creation. His garden is more earthy, but for his sensibilities
the experience in it remains no less disturbing to his soul.

To understand that much about the narrative of the waiter puts one in
a good position to interpret the contrasting Phlebas section. Central to a
textually faithful interpretation is the recognition that Phlebas is not a
sailor. A sailor would not be concerned with "the profits and losses,
and the cargo of tin." Phlebas is engaged on some kind of commercial
enterprise, in keeping with the commercial hegemony of the Phoeni-
cians in the ancient world. Other than that, he is tall and handsome, but
trying. All these characteristics together seem to portray none other
than Eliot himself.

The exact date of composition for "Dans le Restaurant" is unknown, but Grover Smith places it, along with the three other poems in French, between 1916 and 1917. Sometime around March 1917, Eliot gained employment at Lloyd's Bank, which could explain the commercial concerns of Phlebas, but the dating of the composition as well as the connection with the bank is not exact enough to be certain about the autobiographical nature of the commercial aspect of Phlebas's character. Eliot may have only been anticipating his position when he wrote the poem, or the question of employment at the bank may not yet have arisen.

The remainder of the portrait of Phlebas offers firmer ground in identifying it as Eliot. Early photographs testify that Eliot was quite handsome, fine of feature and proper in dress. He was also tall and rather imposing, according to those who knew him. And in "Lines for Cuscuscaraway and Mirza Murud Ali Beg," the last of the "Five-Finger Exercises," he depicts himself as rather trying, indeed. Contrarily, one wonders why he might have wished to depict Jean Verdenal as trying, let alone enmeshed in finances.

One must consider, too, when Eliot wrote the Phlebas lines. It was shortly after his marriage, when he was barely managing to survive— living in quarters not to his liking, on funds insufficient to cover his needs, and with a woman who was providing daily a greater emotional strain. His decisions had run counter to the wishes of his family, and he was not far on his way to proving their judgement wrong and his right. It might well have been a time for reconsiderations, "Passing him through the stages of his former life." Voluntarily he was one of the expatriot writers; "A current under sea" had "carried him far away" from home. Most of the pieces fit easily.

They continue to fit when the lines are viewed in the context of following the shipwreck episode deleted from the original "Death by Water." It is significant that the ship was sailing off the Dry Salvages, the territory that Eliot himself—again, not Jean Verdenal—had sailed many times as a youth. Following the wreck, Phlebas is drawn into a whirl-pool, maelstrom of time in which "He passed the stages of his age and youth," becoming thus a New Englander transformed into an ancient commercial mariner. His origins remain in New England, not France. He shares the same past as Eliot. He asks only to be remembered.

Synopsis: "Death by Water"

Although transplanted from "Dans le Restaurant," this section must be viewed in relation to the deleted shipwreck episode. For that episode, Eliot drew upon the twenty-sixth canto of *The Inferno* in which Ulysses speaks of his death at sea. This narrative was wholly of Dante's own invention, having no counterpart in any classical sources. Dante imagines Ulysses spurning love and duty to pursue adventure to a fateful end. Amplification of this postclassical fabrication was carried forward by Tennyson in his "Ulysses," from which Eliot seems to have absorbed a certain philosophical sustenance for his handling of the same theme altered into a more modern framework.

> All times I have enjoyed
> Greatly, have suffered greatly, both with those
> That loved me, and alone; on shore, and when
> Through scudding drifts the rainy Hyades
> Vexed the dim sea. I am become a name;
> For always roaming with a hungry heart
> Much have I seen and known—cities of men
> And manners, climates, councils, governments,
> Myself not least, but honoured of them all—
> And drunk delight of battle with my peers,
> Far on the ringing plains of windy Troy.[2]

Similarly the codfish schooner in the "Death by Water" episode runs into "foul weather under the Hyades." In Ulysses is much of the likeness of Tiresias. Ulysses says "I have enjoyed / Greatly, have suffered greatly" and "Much have I seen and known," just as Tiresias avers that he has "foresuffered all / Enacted on this same divan or bed."

Ulysses, as depicted by Tennyson, had in common with Eliot a "yearning in desire / To follow knowledge like a sinking star, / Beyond the utmost bound of human thought." This was certainly one of the motives that mixed into the composition of *The Waste Land*, the metaphysical aspect of the quest, an effort to bend Bradleyan idealism to human needs. Undoubtedly this strong identification with Ulysses, who lurked undefined in the shipwreck scene, explains the revival of Phlebas, an imaginary personage from the same almost mythical epoch, from an earlier work. In this regard, it is interesting that Tennyson wrote "Ulysses" in memoriam shortly after the death of his friend Arthur Hallam, while Eliot may have written "Dans le Restaurant" at least within the shadow of melancholy at the death of Jean Verdenal, his friend.

Phlebas, then, seems a complex figure in whom Eliot himself is embedded; the words woven around him are an imaginary spiritual epitaph, an invocation to eternity not to be forgotten nor judged too harshly. Name and origin come naturally from the setting that lay inspirationally behind the deleted shipwreck episode. Eliot more than once in *The Waste Land* contemplated his own spiritual death—nowhere, however, more pointedly than here. As always, he projects this contemplation through a larger framework in which the drowned man is also the effigy of the vegetation god cast into the water that he may rise in the regeneration of life in the spring.

DEATH BY WATER

The implications of this title have been already discussed in the exegesis of line 55, "Fear death by water." Briefly, water in mythology and folklore is a symbol of life. Effigies of certain vegetation gods were cast into the water in hopes that they would absorb the life forces therein to return the following spring in the guise of general fertility over the land. Water was also believed to be purificatory. For Eliot personally, through reference to *The Tempest*, death by water carried implications of his father's demise and perhaps also that of Jean Verdenal. Additionally, drowning was central within the Larisch material.

PHLEBAS THE PHOENICIAN, A FORTNIGHT DEAD,
FORGOT THE CRY OF GULLS, AND THE DEEP SEA SWELL
AND THE PROFIT AND LOSS.

Speculation has run rampant on the origin of the name Phlebas, but to little avail. It seems not to appear anywhere in classical literature. Etymologically, it is related to φλέψ, *vein* or *spring*, most closely through the genitive, φλεβος, or possibly to φλεβις, *penis*. Conceivably Eliot may have combined the two words into a portmanteau word connoting fertility. If Phlebas somehow represents Eliot himself, then it is quite straightforward that in his spiritual death he "Forgot the cry of gulls, and deep sea swell" along the New England coast and escaped "the profit and loss" of his own finances, perhaps of his concerns at the bank.

On another level, as Herbert Knust has pointed out, Phlebas may be identified with the drowned King Ludwig.[3] In the correspondence between the king and the Empress Elizabeth, she was addressed as "the Sea-gull" and he, as "the Mountain Eagle."[4] Gide's Prometheus, we recall, had his eagle; the psychological associations here are tightly interrelated. Elizabeth mused, in a passage previously quoted concerning the "Lady of the Rocks," that "after my death I shall turn into a sea-gull and live on the great spaces of the ocean, or shelter in the crevice of some frowning rock . . ."[5] All this may well have been unconscious, but it may have influenced Eliot to transfer the Phlebas material from "Dans le Restaurant" to "Death by Water."

There is a possibility that Phlebas is not of Greek derivation at all, but a grecification of the Latin, *flebas*, third person imperfect indicative of *flebere,* to weep or lament. Identifying Phlebas with Eliot would make him he who lamented over the deaths of his friend and of his father. Eliot would have been familiar with this verb, since Virgil used it in *The Aeneid.* Looking back to the enigmatic episode recorded in "Dans le Restaurant," it may be that it was no more than an elaboration of an incident between Eliot and Jean Verdenal in some Paris cafe, something trivial yet fraught with personal implications we have no way of sharing.

A CURRENT UNDER SEA
PICKED HIS BONES IN WHISPERS.

Eliot may have modified the original line in "Dans le Restaurant," which simply spoke of carrying Phlebas far away, under the influence of a passage already considered from James Joyce's *Ulysses.* Bloom is gazing at the rat crawling around the crypt of Paddy Dignam: "One of those chaps would make short work of a fellow. Pick the bones clean no matter who it was. Ordinary meat for them. A corpse is meat gone bad."[6] At the graveyard, too, "Gentle sweet air blew round the bared heads in a whisper. Whisper." The same image returns several lines on: "Whispering around you."[7] The setting is suitable for the purposes Eliot had in mind, and he had mined the funeral of Paddy Dignam already for odds and ends of images. Direction may have been imposed for the consolidation of the image under pressure from the "sea change" of the imagined corpse of Ferdinand's father in *The Tempest,* as described in Ariel's song.

AS HE ROSE AND FELL
HE PASSED THE STAGES OF HIS AGE AND YOUTH
ENTERING THE WHIRLPOOL.

Touching upon a common theme, the proverbial review of the events of life preceding the moment of death, these lines remain within the spirit of the original French version, adding only the whirlpool, which did not derive from Joyce. It seems to represent a kind of transfiguration, the whirlpool being the passageway to some new dimension of being.

GENTILE OR JEW
O YOU WHO TURN THE WHEEL AND LOOK TO WINDWARD,
CONSIDER PHLEBAS, WHO WAS ONCE HANDSOME AND TALL AS YOU.

"Gentile or Jew" is an inversion from *Ulysses*—"A merchant, Stephan said, is one who buys cheap and sells dear, jew or gentile, is he not?"[8]—

from a passage bearing also upon the "one-eyed merchant," which helps to explain why Eliot claimed in his notes to line 218 that "the one-eyed merchant, seller of currants, melts into the Phoenician Sailor, and the latter is not wholly distinct from Ferdinand Prince of Naples." His explanation could hardly contribute to the resolution of the complex of associations involved.

First, the "one-eyed merchant," as James Joyce, drew upon the comment of Mr. Deasy to Stephen Bloom that the merchants have "sinned against the light" and therefore "you can see the darkness in their eyes." It was from this passage that came "jew or gentile," linking the merchant with Phlebas. Falling between them, "Mr. Eugenides, the Smyrna merchant," assumes the more unpleasant aspects of the merchants described by Mr. Deasy. And Ferdinand enters the complex of identities through his father's imagined sea-change, a change analogous to Phlebas's. None of this helps to explain the poem, except insofar as it sheds light on the protean character of the personages involved and on the free-associational manner in which one melts into another.

"O you who turn the wheel and look to windward" is a late addition to the original section from "Dans le Restaurant" and seems to indicate a more general identity, probably that of the reader who might be sympathetic to the overall purpose of the poem. Eliot might have originally had in mind the shipwreck of Ulysses described by Dante in the twenty-sixth canto of *The Inferno*, when one considers the speech of Ulysses to exhort his companions to make the final voyage:

> 'O frati,' dissi, che per cento milia
>   perigli siete giunti all' occidente,
>   a queta tanto picciola vigillia
>
> de' vostri sensi, ch'e del rimanente,
>   non vogliate negar l'esperienza,
>   di retro al sol, del mond senza gente.
>
> Considerate la vostra semenza:
>   fatti non foste a vier come bruti,
>   ma per sequir virtute e conoscenza.'

> ["O brothers," I said, "who through a hundred thousand
>   dangers have reached the West,
>   to this so brief vigil
>
> of your senses, such as may remain,
>   wish not to deny the experience,
>   of the unpeopled world behind the sun.

Consider your origin:
>   you were not formed to live like brutes,
>   but to follow virtue and knowledge.][9]

One who did not know of the ultimate connection between this canto and "Death by Water" and who was not aware of Eliot's lifetime devotion to Dante would not think to relate "Considerate la vostra semenza" to "Consider Phlebas," but the temptation is irresistible. It would have firmed Eliot's assimilation of the Phlebas material to the shipwreck episode deriving from *The Divine Comedy*. Also, the diction of the two parallel lines is the same, straightforward and syntactically transparent. In fact, the entire section is notably Dantean in that respect.

As Ulysses exhorted his comrades to adventure, Eliot exhorts those of the future "who turn the wheel and look to windward," who pilot the ship of fate perhaps against the tides of time, to remember him kindly as he may appear in the poetic guise of an ancient quester after "virtue and knowledge," one who would "follow knowledge like a sinking star, / Beyond the bound of human thought."

What the Thunder Said

APPARENTLY the most spontaneously created section of *The Waste Land*, "What the Thunder Said" yields the starkest gallery of portraits of the infernal human condition as Eliot saw it. Varied, indeed, are the images, yet the symbolism is unusually transparent. Since it seems to have been written at white heat, there is a minimum of intervention from deliberate contrivance and obfuscatory censorship. Earlier material from poetic fragments were assimilated into the composition with slight modification but little elaboration. Only one false start, three lines about an "infant hydrocephalous" sitting on a bridge over a dry stream, had to be struck out; the other revisions were minor.

Little wonder that Eliot told Bertrand Russell that this section "is not the best part, but the only part that justifies the whole, at all."[1] Critical reconsiderations had distanced it least from the wellsprings of inspiration, closing the rapprochement between intent and outcome. It reveals most directly what was in his mind as he worked the raw materials into the finished poem. Where he had made oblique passes at fairly ambiguous feelings elsewhere in the poem, here he touches directly upon the quintessential issues. In this sense, many of the strands of the work are gathered together and, if not quite resolved, at least more clearly articulated in this final movement with its coda of complete emotional and ideational cacophony.

Eliot even partially plotted out his course in the notes, announcing that "In the first part of Part V three themes are employed: the journey to Emmaus, the approach to the Chapel Perilous (see Miss Weston's book) and the present decay of Western Europe." Not that these themes might have otherwise been difficult to spot, or that they fully explain the intent of the section, but together they do help to form the skeleton over which the fabric of the poetry is woven. They constitute the allusive ground of the section. Eliot apparently wanted to be sure that readers knew that much. Beyond that, he probably felt that the section could speak for itself. Another note describes an allusion to Bradley; put together with the symbology of the central portion of the section, it clearly suggests that at the uttermost core of the intention, underneath the allusive skeleton, is the realization of solipsism defining the human inferno. Human misery arises fundamentally from the insulary nature of the human ego: even though people do interact, each individual is in the innermost reaches of his feelings an island, unable to reach into the feelings of others, or to have them experience what he or she feels, except in flashes, which can never be sustained. It is almost as if the fruit of Original Sin is not sexual shame, but human consciousness.

As befits the final movement of a work, there is a great diversity in the thematic sources, counterpoint of allusions stretched to the closing scene, encompassing much that appeared in the earlier sections, melodies reviewed for the recapitulation. And, like a musical composition, the tension mounts toward a tonal resolution, which is at last achieved amid a tumult of discord. Images clash against one another until, in an enigmatic silence, there lingers the prolonged last pianissimo that explains, as most it can be explained, the entire mindscape.

Synopsis: "What the Thunder Said"

"What the Thunder Said" begins with a distorted synoptic narration of the fate of Christ, from the vigil in the garden through the trial, crucifixion, and resurrection. All this is told through brief images, like a series of snippets from still shots taken at widely spaced points from a long moving picture of events. Then follows the dispersion of the disciples over the arid plains, except that the disciples become all people, from the historical past to the present. We are the disciples. And the journey takes on proportions of obsession and hallucination, as if across limbo in the dark night of the soul. Water and rock are reiterated as images in a compulsive delirium. Visions appear, and the historical framework is shattered.

Still within the original context of the Passion, Christ appears as the mysterious third figure walking along with his disciples en route to Emmaus, but his identity is blurred with that of a delusional figure seen during an Antarctic expedition and, further, with that of an old woman from an ancient Buddhistic tale. This breakdown of identity becomes the pivot around which the progression of ruminations gradually turns toward the assimilation of a more contemporary landscape. The lamentations of Mary at the cross blend with the overriding cry of mothers whose sons and daughters were lost in World War I. A vision of the destruction of war bursts upon the mindscape with the flare of a bomb, bringing cities ancient and modern crumbling into dust.

As if from the clearing of the dust after the plague of destruction emerges a scene of hell, in which the figure of a woman, charged with the personalities of the duchess of Malfi, the Empress Elizabeth, and Vivien Eliot, is seen half-demented in a Boschean phantasmagoria in which London inexplicably holds within it, within the Tower, the cistern from which the voice of John the Baptist rises with the cries of others left to die. We pass quite naturally to a graveyard, that beside the Perilous Chapel, in which the ill-fated Marie Vetsera was buried. A cock crow dispels the evil apparitions of night, and rain finally comes to the dry land, reviving hope for salvation.

Before salvation can be achieved, however, the terms of the Thunder Sermon must be met: give, sympathize, and control. They are not met. The poet-Fisher King is left alone, struggling with his conscience, still trying to find a beginning to the escape from solipsistic hell—he had neither been able to give nor to sympathize. Self-control would be meaningless. Rationality and the self-consistency of appearance suddenly disintegrate into a polylinguistic mock tragedy become real tragedy, the fulfillment of the obsessive hallucinatory state with which the section had mainly been preoccupied. It is played off against the terms of the Thunder Sermon, and the struggle ends with a closure signifying that it has not been a confession but rather an inquisitive supplication.

Thematically, "What the Thunder Said" deals clearly and exclusively with the spiritual failure of humankind from the beginning of time, with the infernal visions born of that failure, with the slim hopes for escape into salvation, and with the ultimate dilemma that is the human condition, the consciousness of isolation without the ability to achieve, except momentarily or symbolically, and to sustain sympathetic unification with any other person.

WHAT THE THUNDER SAID

Eliot might well have called this section "The Thunder Sermon," as it draws upon a "sermon" at the end of the Brihadaranyaka Upanishad:

> Gods, men, and asuras [devils]—all these descendants of Prajapati [Hindu god of creation]—lived with him for a time as students.
> Then the gods said: "Teach us, sir!" In reply Prajapati uttered one syllable: "Da." Then he said: "Have you understood?" They answered: "Yes, we have understood. You have said to us, 'Damayata— Be self-controlled.'" "Yes," agreed Prajapati, "you have understood."
> Then the men said: "Teach us, sir!" Prajapati uttered the same syllable: "Da." Then he said: "Have you understood?" They answered, "Yes, we have understood. You have said to us. '*Datta*—Be charitable.'" "Yes," agreed Prajapati, "you have understood."
> Then the asuras said: "Teach us, sir!" Prajapati uttered the same syllable: "Da." Then he said: "Have you understood?" They said,

"Yes, we have understood. You told us '*Dayadhwam*—Be compassionate.'" "Yes," agreed Prajapati, "you have understood."
    The storm cloud thunders: "Da! Da! Da!"—"Be self-controlled! Be charitable! Be compassionate!"[2]

In the German translation to which Eliot refers in his notes, evidently the order of the commands was datta, dayadhvam, damayata—give or be charitable, sympathize or be compassionate, and control or be self-controlled. There are numerous such systems of conduct prescribed in Hinduism; this trio is simply one among many. Within Hinduism these admonitions rested upon the assumptions that every action bore fruition or karma—originally an insubstantial clouding of pure vision— and that enlightenment, or unity with the One, could come only with absolutely pure vision. Not entirely metaphysical, there was a definite compromise with ethical imperatives in all this, so that those actions deemed not to contribute to karmatic accumulation turned out to be those least harmful or most beneficial to others. Beyond that was the aim of self-knowledge, or such control over all aspects of the physical self—most strikingly seen in yoga practices—that it could be as if transcended and forgotten. This was a requisite for nirvana, since knowledge of the true self was conceived as knowledge of the self shorn of egoistic boundaries, something difficult for most Westerners to appreciate. It is close to those moments when we become so absorbed in something that we momentarily forget about ourselves, except that in Hinduism and Buddhism such a frame of mind is cultivated. At any rate, the ethical admonitions of the Upanishads are directed toward the achievement of that paradoxical kind of selfless self-knowledge.
    In alluding to these admonitions—datta, dayadhvam, damayata—in the title of this, the final section of *The Waste Land*, Eliot apparently wanted to concretize the human failure to achieve spiritual salvation by singling out specific areas in which he had failed. At the end of the section, Eliot cites poeticized and somewhat dream-distorted instances of the failure to meet each of the three commands, each instance a personal experience projected through the allusive method into something approaching archetypical form. Archetypicality is enhanced, too, by the very choice of ethical framework from the oldest of existing Upanishads.

AFTER THE TORCHLIGHT RED ON SWEATY FACES

Eliot begins his jumbled free-associative reconstruction of the Passion with the moment of betrayal, when Judas brings the soldiers to the garden at Cedron where Christ brought his disciples after he had prayed for them. According to John 18:1–3:

When Jesus had spoken these words, he went forth with his disciples over the brook Cedron, where was a garden, into which he
entered, and his disciples.

And Judas also, which betrayed him, knew the place: for Jesus
ofttimes resorted thither with his disciples.

Judas then, having received a band of men and officers from the
chief priests and Pharisees, cometh thither with lanterns and torches
and weapons.

John B. Vickery, in *The Literary Impact of The Golden Bough*, views
this passage within a larger mythological context. His remarks are
worth quoting (figures in brackets supplant his footnotes with volumes
and page numbers for citations from *The Golden Bough*). "[Frazer's]
description of a pagan festival . . . includes references to gay boating
parties on the river, their licentious conduct, watery rites of purification
and baptism, and concludes that 'the great Midsummer festival has
been above all a festival of lovers and fire' [2:272–73]." The parallels
with "What the Thunder Said" are obvious. There are the royal festivities on the river leading to the consuming fires of Augustine and
Buddha with which the section ends. "A similar developing pattern
may be seen in the fact that, according to Frazer, 'the three great features
of the Midsummer celebration were the bonfires, the procession with
torches round the fields, and the custom of rolling a wheel' into water
[10:161]." The same symbolism is found in the celebration of St. John's
Day for which "Frazer notes the tradition that "this day will have three
persons; one must perish in the air, one in the fire, and third in the
water" [11:27]."[3] Here the parallel may not be perfect, though one may
interpret the crucifixion as death "in the air."

In view of the way *The Waste Land* was composed and the sections
gathered into a single work, it is difficult to go along with everything
that Vickery says. Nevertheless, the parallels that he draws may have
had some bearing upon Eliot's choice of imagery and thematic material
at various places, albeit in a looser and less precise manner than
Vickery suggests. For instance, within the context of the opening episode of "What the Thunder Said," the "torchlight red on sweaty faces"
would seem more firmly to belong to John than to Frazer, in view of the
further details of the Passion contained in the subsequent lines. No
suggestion of a procession is given. Yet the midsummer festivities
described by Frazer may have lingered in Eliot's mind as he contemplated the line, even if not as he composed it. Again, any delinea-
tion between what was contrived and what was construed later is
conjectural. As Eliot moved from considering each section a separate
poem in a series to looking upon them as forming an integral whole, he
undoubtedly came to construe a clarity that had existed before only

behind a fortuitous, partially unconscious adumbration in the composition.

AFTER THE FROSTY SILENCE IN THE GARDENS

This, and the line preceding it, came from a discarded fragment, the full context of which helps to clarify the intent of this whole episode. In it Eliot, using an extended series of lines beginning with "after," referred to the passing of inspired days, praying and crying, a vigil in the garden, judges, advocates and wardens, and the ending of an inspiration.[4] Here is quite manifestly a description of the end of the teaching of Christ, "the inspired days" and "inspired nights," after which "The world seemed futile," "The world was ended." Eliot used silence before, in the hyacinth garden, to describe the moment of struggle for meaning; specifically it recalls the silence of God after Jesus prayed (Luke 22:42), "Father if thou be willing, remove this cup from me: nevertheless, not my will, but thine be done." Reticence of God, challenging the wit of man, offers potent motivation for poetry, explored not only by Eliot but also, among others, by Ingmar Bergman in his 1956 film-play, *Tystnaden (The Silence)*.

AFTER THE AGONY IN STONY PLACES

Probably an oblique reference to the suffering of the disciples as they scattered across the stony plains of Israel, after the Crucifixion, this also continues the theme of sterility of the Waste Land.

THE SHOUTING AND THE CRYING
PRISON AND PALACE AND REVERBERATION
OF THUNDER OF SPRING OVER DISTANT MOUNTAINS

Continuing to loom here is the scene of the Crucifixion, with Roman soldiers and idle witnesses shouting over the weeping of those who came to mourn. Not too far away is the palace of Pontius Pilate, and the prison to which his judgement consigned enemies of the state. Only a symbol of injustice, the prison formed no literal part of the Passion. Thunder over distant mountains came as Christ, embodying all gods of rebirth, was resurrected, signaling the revitalization of the land, a promise earlier announced in "Summer surprised us, coming over the Starnbergersee / With a shower of rain." Peripherally there may be a reminder that in many versions of the Grail legend the quester encounters a storm before reaching the Perilous Chapel.

To return to "Prison and palace and reverberation," it is notable that

Eliot had originally written "Gardens and palaces and reverberation," thus linking the hyacinth garden, Gethsemane, and Calvary, the latter near the palace of Pilate. Interesting is the substitution of "prison" for "gardens," as if in Eliot's mind the garden and prison shared something, probably the intensification of solipsistic isolation.

HE WHO WAS LIVING IS NOW DEAD
WE WHO WERE LIVING ARE NOW DYING
WITH A LITTLE PATIENCE

Christ, the vegetation god, is dead, and we who have lost touch with the wellspring of the religious impulse, one of the mainstays of civilization, are dying slowly from the spiritual inside. "We" are the living dead circling in hell, marching mindlessly over London Bridge. Our death is imperceptibly slow, a falling away from meaning, the ultimate existential angst.

HERE IS NO WATER BUT ONLY ROCK
ROCK AND NO WATER AND THE SANDY ROAD
THE ROAD WINDING ABOVE AMONG THE MOUNTAINS
WHICH ARE MOUNTAINS OF ROCK WITHOUT WATER
IF THERE WERE WATER WE SHOULD STOP AND DRINK
AMONGST THE ROCK ONE CANNOT STOP OR THINK
SWEAT IS DRY AND FEET ARE IN THE SAND

Obsessive repetition of the opposition between dry sand and rock, symbols of sterility, and water, connoting the source of life, characterizes a wandering journey into delirium, a peregrination of one who undertakes the dark night of the soul as also, and paradoxically, one who has forgotten all spiritual origins, echoing "What are the roots that clutch, what branches grow / Out of this stony rubbish," which in turn rests on Job 8 : 11 and 8 : 16–17. In contrast to the desolation depicted in those verses, as Moses was leading his people to freedom out of Egypt and they were caught in the drought of the desert, the Lord said (Exodus 17 : 5–6): "Go on before the people, and take with thee of the elders of Israel; and thy rod, wherewith thou smotest the river, take in thine hand, and go. Behold, I will stand before thee there upon the rock in Horeb; and thous shalt smite the rock, and there shall come water out of it, that the people may drink."

A primeval journey of the soul, it envisages the promise of life out of what is dead, pressing on from desperation to reach something substantial, away from a world of perishing illusions. On another level, it is a grotesque parody or extended metaphor of the journey to Emmaus, in which the answer of the quester was present but unrecognized, Christ disguised from his own disciples in the cloak of truth.

IF THERE WERE ONLY WATER AMONGST THE ROCK
DEAD MOUNTAIN MOUTH OF CARIOUS TEETH THAT CANNOT SPIT
HERE ONE CAN NEITHER STAND NOR LIE NOR SIT

"Dead mountain mouth of carious teeth" encompasses the double image of a tired desert journeyman and the imagined skull of Calvary, called in the Greek text of the Bible κάριον, the skull, because of its cranial shape. "Here one can neither stand nor lie nor sit," because here one is crucified. This is the place of painful death.

THERE IS NOT EVEN SILENCE IN THE MOUNTAINS
BUT DRY STERILE THUNDER WITHOUT RAIN
THERE IS NOT EVEN SOLITUDE IN THE MOUNTAINS
BUT RED SULLEN FACES SNEER AND SNARL
FROM DOORS OF MUDCRACKED HOUSES

Turning upon the earlier "In the mountains, there you feel free," there is neither silence, signaling that precious moment of struggle toward significance, nor solitude in which to approach the silence. We have even passed the vacuity of those vacations that Marie Larisch so loved, sojourns in the mountains where she could find peace of mind. No peace of mind here, there is only the delirium of a self-conscious spiritual death. The dog who seeks out death is supplanted by snarling canine people hardly more than animals, if not vicious, at least mindless.

IF THERE WERE WATER
AND NO ROCK,
IF THERE WERE ROCK
AND ALSO WATER
AND WATER
A SPRING
A POOL AMONG THE ROCK

Shortening of the lines in conjunction with the continued repetition of the rock-water opposition brings the desperation of the journey to Emmaus, across the Waste Land and through space and time, to a climax. Nowhere else in the poem is there such incessant urgency to the rhythm of the words; the mind seems to speak directly from the

page, with no diversion, to this point, from the narrow preoccupation
with which it is temporarily obsessed.

IF THERE WERE THE SOUND OF WATER ONLY
NOT THE CICADA
AND DRY GRASS SINGING
BUT SOUND OF WATER OVER A ROCK
WHERE THE HERMIT-THRUST SINGS IN THE PINE TREES
DRIP DROP DRIP DROP DROP DROP DROP
BUT THERE IS NO WATER

The cicada, often a religious symbol in the Orient, is sometimes
called the harvest-fly, since so many varieties appear in late summer
and early autumn. Thus, there may be suggested here a contrast between the notion of harvest and the barrenness of the Waste Land. But
there is a deeper provocation for Eliot to summon this insect so rare to
poetry. He had come across the cicada in "The Deserted Garden" from
Alan Seeger's *Poems,* which he reviewed in *Egoist* of December 1917.
The context was one that was apt to have stuck in his mind. Seeger
described an idyllic garden in which two lovers met and made their
"bridal bower" in an "old-pleasure-hall." There many flowers bloomed,
"And pink and purple hyacinths exhale / Their heavy fume. . . ." An
"antique tower" stood, and "A crumbling stairway winds to the one
room above":

> And whoso mounts by this dismantled stair
> Finds the old pleasure-hall, long disarrayed,
> Brick tiled and raftered, and the walls foursquare
> Ringed all about with a twofold arcade.[5]

By the "casement" of the bridal bower "A girl might stand and gaze into
green boughs . . . like Vivien, the enchanting fay." Eliot could not have
been insensible to that passing use of his wife's name, not commonly
encountered in poetry. As the lover awaits his beloved, he is:

> Pillowed at ease to hear the merry tune
> Of mating warblers in the boughs above
> And shrill cicadas whom the hottest noon
> Keeps not from drowsy song . . .[6]

Momentarily the mirage of a garden flickers, "Where the hermit-
thrush sings in the pine trees," perhaps a revival from the unconscious
of the idyllic garden in Seeger's poem. It bursts into awareness as if in a
protracted state of delirium, when the longing for water culminates in

hallucinated sounds of dripping, provoked by the singing wind over dry grass, an image dredged from Kipling's *Kim*.

In Kipling's novel, Kimball O'Hara, the orphaned son of a sergeant in an Irish regiment, spends his youth wandering aimlessly until he meets a lama, who is searching for the all-healing River of Arrows, the river of immortality. He joins the lama in this adventurous quest, until he falls into the hands of his father's old regiment, where he is adopted and sent to school. During his vacations he rejoins the lama in the search for the River of Arrows. Set in India, the novel is replete with vivid descriptions of the exotic yet peaceful land. Moving through the Himalaya valleys, Kim and the lama witness many sights both tranquil and awesome: "Except the grey eagle and an occasional far-seen bear grubbing and rooting on the hillside, the vision of a furious painted leopard met at dawn in a still valley devouring a goat, and now and again a bright-coloured bird, they were alone with the winds and the grass singing under the wind."[7]

Eliot had ample reason for latching onto an image from this context, for it dovetailed in more than one respect with the fabric of his poem at this point. First and foremost, the novel depicted in part a quest for water as the symbol of life. In this quest, Kim and the lama "meditated often on the Wheel of life—the more so since, as the lama said, they were freed from its visible temptations."[8] The Wheel of Life is not only one of the tarots figuring in the cartomancy scene with Madame Sosostris, but it is also the wheel upon which Eliot imagined the inhabitants of London to be bound, in his apostrophe to that city, words expunged from the completed text but hardly from his mind.

Further, in the end the lama finds his river at the place of an old lady who had twice before befriended him and Kim. There the "ground was good clean dust—no new herbage that, living, is half-way to death already, but the hopeful dust that holds the seed of all life." Not only a kind of optimistic version of the dead landscape of the waste land, this also links ironically with "fear in a handful of dust," in that throughout the poem the prospect of life, connoting some sort of self-awakening, arouses anxiety.

However, before ending his quest, the lama fasted and meditated: "I took no food. I took no water." All this comes in the last pages of the book. Through a series of layers of meditation the lama comes to the moment of enlightenment: "Then my Soul was all alone, and I saw nothing, for I was all things, having reached the Great Soul." Again reference falls naturally back to the pregnant moment of the search for significance in the hyacinth garden, when the protagonist "knew nothing," and to the taunts of the lady in "A Game of Chess," Do you know nothing? Do you see nothing? Do you remember / Nothing?" Once more, through the allusive technique, a synthesis of oppositions is formed, superimposing the state of living death upon the experience of enlightenment to create an ambivalent composite answering both to Bradleyan metaphysics and to the mechanisms of free-association.

Out of this maze of interrelations came, too, the impetus for that strange repetitive "Drip drop drip drop drop drop drop," onomatopoeic echo from sources yoked together along a common thematic pivot. First there is the image conjured by the lama to explain his experience of enlightenment: "As a drop draws to water, so my soul drew near to the Great Soul which is beyond all Things." It comes, with all the other relevant images previously quoted, from the next to the last page of the novel. Now, remembering the central importance of water in the novel, it is easy to turn to the autobiography of Marie Larisch with its tales of drowning and the various bodies of water around which the lives of the royal family seemed to have revolved. Here is where Eliot found the inspirational nudge necessary to complete the idea for this line imitating dripping water. Aside from the theme of water, Eliot might have been prompted to move between *Kim* and *My Past* by way of the Himalayas. Background for the quest of Kim and the lama, they were also the artificial painted backdrop for the winter garden atop King Ludwig's Residenz in Munich: "There was also an artificial lake with a painted panoramic background of the Himalaya Mountains, and when the King sat in the garden a "property" moon shed its gaseous light above the snow-capped peaks."[9]

More specifically germane to the onomatopoeic line in question, however, was the apparition of King Ludwig to Elizabeth the first night she slept in Bavaria after his death by drowning:

> "It was no dream," replied the Empress. "I had gone to bed, but I could not sleep, although the room was in darkness and everything outside was perfectly still.
>
> "As I lay awake in the lonely hours thoughts assailed me, and suddenly I heard a monotonous drip, drip, of water.
>
> " 'It must be raining,' I said to myself, 'and the drops are falling on the leaves close to my window,' so I took no further notice until the noise was succeeded by the unmistakable ripple of water when it kisses the shore.
>
> "You know that sound, Marie. We have heard it often as we rode by Lake Starnberg. As the gentle, rippling sound continued it gradually filled the room, and I began to experience all the sensations of drowning. I choked and gasped as I struggled for air; but the terror passed, and with an effort I sat up in bed and breathed freely.
>
> "The moon had now risen, and its radiance made the room as light as day. Then I saw the door open very slowly, and Ludwig came within.

"His clothes were very heavy with water, which dripped from them and made little pools on the parquet. His damp hair lay close round his white face, but it was Ludwig much as he had looked in life."[10]

Ludwig tells her about the strange burning lady to whom Eliot alludes at the close of "The Fire Sermon"; Elizabeth asks if she will suffer when she dies, and he assures her that she will not; she asks him to join her in a prayer for peace: "But as I spoke the figure vanished, and again I heard the drip of the invisible water succeeded by the ripple of the lake around the reeds. Panic seized me, for I felt I was very near the dwellers in that other world who stretch out their shadowy arms and beseech consolation from the living."[11]

The "monotonous drip, drip, of water" suggests the extended repetition to which Eliot resorted, while "the drip of the invisible water" suits the phenomenon perfectly to the hallucinatory context of the episode in the poem. At the same time, blending with the water-drop image of enlightenment put forth by the lama, both images of Elizabeth contribute to another Bradleyan synthesis: this time not opposites but disparates. "But there is no water" finalizes the whole episode as ultimately delusional.

WHO IS THE THIRD WHO WALKS ALWAYS BESIDE YOU?
WHEN I COUNT, THERE ARE ONLY YOU AND I TOGETHER
BUT WHEN I LOOK AHEAD UP THE WHITE ROAD
THERE IS ALWAYS ANOTHER ONE WALKING BESIDE YOU
GLIDING WRAPT IN A BROWN MANTLE, HOODED
I DO NOT KNOW WHETHER A MAN OR A WOMEN
—BUT WHO IS THAT ON THE OTHER SIDE OF YOU?

Peak of the delirium seemingly passed, the flow of the mindscape runs toward a distracted, almost febrile but low-keyed questioning, which Eliot in his notes explains as having been "stimulated by the account of one of the Antarctic expeditions (I forget which, but I think one of Shackleton's): it was related that the party of explorers at the extremity of their strength, had the constant delusion that there was *one more member* than could actually be counted." Sir Ernest Shackleton, famous for his explorations of the south polar region, published acounts of his adventures in *The Heart of the Antarctic* (1909) and *South* (1919).

As usual, in his notes Eliot only spiked the guns of his critics; he did not begin fully to explain himself. He left it to the reader to make the connection with the journey to Emmaus, as told in Luke 24:13–15:

And, behold, two of them went that same day to a village called
Emmaus, which was from Jerusalem about threescore furlongs.
And they talked together of all these things which had happened.
And it came to pass, that, while they communed together and
reasoned, Jesus himself drew near, and went with them.
But their eyes were holden that they should not know him.

Grover Smith has called attention to still another source for this
episode, a Buddhist story told in H. C. Warren's *Buddhism in Translation* (to which Eliot refers readers for the text of the Fire Sermon of
Buddha):

> According to the story, a wise man, meeting a woman on the
> highway, begged alms of her. She only laughed at him, but since as
> she did so she displayed her teeth, he was enabled to achieve
> sainthood through realizing the essential impurity of her body, whose
> naked bones he had glimpsed; and a little later, meeting her husband
> in search of her, the saint replied to his question:
> > 'Was it a woman, or a man,
> > That passed this way? I cannot tell.
> > But this I know, a set of bones
> > Is traveling upon this road.'[12]

Insofar as the episode of the third figure derives from Shackleton, the
hallucinatory aspect is emphasized; replicating the journey to Emmaus,
it continues a weaving theme of the whole section, representing failure
to discern the significant pattern in appearance. From the Buddhist
story comes the ambiguous sex of the figure, identifying him on one
level with the dual-sexed Tiresias. Altogether the figure seems to challenge the protagonist, to disturb any inner peace that might come of
mindlessness. He resembles the Stranger in the third chorus from "The
Rock," of whom Eliot writes, "O my soul, be prepared for the coming of
the Stranger, / Be prepared for him who knows how to ask questions,"
for "Life you may evade, but Death you shall not. You shall not deny the
Stranger."[13] Transmutation of this figure continued in *The Cocktail
Party*, in the guise of the Unidentified Guest, who later turned out to be
the psychiatrist Sir Henry Harcourt-Reilly, identified with the healer in
ancient or primitive folklore.

Still another interpretation identifies the third figure with any one of
Vivien's rumored lovers, placing him on her other side. If that were so—
and it is pure speculation—"I do not know whether a man or a woman"
would raise more questions than it answered.

WHAT IS THAT SOUND HIGH IN THE AIR
MURMUR OF MATERNAL LAMENTATION

WHO ARE THOSE HOODED HORDES SWARMING
OVER ENDLESS PLAINS, STUMBLING IN CRACKED EARTH
RINGED BY THE FLAT HORIZON ONLY

Eliot in his notes asks readers to compare this episode, running to "Unreal," with a quotation he cites in the original German from Hermann Hesse's *Blick ins Chaos* (Glimpse into Chaos). A translation of the passage is as follows: "Already half of Europe, already at least half of Eastern Europe is on the way to Chaos, driving drunken in sacred folly along the edge of the abyss and, drunken, singing hymn-like songs as Dimitri Karamazov sang. Offended by these songs the burgher laughs, while the saint and seer listen to them with tears."[14] Eliot borrowed nothing verbally from this; it simply expresses a sentiment that he explores throughout this whole stanza, a prescience of the decline of Europe projected historically as humankind falling away from inner core values toward a senseless materialism. He saw the disintegration of civilization around him in the disheartening aftermath of World War I, and he used that as his starting point, but he did not forego the search for parallels in the distant past.

As Dante was exiled from Florence, Eliot found himself alienated spiritually and, in a political sense, ideologically from the whole of Western Europe. In this mood, he came upon Hesse's slim volume of essays; its impact upon him was tremendous:

> In May 1922, T. S. Eliot visited Hermann Hesse in Montagnols, the isolated Swiss village above Lugano where Hesse had recently settled and where he was to live until his death in 1962. But it was not the author of the recently sensational novel *Demian* (1919) to whom Eliot was paying his respects. Nor was it the fashionable writer of popular pre-war fiction from whom he hoped to elicit contributions to his journal *Criterion*. Rather, as Eliot had explained in an earlier letter of introduction, a slender volume of essays entitled *Blick ins Chaos* (1920; *In Sight of Chaos*) had aroused his admiration. "In your book *Blick ins Chaos* I detect a concern with serious problems that has not yet penetrated to England, and I should like to spread its reputation." It is a fact of literary history that Eliot attempted to do precisely this by citing *Blick ins Chaos* in his Notes to *The Waste Land*. Yet this publicity effort obviously failed, for fifty years later Hesse's essays constitute an aspect of his writing that is virtually unknown in the English-speaking world, even among his most fervent devotees, and that is still too little appreciated even in Germany.[15]

The essay that apparently most caught the interest of Eliot was "The Brothers Karamazov, or The Decline of Europe," from the last paragraph of which Eliot took the quotation cited in his notes. Hesse's point of departure in this essay was "that in the works of Dostoevsky, and in its most concentrated form, *The Brothers Karamazov*, what I call to myself the "decline of Europe" is foretold and preclaimed with frightful clarity."

> . . . the "new ideal," which threatens the European spirit at its root, appears to be an amoral way of thinking and feeling, an ability to perceive the divine, the necessary, the fated, even in what is most wicked and ugly, and also to pay it reverence and worship in this guise, yes, especially in this guise.[16]

Certainly this passage would have struck in him a sympathetic note, recalling lessons he had learned from the writings of Charles Baudelaire, which he himself summed up most succinctly: "the essential advantage for a poet is not, to have a beautiful world with which to deal: it is to be able to see beneath both beauty and ugliness; to see the boredom, and the horror, and the glory."[17]

Hesse pursued the Baudelairean malaise and proclaimed that "this decline is a turning back to Asia, a return to the mother, to the sources, to the Faustian "Mothers," and of course will lead like every earthly death to a new birth." Referring more particularly to *The Brothers Karamozov*, he gave a more specific diagnosis and prognosis:

> . . . the holy Alyosha becomes more and more worldly, the worldly brothers more holy, and it is precisely the most criminal and unrestrained brother, Dimitri, who becomes the holiest, most sensitive, most profound possessor of a presentiment of a new holiness, a new morality, a new humanity. This is very strange. The more Karamazovian things become—the more vicious and drunken, the more unrestrained and rowdy—the much nearer shimmers through these rough physical phenomena, these men and deeds, a new ideal; inwardly they become all the more holy, more spiritualized. And compared to Dimitri, drunkard, killer, man of violence, and the cynical intellectual Ivan, the honest highly respected types—the public prosecutor and the other representatives of society—become shabbier, emptier, more worthless, the greater their outward triumph.

The "Karamazovian element" sweeping over Europe Hesse described as an "Asiatic, chaotic, wild, dangerous, amoral element," but paradoxically he claimed that it "can be evaluated positively as well as negatively."[18] It was not such a paradox within the Bradleyan metaphysics that Eliot had adopted. According to that metaphysics, as viewed through a deep-colored Baudelairean glass, "damnation itself is an immediate form of salvation—of salvation from the ennui of modern life, because it at least gives some significance to living."[19] By this reasoning, even the decline of Europe could be construed as the prelude to a new rebirth. The difference was that Hesse regarded the contemporary world socially and historically, whereas Bradley's perspective was more purely philosophical. Eliot shared both viewpoints: he was caught in the pain of a distressing world situation and, although he could rationalize it à la Bradley, that intellectual distancing did not fully insulate him from the trauma of it.

For his method, Eliot has chosen to syncretize the decline of Europe, embodied in the destruction of war and even natural catastrophe, with the tragedy of the Crucifixion and its aftermath. Heard again are the crowds of homeless victims scurrying through the streets during the Great Fire of London, as reflected in stanza 227 of *Annus Mirabilis*:

> Their cries soon waken all the dwellers near;
> Now murmuring noises rise in every street;
> The more remote run stumbling with their fear,
> And in the dark men justle as they meet.[20]

reinforced by the ominous description of the night of death given by Lennox in *Macbeth*, 2.3.55–62:

> The night has been unruly; where we lay,
> Our chimneys were blown down; and, as they say,
> Lamentings heard i' th' air; strange screams of death;
> And prophesying, with accents terrible,
> Of dire combustion and confused events
> New Hatcht to th' woeful time: the obscure bird
> Clamour'd the livelong night: some say, the earth
> Was feverish and did shake.[21]

That was the night upon which Macbeth had done his horrid deed. From "murmuring noises rise in every street" and "Lamentings heard i' th' air," mixed with other allusive material, came "What is that sound high in the air / Murmur of maternal lamentation." Sounds "high in the air" suggest also war planes that drop bombs that flash light that "bursts in the violet air." These sounds mingle with the "Murmur of maternal lamentation," the wailing of mothers for their dying children, the weeping of Mary for Jesus, and the cries of women for Tammuz, Osiris, and Attis.

To appreciate fully the implication of the lines following, one should turn to the original draft, where the plains over which the "hooded hordes" were "swarming" were first conceived as Polish. Eliot had something then quite current in mind. The boundaries of Poland were established by the Treaty of Versailles on 28 June 1919, but not to the satisfaction of the Polish nationalists, who wanted the frontiers to be those of the first partition of 1772. This precipitated the Russian-Polish

War, during which Poland regained a substantial part of its claim, and also took Vilna, a city of Lithuania—a fact also related to "Bin gar kein Russin, stemm' aus Litauen, echt deutch." For reasons that may never be understood, Eliot latched onto this series of events to illustrate the thesis of European decline enunciated in the Hesse passage appended to these lines in the notes.

"Hooded hordes" appear as a dream-multiplication of the "hooded" stranger in the previous episode. They also identify with the swarms stumbling over the barren plains in *The Inferno*, those who were never alive because they had had no faith in God. They move like those fleeing the burning London, they "run stumbling with their fear," "stumbling in cracked earth." While the damned, encounted in one of Eliot's favorite sources, the third canto of *The Inferno*, moved in such a train that Dante "should never have believed that death had undone so many," and "Quivi sospiri, pianti, e alti guai / risonavan par l'aer senza stelle" [Here sighs, plaints, and deep wailings resounded through the starless air].[22] "Ringed by the flat horizon only" certainly mirrors the circular landscape encountered at each level of hell.

Vickery calls attention to Frazer's description of Egypt as one source for the landscape here, as well as elsewhere in *The Waste Land*. Egypt, Frazer says, is "scorched by the sun, blasted by the wind that has blown from the Sahara for many days." More pointedly, the "plain appears to pant in the pitiless sunshine, bare, dusty, ash-coloured, cracked and seamed as far as the eye can see with a network of fissures."[23] There certainly are the seeds of "cracked earth," with the close juxtaposition of "plain" and "cracked" helped by "a network of fissures." As one of the cradles of ancient religion, Egypt, as seen by Frazer, could only complement the composite Eliot was forging.

WHAT IS THE CITY OVER THE MOUNTAINS
CRACKS AND REFORMS AND BURSTS IN THE VIOLET LIGHT
FALLING TOWERS
JERUSALEM ATHENS ALEXANDRIA
VIENNA LONDON
UNREAL

Destruction of war, crumbling walls, "Falling towers," Jerusalem, Athens, Alexandria, Vienna, and, of course, London itself, now and through history, the "city over the mountains" of which all cities are examples, is leveled to dust in the "violet air" of bombs and hellfire. This is a double image of earth and hell converging to the eternal timeless and spaceless point about which the illusion of appearance revolves. More simply, all this real historical and present devastation is portrayed against the fires of war and hell at once, that is, if there is a clear distinction between the two. It is all "Unreal" both in that it is nightmarish and in that appearance, in the Bradleyan sense, is not reality.

True to the hallucinatory quality of this passage, striking for the third time in the poem the note of *unreality*, Eliot may have been conjuring the effects of a *fata Morgana* as described by Shackleton. In his *South: The Story of Shakleton's Last Expedition 1914–1917*, the explorer alludes to mirages continually lurking in the polar landscape, mirages that cast the illusion of cities, "white and golden cities of Oriental appearance at close intervals along these cliff-tops," like the "city over the mountains," and "[f]loating above these are wavering violet and creamy lines of still more remote bergs and pack,"[24] echoing, however remotely, "the violet air" and more distantly "the violet hour." At one point, Shackleton says, "We seem to be drifting helplessly in a strange world of unreality," and elsewhere, "Everything wears an aspect of unreality."[25] Such subconscious associations reinforce the impression of the visionary aspect of an arduous journey, spiritual, physical, or both.

"Falling towers" functions not only descriptively within the context but as an associative bridge to "upside down in air were towers," itself from Virgil's picture of the underworld, and to "London Bridge is falling down," in which song the lady is to be locked up in the tower. Of course, it looks back to a prior allusion to the Tower of London in "A Game of Chess." And, probably embedded in a web of unconscious association, it relates to the tower in which Ugolino of Pisa is imprisioned (encountered by allusion at the "dayadhvam" episode), and to "*la tour abolie*" of "*Le Prince d' Aquitaine*."

A WOMAN DREW HER LONG BLACK HAIR OUT TIGHT
AND FIDDLED WHISPER MUSIC ON THOSE STRINGS

Conrad Aiken attests to having seen these lines back in the days when he and Eliot were attending Harvard. Valerie Eliot, including in her facsimile edition of *The Waste Land* drafts the whole fragment from which they were taken, places the date of composition at 1914 or possibly earlier. In that fragment, "the violet air" is simply the atmosphere at dusk, when the protagonist is given over to "tortured meditation" and "A chain of reasoning," from which the "sense" or "thread" was "gone," causing him to gather "strange images" in his distraught mind. He is given over to hallucinations of bats whining in the air and of a man, contorted or withered by a mental "blight" but possessing supernatural powers, crawling head downward down a wall, then suffers a second vision of a dead man who proclaims that the world has passed through many strange revolutions since he died. Finally he goes "out from town" in a confusion reminiscent of a blind man swimming deep below the sea, knowing neither up nor down—tying in both with the Phlebas episode and with the discarded on-the-town narrative with which "The Burial of the Dead" orignally began.[26]

Despite the tentative form in which this unfinished—or, at any rate, unrevised and editorially incompleted—poem has been left, it still can shed considerable light on this surrealistic visionary episode. It takes little imagination to see that the woman is again the duchess of Malfi, and that the "strange images" Eliot was contemplating here were spun out from the same scene mined in "A Game of Chess," the scene in which the duchess sits in her bedroom combing out her hair and bantering with her husband until he withdraws to tease her and she is discovered by her brother Ferdinand. Ferdinand is the man "distorted by some mental blight / Yet of abnormal powers." Parallel to Ferdinand's attempting to drive his sister mad before ending her life, Eliot created a kind of deranged pastiche to simulate the achievement of that intention.

AND BATS WITH BABY FACES IN THE VIOLET LIGHT
WHISTLED, AND BEAT THEIR WINGS
AND CRAWLED HEAD DOWNWARD DOWN A BACKENED WALL

Eliot attests in the French edition of his poems that his image was suggested to him by one panel, that depicting hell, of a diptych by Hieronymus Bosch, *The Deluge*. In this panel appear bats literally with baby faces flying upside down against a wall. Considering the earliest version of these lines, it is impossible to dismiss them simply as descriptive of the Bosch painting, in as much as there is involved the transformation of the original male figure into bats. Lee J. Richmond believes that Eliot may have drawn upon the 1897 gothic novel by Bram Stoker, *Dracula*.[27] Pointing out that James Joyce also used that novel as a source, Richmond calls attention to the appropriateness of the master of the undead to the tone of *The Waste Land*. Though there is no hard evidence that Eliot had in fact read Stoker, the speculation is interesting for the way in which the theme of *Dracula* parallels Eliot's vampire transformation of the original Ferdinand character. Richmond supports his contention with the following passage from the third chapter of *Dracula*:

> What I saw was the Count's head coming out from the window. I did not see the face, but I knew the man by the neck and the movement of his back and arms. In any case I could not mistake the hands which I had had so many opportunities of studying. I was at

first interested and somewhat amused, for it is wonderful how small a matter will interest and amuse a man when he is a prisoner. But my very feelings changed to repulsion and terror when I saw the whole man slowly emerge from the window and begin to crawl down the castel over the dreadful abyss, *face down* with his cloak spreading out around him like great wings. At first I could not believe my eyes. I thought it was some trick of the moonlight, some weird effect of shadow; but I kept looking, and it could be no delusion. I saw the fingers and toes grasp the corners of the stones, worn clear of the mortar by the stress of years, and by thus using every projection and inequality move downwards with considerable speed, just as a lizard moves along a wall.[28]

Richmond continues: "Later in Chapter IV, Harker remarks that near the Count's quarters is "an old, ruined chapel, which had evidently been used as a graveyard." This turns out to be the ground of vampires, creatures who are dead and yet still living."[29]

Suggestive as the verbal parallels are, one can assume only that the vampire idea undoubtedly influenced Eliot in his revision. Whether it came from a reading of *Dracula*, from some heresay regarding the story, or from quite other sources, one cannot say. After all, the vampire theme has a long history in literature and folklore, and Eliot could have imaginatively responded to the idea just as Stoker did when writing his novel.

Plainly, in dispensing with the Ferdinand figure, Eliot made much more tenuous any relation with *The Duchess of Malfi*, so that the whole scene takes on a more diffuse nightmarish quality. Nevertheless, it would hardly violate the character of Ferdinand to turn him into a bat or vampire; yet even this alteration is partly vitiated by the fact that not one bat but many invade the mindscape. One is left with an abstract delusion of hell. In this regard, perhaps one ought to consider certain remarks Jessie Weston made on the Perilous Chapel:

Students of the Grail romances will remember that in many of the versions the hero—sometimes it is a heroine—meets with a strange and terrifying adventure in a mysterious Chapel, an adventure which, we are given to understand, is fraught with extreme peril to life. The details vary: sometimes there is a Dead Body laid on the altar; sometimes a Black Hand extinguishes the tapers; there are strange and threatening voices, and the general impression is that this is an adventure in which supernatural, and evil, forces are engaged.[30]

Adjacent to the Perilous Chapel is a haunted cemetery, providing all the ingredients of the present nightmare vision. But to say that it belongs to the Perilous Chapel adventure, or to a phantasm of the undead, or to any other specific source would be to restrict unduly its import and impact. All these sources merely contribute ingredients for the synthesis of a new experience undoubtedly closer to the dark night of the soul questing for significance than to the specifics of any of the sources.

AND UPSIDE DOWN IN AIR WERE TOWERS
TOLLING REMINISCENT BELLS, THAT KEPT THE HOURS
AND VOICES SINGING OUT OF EMPTY CISTERNS AND EXHAUSTED WELLS.

These images must have carried special and profound meaning for Eliot, since he continued to amplify them in his later poetry. In the seventh chorus from "The Rock," he wrote straightforwardly of the loss of faith in modern man:

> But it seems that something has happened that has never happened
>   before: though we know not just when, or why, or how, or where.
> Men have left GOD not for other gods, they say, but for no god; and this
>   has never happened before
> That men both deny gods and worship gods, professing first Reason,
> And then Money, and Power, and what they call Life, or Race, or
>   Dialectic.
> The Church disowned, the tower overthrown, the bells upturned,
>   what have we to do
> But stand with empty hands and palms turned upwards
> In an age which advances progressively backwards?[31]

Tower and bells surely were closely allied in Eliot's mind with churches, and the tolling of bells were a kind of proclamation of faith. As he wrote in "The Dry Salvages," "The tolling bell / Measures time not our time . . . / . . . a time older than the time of chronometers." They are voices of eternity, a symbolism not difficult to accept. And their ringing suggests that a significant order prevails.

It is not known when Eliot first read Edward Arthur Waite's *The Pictorial Key to the Tarot*, but it may have been in his student days when he first penned these lines; the book would certainly have provided him with the basis for the symbolism that he seems to have ascribed to the tower. The Tower is the sixteenth trump in the tarot deck, and of it Waite wrote:

> Occult explanations attached to this card are meagre and mostly disconcerting. It is idle to indicate that it depicts ruin in all its aspects, because it bears this evidence on the surface. It is said further that it contains the first allusion to a material building, but I do not conceive that the Tower is more or less material than the pillars which we have met with in three previous cases. I see nothing to warrant Papus in supposing that it is literally the fall of Adam, but there is more in favor of his alternative—that it signifies the mate-

rialization of the spiritual world. The bibliographer Christian imagines that it is the downfall of the mind, seeking to penetrate the mystery of God. I agree rather with Grand Orient that it is the ruin of the House of Life, when evil has prevailed therein, and above all that it is the rending of a House of Doctrine. I understand that the reference is, however, to a House of Falsehood.[32]

As illustrated by Pamela Colman Smith for the Waite book, the card depicts a tower struck by lightning. Two figures are seen hurtled down from the top. If Eliot did not derive his symbolism from Waite, then both men seem to have shared similar feeling toward the tower as a mystical emblem: that it represents civilization in spiritual disorder.

For specific elements of his image, Eliot may have remembered the "pleasure-dome" of Khubla Khan, "that dome in air," as well as the tower that Aeneas saw at the entrance of the underworld, "Ferrea turris stat ad auras," [An iron tower stands in the air].[33] Needless to say, these towers "upside down in air" are not separate and distinct from the other towers that occur throughout the poem.[34]

From Shackleton, too, there may have lingered in Eliot's mind the account of a polar mirage in which "[i]cebergs hang upside down in the sky,"[35] especially since it immediately followed the statement, "Everything wears an aspect of unreality."

Tolling of the bells refers in part to "where Saint Mary Woolnoth kept the hours / With a dead sound on the final stroke of nine." Other than the emblematic value assigned to them, they also ring out of the depth of the despair felt by Marie Larisch upon hearing of the death of Rudolph:

> We travelled at night, and when we arrived at Vienna we found a city of sorrow. I cannot describe my feelings when I saw the black crowds and the signs of universal mourning; and sombre stillness hung like a funeral pall over everything and everybody, and there was a sense of horror and mystery in the very air we breathed.

She had not learned yet the details of the double death.

> And then the air outside vibrated with the deep and solemn tolling of bells. Each stroke made my heart quiver, and fell like a sledgehammer on my tired brain. Would they never stop? One—two—three—Rudolph was now lying in the Augustina Kirche . . . where was his spirit? Near me, I felt sure . . . what touched my cheek just then? . . . the last kiss . . . yes, that's what I felt . . . one—two—three—the bells again; I shall hear them for ever in my dreams.
>
> I flung myself on the couch; I put my fingers in my ears to deaden the haunting noise; I buried my head in the cushions; I felt I should die if I had much more to hear.[36]

If Eliot had not read that account before writing the original early draft from which these lines were incorporated, as revised, into his finished poem, he could hardly have kept from construing them partly within the emotionally charged reminiscences of Countess Larisch.

Finally, the "voices singing out of empty cisterns and exhausted wells" are scored from the monody of St. John in the cistern in Oscar Wilde's *Salome*, his voice prophesying the doom of Herodiade and the coming of Christ. Eliot has altered the underlying substratum of the allusive meaning so that it conforms to a more generalized atmosphere of terror. Assimilation of specific personal material, including recollections of things read as well as events experienced, to monstrous distortion, to visions difficult to conquer through ordinary comprehension, supposedly characterizes the dark night of the soul—a state toward which Eliot seemed to be aiming when he initially wrote of this whole nightmare sequence as "strange images" emerging from "tortured meditation" and reason from which all purpose seemed to be voided.

> IN THIS DECAYED HOLE AMONG THE MOUNTAINS
> IN THE FAINT MOONLIGHT, THE GRASS IS SINGING
> OVER THE TUMBLED GRAVES, ABOUT THE CHAPEL
> THERE IS THE EMPTY CHAPEL, ONLY THE WIND'S HOME.
> IT HAS NO WINDOWS, AND THE DOOR SWINGS,
> DRY BONES CAN HARM NO ONE.

As nightmare slowly dissolves, fading into reality, the hallucinatory aspect of the previous episode wanes, though it does not entirely vanish. Perhaps with the return of the Larisch material at the end of the previous episode, the matrix of rumination, like a mirror, rotates slightly back around to reflect again the Kipling saga thematically linked with images from *My Past*. The scene returns to the foothills at the base of the Himalayas, where there is the "grass singing under the wind," this time in a moonlight illuminating the nightingale seen offstage, as it were, through allusive implication with Matthew Arnold's "Philomela":

> Hark! ah, the nightingale—
> The tawny-throated!
> Hark, from that moonlit cedar what a burst!
> What triumph! hark!—what pain!
>
> O wanderer from a Grecian shore,
> Still, after many years, in distant lands,
> Still nourishing in thy bewildered brain
> That wild, unquenced, deep-sunken, old-world pain—

Say, will it never heal?
And can this fragrant lawn
With its cool trees, and night,
And the sweet, tranquil Thames
And moonshine, and the dew,
To thy racked heart and brain
Afford no balm.

Dost thou tonight behold,
Here, through the moonlight on this English grass,
The unfriendly palace in the Thracian wild?[37]

If this, indeed, contributed to "In the faint moonlight, the grass is singing," by way of "through the moonlight on this English grass," it must certainly have been through the Philomel connection reinforced by "sweet, tranquil Thames," echoing "Sweet Thames, run softly till I end my song." Dovetailing of so many images and themes would have raised these lines from the unconscious to participate in the wrought-ing of verbal detail in the poem.

In this setting is placed the Perilous Chapel or its equivalent, a chapel and cemetery embodying the atmosphere of death, also a suitable final backdrop against which the previous nightmare scenes could be imag-ined. "Dry bones," from the well-known song text and earlier references based on Ezekiel, enhances the atmosphere of death, but it is death deprived of real terror, since the bones "can harm no one."

ONLY A COCK STOOD ON THE ROOFTREE
CO CO RICO CO CO RICO
IN A FLASH OF LIGHTNING. THEN A DAMP GUST
BRINGING RAIN

Well known is the prophesy of Jesus to Peter at the Last Supper, quoted in Mark 14:30: "And Jesus said unto him, Verily I say unto thee, That this day, even in this night, before the cock crows twice, thou shalt deny me thrice." The prophesy is fulfilled in "What the Thunder Said," though in a characteristically transformed manner. First, the time-sequence is reversed: the three denials occur after the cock crows. Second, they are not precisely denials but rather spiritual failures to meet the divine commands. And third, they are negations directed not at Christ nor at the Christian god but at a divinity conceived more broadly as that toward which the human religious impulse moves to satisfy itself. They are, of course, the failures to meet the three com-mands of the Thunder: datta, dayadhvam, damyata.

Cock crows, introduced here, not only suggest the biblical prophesy, they also act as the traditional herald of dawn, at the sound of which, according to folklore, all the evil spirits and terrifying visions of the night are dispelled. This they do, for thereafter and until the final sequence the form of the poem becomes more logical and discursive. Grover Smith claims that the cock crows in Portuguese, but the crow is as likely a variant of the French *cocorico*.[38] Whether it conceals an allusion is not known. However, Eliot may have used it simply for the sound—*cock-a-doodle-doo* would have been ludicrous.

Lightning, aside from the literal significance throughout the Bible and in ancient mythology, represents the divine will, amplifying the import of the cock crow, framing it more archetypally. And the ensuing "damp gust / Bringing rain" has no more real effect than the storm over the Starnbergersee. Just as there is a failure to fulfill the commands of what the Thunder says, there is no revitalization of the spirit from the rain. In fact, had Eliot been following the Frazer-Weston line, as he successfully led critics to believe, this rain, being neither clearly illusory nor inducing regeneration, would be a nonsensical violation of the plan. Instead, not originally thinking of any strict adherence to the Grail narrative, he felt free to use the rain as a means for ushering in the Thunder with its spiritual admonitions.

> GANGA WAS SUNKEN, AND THE LIMP LEAVES
> WAITED FOR RAIN, WHILE THE BLACK CLOUDS
> GATHERED FAR DISTANT, OVER HIMAVANT
> THE JUNGLE CROUCHED, HUMPED IN SILENCE.

Ultimate unconscious sources for Eliot's inspiration may, as Herbert Knust suggests, include another passage from Frazer.[39] It concerns not Prajapati, speaker in the Fire Sermon, but Indra, Hindu god of thunder, and the cult surrounding him:

> It has been plausibly interpreted as a description of the bursting of the first storms of rain and thunder after the torrid heat of an Indian summer. At such times all nature, exhausted by the drought, longs for coolness and moisture. . . . The cloud-dragon has swallowed the waters and keeps them shut up in the black coils of his sinuous body; the god cleaves the monster's belly with his thunder-bolt, and the imprisoned waters escape, in the form of dripping rain and rushing stream.[40]

A substratum of feeling and a vein of imagery present in the passage could easily have provided part of the matrix out of which Eliot's lines sprang. The elements are there: "all nature, exhausted by the drought, longs for coolness and moisture," "the limp leaves / Waited for rain," "rain descends in sheets, drenching the parched earth and flooding the rivers," "Ganga was sunken," "sight of clouds that gather and then pass away," "the black clouds / Gathered far distant."

Ganga is the Hindu name for the Ganges River, the most sacred river in India. Into its waters the ashes of the cremated dead are cast, and it is thought to have a healing powers. Choice of the Ganges and the Himavant, a sacred mountain in the Himalaya range, would have been dictated by the need for an Indian setting against which to stage the commands of Prajapati as well as by the reverberations from the earlier allusions to *Kim*.

"The jungle crouched, humped in silence" revives the impenetrable mystery of *The Heart of Darkness*, for this is Conradian diction. It is as if the world waited for relief: literally for rain, symbolically for significance.

THEN SPOKE THE THUNDER
DA
DATTA: WHAT HAVE WE GIVEN?
MY FRIEND, BLOOD SHAKING MY HEART
THE AWFUL DARING OF A MOMENT'S SURRENDER
WHICH AN AGE OF PRUDENCE CAN NEVER RETRACT
BY THIS, AND THIS ONLY, WE HAVE EXISTED
WHICH IS NOT TO BE FOUND IN OUR OBITUARIES
OR IN MEMORIES DRAPED BY THE BENEFICENT SPIDER
OR UNDER SEALS BROKEN BY THE LEAN SOLICITOR
IN OUR EMPTY ROOMS

Each, in the most intimate sense, has only himself to give, which means an unspoken gesture that totally opens the self to another, with the implicit expectation or hope that the exchange will be one of understanding. Of course, that would be in defiance of solipsism; in fact, solipsistic isolation can be transcended only symbolically or through an act of faith, in as much as communication can never be verified. There is no way to get into the other person's mind to see whether or not we have really been understood. We must rely on what the other tells us, which is to say we must find substantiation in appearance only. Finally, we must have faith that appearance, that what the other person tells us in word and action, is what we think it is.

To test that faith, we abandon reason and enter "The awful daring of a moment's surrender / Which an age of prudence can never retract." Such a commitment can either succeed, at least theoretically, or make us feel foolish or guilty. It is no good speculating about the personal core of experience on which Eliot may have built this episode; there simply is not sufficient biographical material available. Miller makes much of the fact that in the original draft Eliot began, "we brother, what have we given," taking it to support his hypothesis that a homosexual liaison between Eliot and Verdenal formed the inspirational basis of the poem.[41] However, the apostrophic "we brother" is of too common a literary currency to validate such an interpretation. Even if it indicated a comraderie between two males, there is no secure elucidation of it. Even if the tone of the whole passage seems to suggest a homosexual exchange, one certainly cannot conclude a homosexual relationship took place. Considering that about a third of all males experience at least one homosexual encounter during their lifetime, and that most such encounters occur during youth, this one supposed episode for Eliot would bear little upon his overall sexual proclivity. Further, it is not known whether, if the encounter occurred, Eliot or the other party (and there is no evidence that it was Jean Verdenal) was the initiator, or even whether the act, whatever it was, was consummated. The passage is simply an attested surrender of one person to another in something that was only "momentary" and therefore not ultimately redemptive— because had it been redemptive, the poem could not meaningfully proceed as it does.

It is clear that an act of giving, so profound that it causes the heart to quiver, is that by which we know we have existed, for only in such moments—and these must also include creative and religious acts of complete involvement—do we forget ourselves, and in so doing are released from being only finite centers. With the momentary dissolution of the boundaries of the self, we become one with existence, at least within the philosophical frameworks of Bradley, Hinduism, and Buddhism. This is so personal an experience that it will not appear "in our obituaries," nor in a last will and testament "under seals broken by the lean solicitor / In our empty rooms." Nor will it be found in any epitaph upon a gravestone "draped by the beneficent spider." For this last image Eliot refers in his notes to words spoken by Flamineo in John Webster's *The White Devil*, 5.6. It is a play of seduction and murder, in which Flamineo helps abduct his own sister. At this particular point in the play, one of Flamineo's plots has backfired; he lies apparently shot by his sister and her maidservant, but then reveals that the gun was not loaded and he is not hurt; nevertheless he rails against the treachery of women:

> O men
> That lie upon your deathbeds, and are haunted
> With howling wives, ne'er trust them! they'll remarry
> Ere the worm pierce your winding sheet, ere the spider
> Make a thin curtain for your epitaph.[42]

It is interesting that Eliot should have divulged his source in Webster, for it rather obviously directs attention toward his own shabby marital status. It suggests that between him and his wife there were no moments of giving in which each fully understood the other. For that, he had to await a second marriage, the joy of which he celebrated in *The Elder Statesman.*

However reprehensible he may have felt the act confessed here, Eliot could have placed it here only in the conviction that it was a moment during which salvation was glimpsed, whether through purification or through damnation, for to him damnation itself could be the starting point of salvation.

DA

DAVADHVAM: I HAVE HEARD THE KEY
TURN IN THE DOOR ONCE AND TURN ONCE ONLY
WE THINK OF THE KEY, EACH IN HIS PRISON
THINKING OF THE KEY, EACH CONFIRMS A PRISON

No doubt is left by the note to these lines that Eliot specifically had in mind the quandary that solipsism forbids sympathy except as a subjective experience. He quotes Bradley's *Appearance and Reality:*

> My external sensations are no less private to myself than are my thoughts or my feelings. In either case my experience falls within my own circle, a circle closed on the outside; and, with all its elements alike, every sphere is opaque to the others which surround it. . . . In brief, regarded as an existence which appears in a soul, the whole world for each is peculiar and private to that soul.

But sympathy is useless unless it touches the person to whom it is directed. That is the problem with which Eliot seems to have been wrestling. On the one hand, Bradley was saying that the mind or soul is closed upon itself, making giving and sympathy theoretically impossible; yet, in communicating this, Bradley was taking on faith the existence of other finite centers to whom his words were directed. No bridge exists between the facts of the position—namely, that each person is a totally insular being, and that each is consequently incapable of proving the external existence of any other, since all others can be known only as percepts—and the implicit assumption made in enunciating the position, that there *are* others to whom to enunciate it.

Instead of attacking the quandary, Eliot simply acknowledged it by drawing in the passage from Bradley. It forms part of the illusion of appearance that the soul must face in the dark night of struggle to comprehend reality. Eliot allowed the picture to form itself upon certain allusive sources in which the feeling of the terror and alienation of isolation is underscored.

First among these sources is the thirty-third canto of *The Inferno*, in which the story of Ugolina of Pisa is told. In 1288 Pisa was under the rule of the Guelfs, who were divided into two parties, one led by Ugolino della Gherardesca, the other by his grandson, Nino de' Visconti. Ruggieri degli Ubaldini, archbiship of the city, was head of the Ghibellines; Ugolino conspired with him to oust Nino so that he could gain supreme control of Pisa. He was, however, betrayed by Ruggieri who, seeing that the Guelfs had been weakened through this internal strife, had him imprisoned with four of his sons and grandsons. When Guido of Montefeltro took command of the forces in Pisa the following year, he had the keys to the prison thrown into the river, leaving the prisoners to starve. That last condemnatory act of fate Ugolino records as he tells Dante that "io senti chiavar l'uscio di sotto / all orribile torre" [I heard below the key turn in the door / of the horrible tower].[43]

This gruesome tale bears upon the later reiteration of the London Bridge reference, this time in the form of the well-known children's song that remembers the primitive rite of the foundation sacrifice, the slaughter of a victim to avert evil from a newly built bridge or other structure. The scapegoat is represented in the song by the prisoner behind the stones:

> Take the key and lock him up, lock him up, lock him up,
> Take the key and lock him up, my fair lady.

Less macabre is Baudelaire's prose poem, "À une Heure du Matin" [At One O'Clock in the Morning], which it is likely that Eliot would have read, since it is an autobiographical piece of an author from whom he collected great inspiration:

> Enfin seul! On n'entend plus que le roulement de quelques fiacres attardés et éreintés. Pendant quelques heures, nous possederons le silence, sinon le repos. Enfin! la tyrannie de la face humaine a disparu, et je ne souffriarai plus que par moi-même.
> Enfin! Il m'est donc permis de me délasser dans un bain de ténèbres! D'abord, un double tour à la serrure. Il me semble que ce tour de clef augmentera ma solitude et fortifiera les barricades qui me séparent actuellement du monde.
> Horrible vie! Horrible ville!. . .
> Mécontent de tous et mécontent de moi, je voudrais bien me racheter et m'enorgueillir un peu dans le silence et la solitude de la nuit. Âmes de ceux que j'ai aimes, ames de ceux que j'ai chantés, fortifiez-moi, soutenez-moi, éloignez-moi le mensonge et les vapeurs corruptrices du monde; et vous, Seigneur mon Dieu! accordez-moi la

grace de produire quelques beaux vers qui me prouvent a moi-meme que je ne suis pas le dernier des hommes, que je ne suis pas inférieur à ceux que je méprise.

[At last alone! There is no longer to be heard but the passage of some belated and weary carriages. For a few hours, we shall possess silence, if not repose. At last! the tyranny of the human face has disappeared, and I no longer suffer but by myself.

At last! I am permitted to relax in a bath of shadows! First, a double turn of the lock. It seems to me that this turn of the key will increase my solitude and fortify the barriers which presently separate me from the world.

Horrible life! Horrible town!. . .

Discontented with everyone and discontented with myself, I should like to redeem myself and feel a little pride in the silence and solitude of the night. Spirits of those whom I have loved, spirits of those whom I have sung, fortify me, sustain me, take away from me the lying falsehood and the corrupting vapors of the world; and you, Lord my God! accord me the grace to produce some beautiful verses which may prove to me that I am not the last of men, that I am not inferior to those whom I despise.][44]

At Margate Eliot could hardly have expressed his own predicament more bluntly, but he must have taken some solace in that others, like Baudelaire, suffered the same sense of alienation. It is not an uncommon feeling; many authors have dealt with it. Consider, as a further example and possible literary source, Stephen Daedelus in a *Portrait of the Artist as a Young Man*. After confessing his sins to a priest following a hellfire and brimstone sermon, which roused in him the fear of judgement:

He went up to his room after dinner in order to be alone with his soul: and at every step his soul seemed to sigh: at every step his soul mounted with is feet, sighing in the ascent, through a region of viscid gloom.

He halted on the landing before the door and then, grasping the porcelain knob, opened the door quickly. He waited in fear, his soul pining within him, praying silently that death might not touch his brow as he passed over the threshold, that the fiends that inhabit darkness might not be given power over him. He waited still at the threshold as at the entrance to some dark cave. Faces were there; eyes: they waited and watched.[45]

The literature of solitude is great, and I have touched upon only some few instances of it with which Eliot was certainly familiar. Examples even there could be multiplied, but enough has been cited to evoke the aura of feeling that no doubt surrounded the composition of these few lines of extreme solipsism.[46]

ONLY AT NIGHTFALL, AETHEREAL RUMOURS
REVIVE FOR A MOMENT A BROKEN CORIOLANUS

Elsewhere, in "Coriolan: Triumphal March," Eliot explained by implication his choice of Coriolanus as an objective correlative for the feeling of not being able to sympathize:

> There is no interrogation in his eyes
> Or in his hands, quiet over the horse's neck,
> And the eyes watchful, waiting, perceiving, indifferent.

Coriolanus, in Shakespeare's play of the same name, after having had the populace stirred against him by enemies in the senate, refuses to placate "the mutable, rank-scented many," and joins the Volsces in a siege against his own Rome; but he is in turn killed by a jealous leader among the Volsces. Although "his nature is too noble for this world," Coriolanus is unable to sympathize with others, and so he brings upon himself his own downfall. He is the epitome of Western pride or hubris, as opposed to the Buddhist saint who joins others by transcending the boundaries of the self.

DA
DAMYATA: THE BOAT RESPONDED
GAILY, TO THE HAND EXPERT WITH THE SAIL AND OAR
THE SEA WAS CALM, YOUR HEART WOULD HAVE RESPONDED
GAILY, WHEN INVITED, BEATING OBEDIENT
TO CONTROLLING HANDS

For self control (damyata), Eliot goes back to his training in sailboating when he was a youth vacationing along the New England coast. Boat and sailor become as one, and to control oneself, therefore, is to control the boat. To complete his metaphoric development, he recalls a near romantic encounter, evidently also in those early days at Gloucester, by the testament of indecision writ in the original draft. Most spontaneously he had written "your heart responded," only to change the verb to the past conditional on second thought. As a bridge to the following lines, "I sat upon the shore / Fishing, with the arid plain behind me," he considered several possibilities describing the beloved left behind upon the shore, while the protagonist clasps "empty hands."

Considering the closeness with which these lines touch upon his youthful background, they clearly seem to recall an experience conceived as having happened, even if only in fantasy. Furthermore, the experience is much akin to that in the hyacinth garden sequence;

similarly, death is the thought that comes to mind as the failure or irresolution of the event is contemplated—which becomes clear in the biblical reference three lines later.

                    I SAT UPON THE SHORE
FISHING, WITH THE ARID PLAIN BEHIND ME

These lines originally belonged at the end of the previous episode. They reflect back to "While I was fishing in the dull canal / On a winter evening round behind the gashouse," and so to the funereal background from whence it came in *Ulysses*. Given that this figure is associated with the Fisher King, it would merely be substituting infirmity for death. In either case, the implications are unpleasant. Even without knowing that the image grew out of the damyata episode, it is clear enough that the figure is solitary, cut off from significance, "with the arid plain behind" him.

SHALL I AT LEAST SET MY LANDS IN ORDER?

During the reign of Hezekiah, Palestine was threatened by Assyria. Hezekiah favored an alliance with Egypt, but Isaiah, the prophet, opposed this. At that point Hezekiah was stricken with an illness, as was the Fisher King, and sent for the prophet. "In those days was Hezekiah sick unto death. And Isaiah the prophet the son of Amoz came unto him, Thus saith the Lord, Set thine house in order: for thous shalt die, and not live"[47] On the face of it, to set one's lands in order would mean to prepare for death; but Hezekiah did not die. He prayed to God, saying, "I have walked before thee in truth and with a perfect heart, and have done that which is good in thy sight," and he lived for fifteen more years. Still, "Shall I at least set my lands in order?" shows that the protagonist is entertaining premonitions of death, whether or not they prove to be false.

LONDON BRIDGE IS FALLING DOWN FALLING DOWN FALLING DOWN

Here begins what some critics have taken to be a kind of final madness, a final giving in to chaos, as the poem ends in a sudden burst of allusions in different languages. Such interpretations are superficial, however. Eliot proceeds along two disparate paths in this polyglot undertaking, each moving along a direction that can be clearly delineated.

A children's song sets the stage. Psychologically, the song arises by association from the recollections of youth rehearsed in the previous episode. Taken in the larger context of the poem, London Bridge has already been established in "The Burial of the Dead" as carrying the living dead back and forth over the Thames, as they move mindlessly through their daily repetitive routines. That it is now falling down has nearly apocalyptic connotations. Seen literally, it would belong to the dreamlike structure of the whole work.

"London Bridge is falling down," as a children's song, fulfills another function: it establishes a kind of innocence of mind. This is necessary to one aspect of the polyglot pastiche to follow. Milton Miller has advanced the highly supportable contention that this multilingual passage represents glossolalia, the gift of tongues, "the peculiar mark and manifestation of the outpouring of the Spirit and . . . the tangible sign of spiritual baptism."[48] Described mainly in Acts, glossolalia was in early Christianity associated mainly with conversions achieved during the Pentecost. Further, within the narrative of the Passion found fragmentarily in "What the Thunder Said," this would fit into a natural chronology—the Pentecost following a week upon the Resurrection—placing any consideration of it most properly at the end of the section. To see how the innocence of mind suggested by "London Bridge is falling down" is related to the Pentecostal glossolalia, one has only to revert to biblical texts.

Christ himself said in Mark 16:17: "And these signs shall follow them that believe; In my name shall they cast out devils; they shall speak with new tongues." Belief in or acceptance of Christ is spiritual baptism, by which the converted may then upon physical death enter heaven. But Christ also said, in Matthew 18:3: "Except ye be converted, and become as little children, ye shall not enter into the kingdom of heaven." Hence the transitional connection between childlike innocence of mind and the gift of tongues as a sign of conversion.

Straightforward conversion, as a denouement to the poem, would have been a violation of the whole Bradleyan structure; Eliot cues us to an alternative consideration with "Why then Ile fit you," a line he pointedly identifies in his notes as from The Spanish Tragedy by Thomas Kyd, possibly because he knew it was the sort of thing to be discovered quickly anyway. The context of the quotation should be examined rather carefully.

The political background of the play is the victory of Spain over Portugal in 1580. The characters are several and their involvements, complex. Don Cyprian, duke of Castile, brother of the king of Spain, has a son, Lorenzo, and a daughter, Bel-imperia. Additionally, there is Hieronimo, marshall of Spain, his son, Horatio, and the son of the viceroy of Portugal, Balthazar, who has been taken prisoner by Lorenzo and Horatio during the war. Balthazar courts Bel-imperia, and his suit is favored by Lorenzo and also the king of Spain for political reasons. However, Lorenzo and Balthazar discover that Bel-imperia loves Horatio. Coming upon Horatio in his father's garden at night, they slay him and hang him to a tree. When Hieronimo finds his dead son, he is stricken with violent grief. He soon finds out who the murderers are and plots their death with Bel-imperia. He lures them into playing parts in a play staged before the court, a play in which the characters whom they portray are to be killed during the action. His plan, of course, is to make the killings real, and this he does. Moreover, over the course of the play, Bel-imperia stabs herself, and Hieronimo too ends his own life.

After Hieronimo finds his son dead and hanging from a tree, he is distraught and begins to act strangely, exhibiting fits of madenss. He is approached by Lorenzo to present a play at court:

> Bal.: *It pleased you*
>   At the entertainment of the ambassador,
>   To grace the king so much as with a show.
>   Now, were your study so well furnished,
>   As for the passing of the first night's sport
>   To entertain my father with the like,
>   Or any such-like pleasing motion,
>   Assure yourself, it would content them well.
> Hier. *Is this all?*
> Bal.: *Ay, this is all.*
> Hier.: *Why, then I'll fit you: say no more.*
>   When I was young, I gave my mind
>   And plied myself to fruitless poetry;
>   Which though it profit the professor naught,
>   Yet is it passing pleasing to the world.[49]

Hieronimo explains that he has written a tragedy based upon an incident in Spanish history. He then assigns to his enemies those characters in the play who are murdered. And later, still in act 4, scene 1, he stipulates:

> Hier.: *Each of us*
>   Must act his part in unknown languages,
>   That it may breed the more variety:
>   As you, my lord, in Latin, I in Greek,
>   You in Italian, and for because I know
>   That Bel-imperia hath practiced the French,
>   In courtly French shall all her phrases be.
> Bel.: *You mean to try my cunning then, Hieronimo?*
> Bal.: *But this will be a mere confusion,*
>   And hardly shall we all be understood.
> Hier.: *It must be so; for the conclusion*
>   Shall prove the invention and all was good;

And I myself in an oration,
And with a strange and wondrous show besides,
That I will have there behind a curtain,
Assure yourself, shall make the matter known:
And all shall be concluded in one scene,
For there's no pleasure ta'en in tediousness.[50]

Eliot, in fact used all the mentioned languages, except Greek, in these closing lines. Insofar as he followed the promptings from the play, he was aware that the polyglot presentation was a deception. Therefore, for him at this point there could be no hard and fast distinction made between genuine conversion by glossolalia and a deception of conversion. Further corroboration of this conclusion emerges from the convergence of "Hieronymo's mad againe," the subtitle of Kyd's tragedy, with I Corinthians 14:23: "If therefore the whole church be come together in one place, and all speak with tongues, and there come in those that are unlearned, will they not say that ye are mad?" Eliot had originally placed "Why then Ile fit you. Hieronymo's mad againe" after "*Quando fiam uti chelidon*—O swallow swallow," but then moved it to the end of the pastiche, where it reinforces the ambiguous nature of the conversion through the allusive convergence just discussed.

POI S'ASCOSE NEL FOCO CHE GLI AFFINA

[THEN HE DIVED BACK INTO THE FIRE THAT REFINES THEM.]

Dante has come upon those who indulged in carnal lust, among whom he spots the medieval poet of the famous obscure style, Arnaut Daniel, who willingly suffers the refining fire so that he may enter heaven. The line quoted—*Purgatory*, 26.148—Daniel speaks after describing himself. This involves yet another Bradleyan opposition: fire as an all-consuming passion of the flesh versus fire as a purifying agent.

QUANDO FIAM UTI CHELIDON—

[WHEN SHALL I BE AS THE SWALLOW]

This line is from the *Pervigilium veneris* (Vigil of Venus), of which that venerable scholar J. W. Mackail wrote:

Its author is unknown, nor can its date be determined with certainty. The worship of Venus Genetrix, for whose spring festival the poem is written, had been revived on a magnificent scale by Hadrian; and this fact, together with the internal evidence of the language, make it assignable with high probability to the age of the Antonines. The use of the preposition *de*, almost as in the Romance languages, where case-inflexions would be employed in classical Latin, has been held to argue an African origin; while its remarkable medievalisms have led some critics, against all the other indications, to place its date as low as the fourth or even the fifth century.[51]

The poem is full of lush descriptions of nature quite in the bucolic tradition of late Latin verse. It depicts the awakening of all living things upon the eve of the festival devoted to the goddess of love. Running through it is the refrain, "Cras amet qui nunquam amavit, quique amavit eras amet" [Tomorrow loves he who never loved, and who loved tomorrow loves].[52] Even the nightingale sings, as if Tereus had never raped her:

> Illa cantat, nos tacemus: quando veritenit meum?
> Quando fiam uti chelidon ut tacere desinam?
>
> She sings, we remain silent: when will my spring come?
> When will I be as the swallow that I may desist my silence?][53]

While all the world rejoices at coming of spring, the poet is left forlorn, another fragment of Eliot's conscience at the time.

O SWALLOW SWALLOW

A further extension of the previous fragmentary line, this echoes a fervent longing to be as the swallow, having suffered but to rise once more to song, a feeling identical with that expressed by Baudelaire in "À une Heure du Matin." At the end of the *Pervigilium veneris*, too, the poet complains that he has lost his muse in silence and that Apollo no longer looks upon him. Immediate source for the apostrophe is the opening lines from the love song from *The Princess* by *Tennyson*:

> O Swallow, Swallow, flying, flying south,
> Fly to her, and fall upon her gilded eaves,
> And tell her, tell her, what I tell to thee.[54]

The song goes on to tell that the poet loves his lady and that he shall fly to her, following the messenger swallow. A variant is found in Swinburne's "Itylus," in which Philomela laments her tragedy to her sister, Procne (who was turned into a swallow):

> Swallow, my sister, O sister swallow,
> How can thine heart be full of the spring?
> A thousand summers are over and dead.
> What hast thou found in the spring to follow?

> What has thou found in thine heart to sing?
> What wilt thou do when the summer is shed?[55]

LE PRINCE D'AQUITAINE À LA TOUR ABOLIE
[THE PRINCE OF AQUITAINE WITH THE RUINED TOWER]

Final glossolalic utterance, this line comes from "El Desdichado" [The Wretch], a French poem with a Spanish title by Gerard de Nerval:

> I am the tenebrous—the widower—the unconsoled,
> The Prince of Aquitaine with the ruined tower:
> My only *star* is dead—and my constellated lute
> Bears the black *sun* of *Melancholy*.
>
> In the night of the tomb, you who consoled me,
> Give me back Posilipo and the Italian sea,
> The *flower* which so much pleased my desolate heart,
> And the arbor where the vine is to the rose allied.
> Am I Eros or Phoebus? . . . Lusignan or Biron?
> My brow is red still from the kiss of the queen;
> I have dreamed in the arbor where the siren swims . . .
>
> And I have two times victorious crossed Acheron:
> Modulating by turns on the lyre of Orpheus
> The signs of the saint and the cries of the fairy.[56]

Gerard de Nerval, whose real name was Gerard Labrunie, was a French poet of the first half of the nineteenth century whose talents remained largely unappreciated until his rediscovery in this century. Little wonder that Eliot turned to him as a source, for his genius was to objectify his own personal life through allusions and mystic symbolism, not at all unlike the genius of Eliot. "El Desdichado" can hardly be understood, let alone appreciated, without an intimate familiarity with obscure occultism and symbolism.[57]

It is certainly to be noted that Nerval employed here, as elsewhere, several references to the tarot. He had traced his family to the region of Aquitaine, a political division of Roman Gaul, and he believed that his family name meant *tower*, so that he could poetically declare himself "The Prince of Aquitaine with the ruined tower," the "ruined tower" referring not only to his familial identity but to the Tower, sixteenth major trump of the tarot, previously described in relation to "And upside down in air were towers." He construed the tower in ruin, depicted on the tarot card, as his own fallen nobility. His "star" had been Jenny Colon, an actress with whom he had fallen passionately in love in 1836. Two years later she married someone else, and in 1842 she died. He therefore considered himself a "widower" from her. His "constellated lute" was simply himself, the lute being a symbol of the human microcosm, and that it may be "constellated" signified that he was under the influence of specific zodiacal signs. The "black sun" is an astrological position of the sun, auguring inevitable suffering and melancholy.

It would lead too far astray to explicate the poem in sufficient detail to clarify it fully, but it may be noted in passing that his longing for Posilipo and the Italian sea recalled for him two former sojourns in Naples, and that Posilipo, a mountainous promontory near Naples, is thought to have on it, a grotto, the tomb of Virgil. This Virgilian association would help to sustain at least a mnemonic link with the Dantean allusion two lines back.

When one looks back on the glossolalic fragments, one can see suddenly how they all fit together. Thematic continuity, as throughout the poem, is the key. First came the words of the troubadour Arnaut Daniel, a poet who, for his dedication to the praise of earthly love, had to suffer the refining fire of purgatory so that he might be saved, paralleling Eliot's own purgatorial damnation for his subservience to passion in his relationship with Vivien. Next, an unknown poet bemoans his loss of inspiration as the festivals of regeneration close around him, much as Eliot at Margate could "connect / Nothing with nothing," fitfully putting together a series of poems that, apparently for momentary lack of faith in his own muse, he did not trust himself solely to revise. Both he and the unknown poet in the *Pervigilium veneris* admired the swallow for her ability to rise through suffering to renew her vernal song. And finally, still another poet, Nerval, reinforces this train of complaints of the poets, declaring himself fallen and desolate, condemned by cosmic fate to ultimate melancholy, again a feeling echoing Eliot's at that time. In short, what looked like a pastiche turns out to be a coherent cry of the poet for his misfortune, which is suffering and loss of inspiration due to entanglements of love. Such cannot be the content of true spiritual conversion; it is a mockery of conversion, painful and sardonic, part of a ruse, in the manner of Hieronimo's play, to conceal the true feelings and intent of the poet. It is yet another mask for him to hide behind, but it is a mask that can be penetrated.

THESE FRAGMENTS I HAVE SHORED AGAINST MY RUINS

Eliot's "ruins" are, as with the "ruined tower" of Nerval, the condition of life as he was writing *The Waste Land*. He had not yet put together the pieces of his life. He still could not connect them together. He could only shore them against his condition. Obliquely the fragments were reflected in the images that together comprised the poem.

WHY THEN ILE FIT YOU. HIERONYMO'S MAD AGAINE.

Balthazar requested an entertainment; in saying that he would "fit" the request, Hieronimo implies not only that he will comply with the wishes of murderers but that he will do so in a *fitting* manner. Appearance and reality, play-acting and real life, are inextricably synthesized in the tragedy that he proposes. It is Bradleyan unity achieved symbolically. Similarly, in *The Waste Land* Eliot fused together the events and experiences of his own life with the appearance of poetic fiction, transmutations of personal details into allusive symbols. Just as Paul wrote to the Corinthians, if those who are unlearned enter where many tongues are being spoken, where the levels of experience do not appear of a single mind, they will call it madness—"Hieronymo's mad againe." It is all a deception, but a deception in which reality is caught, or perhaps reality too is a deception.

DATTA. DAYADHVAM. DAMYATA.

These are the keys by which to escape the illusions of the physical world, if only we could master them. We hold them before us, repeat them ritualistically in the hour of madness, like clutching at straws, desperate for salvation. This is the summation, almost the end of the ritual, which must be repeated over and over unto the final extinction of the self.

SHANTIH   SHANTIH   SHANTIH

Commentators have usually confined themselves to a consideration of the meaning of this word, rather than of the function that it serves. Eliot calls attention to both aspects in his notes. He gives the meaning as the "peace which passeth understanding." *Shantih* (also spelled *santi*) in Vedantic thought is the fundamental emotion from which all others spring, just as Brahman is the One from which the Many of appearance arise. It encompasses all emotions and as such cannot be conceived; it "passeth understanding."

More important—and Eliot calls attention to this in his notes—this word closes the Upanishads. Strangely, no one seems to have followed this implication. A Upanishad is a speculative treatise attached to the end of a Veda. The Veda expresses its mystic doctrine in poetic form, and the Upanishad supplies a commentary that seeks to explore and expatiate upon the Vedic content. That is why Upanishadic doctrine is not unified: it contains the opinions of many people, similar to the Talmudic body. So, primarily, the Upanishad is a work of speculation.

And Upanishadic speculation centers around various aspects of a single problem: how appearance is related to reality, how the individual self is related to Brahman. Further, the Upanishads were to be passed on to initiates who were about to withdraw into hermitage, so that they might meditate upon them in their isolation.

Applying this to *The Waste Land* leads back around to the position from which I began this exegesis. It is a poem containing the speculations of Eliot upon his own condition as projected through the Bradleyan metaphysics of appearance versus reality. It is in itself not unified, just as the Upanishads are not. Eliot wrote it as he was contemplating withdrawal into the hermitage of a Buddhist monastery. In a sense, when he published it, it too, like the Upanishads, was intended for the initiates; few others would have been able to understand it.

Finally, both the meaning and the function of the word *shantih* require one to read it in the subjunctive mode of closing invocation, not entirely dissimilar to the Hebrew *amen;* accordingly translated *May there be peace.* And so the peace with which the poem ends is not achieved, but longed for, a peace sought out of anguish. That was the final testament of Eliot at Margate, to find the full significance of silence.

Notes

Introduction

1. Horace Gregory and Marya Zaturenska, *A History of American Poetry 1900–1940* (New York, 1946), 413.
2. Kenneth Rexroth, *American Poetry in the Twentieth Century* (New York, 1971), 56.
3. Ibid.
4. Quoted in John Unterecker, *Voyager: A Life of Hart Crane* (New York, 1969), 282.

Chapter 1. A Couple of Feelers down at Tom's Place

1. Letter to John Quinn, 5 November 1919. Quoted in T. S. Eliot, *The Waste Land: A Facsimile and Transcript of the Original Drafts Including the Annotations of Ezra Pound*, ed. Valerie Eliot (New York, 1971), xviii (hereafter cited as *Facsimile*).
2. Ibid., xix–xx. Letter to his mother.
3. Ibid., xxi. Letter to his mother, 9 May 1921.
4. Grover Smith, *T. S. Eliot's Poetry and Plays: A Study in Sources and Meaning*, 2d ed. (Chicago, 1974), 300–314.
5. Hugh Kenner, "The Urban Apocalypse," in *Eliot in His Time: Essays on the Occasion of the Fiftieth Anniversary of "The Waste Land,"* ed. A. Walton Litz (Princeton, N.J. 1973), 23–49.
6. Ibid., 35.
7. Ibid., 28–29.
8. Ibid., 27.
9. Monroe Stearns, *Dante: Poet of Love* (New York, 1965), 222.
10. Quoted in T. S. Matthews, *Great Tom: Notes toward the Definition of T. S. Eliot* (New York, 1973), 48.
11. Herbert Read, "T. S. E.—A Memoir," in *T. S. Eliot: The Man and His Work*, ed. Allen Tate (New York, 1966), 31.
12. Dante Alighieri, *La Divina Commedia*, *Inferno*, 1.1–12. Translation adapted from that of John Aitken Carlyle (New York, 1899–1901: reprint, New York 1933).
13. Letter to William Carlos Williams, 18 March 1922. Quoted in Roger Kojecky, *T. S. Eliot's Social Criticism* (New York, 1972), 51.
14. *Transatlantic Review* 1 (January 1924): 95. This is a message from Eliot,

as editor of the *Criterion*, to Ford Madox Ford, helping him to launch the first issue of his new journal.

15. T. S. Eliot, "A Commentary," *Criterion* 13 (April 1934): 451.

16. Ezra Pound, *The Spirit of Romance* (New York, n.d.), 127.

17. Ernest Hatch Wilkins, *A History of Italian Literature* (Cambridge, Mass, 1954), 71.

18. Thomas G. Bergin, *Dante* (New York, 1965), 258–59.

19. George Santayana, *Three Philosophical Poets* (Cambridge, Mass., 1910), 91.

20. Ibid.

21. T. S. Eliot, *The Use of Poetry and the Use of Criticism* (Cambridge, Mass., 1933), 131.

22. T. S. Eliot, "The Three Voices of Poetry," in *On Poetry and Poets* (New York, 1957), 107. There are several other notable instances in which Eliot discussed the creative process in tellingly personal terms:

> . . . some forms of ill-health, debility or anaemia, may (if other circumstances are favourable) produce an efflux of poetry in a way approaching the condition of automatic writing—though, in contrast to the claims sometimes made for the latter, the material has obviously been incubating within the poet, and cannot be suspected of being à present from a friendly or impertinent demon. What one writes in this way may succeed in standing the examination of a more normal state of mind; it gives me the impression, as I have just said, of having undergone a long incubation, though we do not know until the shell breaks what kind of egg we have been sitting on. To me it seems that at these moments, which are characterized by the sudden lifting of the burden of anxiety and fear which presses upon our daily life so steadily that we are unaware of it, what happens is something *negative*: that is to say, not "inspiration" as we commonly think of it, but the breaking down of strong habitual barriers—which tend to re-form very quickly. Some obstruction is momentarily whisked away. The accompanying feeling is less like what we know as positive pleasure, than a sudden relief from an intolerable burden. (*Use of Poetry and Use of Criticism*, 137–38)

Having said that much, Eliot goes on to add: "I am not even sure that the poetry which I have written in this way is the best that I have written; and so far as I know, no critic ever identified the passages I have in mind." (ibid.)

In "The *Pensees* of Pascal," he wrote in a similar vein:

> . . . it is a commonplace that some forms of illness are extremely favourable, not only to religious illumination, but to artistic and literary composition. A piece of writing meditated, apparently without progress, for months, may suddenly take shape and word; and in this state long passages may be produced with little or no retouch. I have no good word to say for the cultivation of automatic writing as the model of literary composition; I doubt whether these moments *can* be cultivated by the writer; but he to whom this happens assuredly has the sensation of being a vehicle rather than a maker. No masterpiece can be produced whole by such means: but neither does even the higher form of religious inspiration suffice for the religious life. . . . (*Selected Essays*, 2d ed. [New York, 1950], 358)

Of course, Valerie Eliot attested that it was "What the Thunder Said" that Eliot had written under these conditions of unbridled spontaneity.

23. Ibid., 108.

24. Paul Valery, "Remarks on Poetry," in *The Art of Poetry* (New York, 1958; New York, 1961), 198. His italics.

25. Ibid. His italics.

26. T. S. Eliot, "The Art of Poetry," an interview, *Paris Review* 21 (Spring–Summer 1959): 63–64.

27. David Foulkes, *The Psychology of Sleep* (New York, 1966), 136.

28. Edward S. Tauber and Maurice R. Green, *Prelogical Experience: An Inquiry into Dreams and Other Creative Processes* (New York, 1959), 171.

29. Lewis R. Wolberg, *The Technique of Psychotherapy*, 2d ed. (New York, 1967), 1:634.

30. Ibid.

31. *Waste Land*, 346–58, in *Complete Poems and Plays* (New York, 1950), 47–48. (Hereafter cited as WL.)

32. Mardi J. Horowitz, *Image Formation and Cognition* (New York, 1970), 87.

33. T. S. Eliot, "Dante," in *Selected Essays*, 2d ed. (New York, 1950), 204.

34. Tauber and Green, *Prelogical Experience*, 274–75.

35. Ibid., 275.

36. T. S. Eliot, preface for Saint-John Perse, *Anabasis: A Poem*, 3d ed. (New York, 1949), 10.

37. Stephane Mallarmé, *Oeuvres Complètes*, ed. H. Mondor and G. Jean-Aubry (Paris, 1945), 869.

38. Henry W. Wells, *Poetic Imagery* (New York, 1924), 31.

39. Cleanth Brooks, *The Well Wrought Urn* (New York, 1947), 198.

40. F. H. Bradley, *Appearance and Reality*, 2d ed. (London, 1897), 29.

41. Ibid. 405.

42. Ibid., 120.

43.

Satori may be defined as an intuitive looking into the nature of things in contradistinction to the analytical or logical understanding of it. Practically, it means the unfolding of a new world hitherto unperceived in the confusion of a dualistically-trained mind. Or we may say that with satori our entire surroundings are viewed from quite an unexpected angle of perception. Whatever this is, the world for those who have gained a satori is no more the old world as it used to be; even with all its flowing streams and burning fires, it is never the same one again. Logically stated, all its opposites and contradictions are united and harmonized into a consistent organic whole. (D. T. Suzuki, *Zen Buddhism*, ed. William Barrett [Garden City, N.Y., 1956], 84)

44. F. H. Bradley, *Essays on Truth and Reality* (London, 1914), 426.

45. F. H. Bradley, *Appearance and Reality*, 190–91.

46. F. H. Bradley, *Truth and Reality*, 407.

47. Ibid., 405.

48. David Hume, *A Treatise on Human Knowledge*, 1.4.6.

49. F. H. Bradley, *Truth and Reality*, 248.

50. Ibid., 250–51.

51. F. H. Bradley, *Appearance and Reality*, 466.

52. Ibid., 223.

53. Kenneth W. Morgan, ed., *The Religion of the Hindus* (New York, 1953), 254.

54. Quoted in John D. Margolis, *T. S. Eliot's Intelectual Development* (Chicago, 1972), 142.

55. Letter from T. S. Eliot to Paul Elmer More, 2 June 1930, ibid., 144.

Chapter 2. Synthesis toward an Interpretation

1. WL, 385–90.

2. Gertrude Patterson, *T. S. Eliot: Poems in the Making* (New York, 1971), 93.

3. I. A. Richards, "The Poetry of T.S. Eliot," in *Principles of Literary Criticism* (New York, n.d.), 190–91.

4. Julius Laffal, *Pathological and Normal Language* (New York, 1965). Extensive bibliography.

5. T. S. Eliot, "William Blake," in *Selected Essays*, 2d ed. (New York, 1970), 278.

6. T. S. Eliot, "A Commentary," *Criterion* 2 (April 1924): 232.

7. John Butler Yeats, *Passages from the Letters*, ed. Ezra Pound (Churchtown, Dundrum, 1918), 5.

8. Eliot, *Use of Poetry and Use of Criticism*, 151.

9. Wilhelm Wundt, *Elements of Folk Psychology*, trans. Edward Leroy Schaub (London, 1916), 93.

10. Ibid., 92–93.

11. T. S. Eliot, *Knowledge and Experience in the Philosophy of F. H. Bradley* (New York, 1964), 138.

12. T. S. Eliot, "The Idea of a Literary Review," *Criterion* 4 (January 1926): 5.

13. T. S. Eliot, *After Strange Gods* (London, 1934), 28.

14. Angelo Bertocci, *From Symbolism to Baudelaire* (Carbondale, Ill., 1964), 164.

15. Arthur Symons, *The Symbolist Movement in Literature* (New York, 1919), 94–95.

16. Eliot, "Tradition and the Individual Talent," in *Selected Essays*, 10.

17. T. S. Eliot, preface to Perse, *Anabasis*, 10.

18. Brooks, *Well Wrought Urn*, 207.

19. M. L. Rosenthal, "T. S. Eliot and the Displaced Sensibility: *The Waste Land*," in *The Merrill Studies in "The Waste Land"* (Columbus, Ohio, 1971), 82.

20. T. S. Eliot, "Dante," in *The Sacred Wood* (1920; reprint, London and New York, 1960), 166.

21. Frederick J. Streng, *Emptiness: A Study in Religious Meaning* (Nashville and New York, 1967), 19.

Chapter 3. The Burial of the Dead

1. Charles Dickens, *Our Mutual Friend* (New York, 1957), 191.

2. Eliot, "William Blake," in *Selected Essays*, 278.

3. George L. K. Morris, "Marie, Marie, Hold on Tight," *Partisan Review* 21 (March–April 1954): 231–33. Reprinted in *T. S. Eliot: A Collection of Critical Essays*, ed. Hugh Kenner (Englewood Cliffs, N.J., 1962), 86–88.

4. Eliot, *Facsimile*, 125–26.

5. Countess Marie Larisch, *My Past* (New York, 1913), 113.

6. Ibid., 123.

7. Ibid., 121.

8. Ibid., 113.

9. Ibid., 310.

10. Ibid., 152–53.

11. T. S. Eliot, *The Cocktail Party* in *The Complete Poems and Plays: 1909–1950* (New York, 1952), 360 (hereafter cited as CPP).

12. Ibid., 361.

13. Ibid., 360.

14. Joseph Conrad, *A Heart of Darkness*, in *Conrad Argosy* (Garden City, New York, 1942), 72.

15. Ibid., 75.

16. Ibid., 73.

17. William York Tindall, *Forces in Modern British Literature: 1885–1956* (New York, 1956), 287–88.

18. 1. Corinthians 15:52.

19. Guillaume de Lorris and Jean de Meun, *The Romance of the Rose*, trans. Charles Dahlberg (Princeton, N.J. 1971), 31–32.

20. Chaucer, "Prologue," *Canterbury Tales*, in *Works*, ed. F. N. Robinson (Boston, 1957), 17, lines 1–18.

21. William Shakespeare, *Anthony and Cleopatra*, 3.2.

22. Larisch, *My Past*, 291.

23. Charles-Louis Philippe, *Bubu of Montparnasse*, with an introduction by T. S. Eliot (New York, 1951), 15.

24. Geoffrey Faber, "Loyalty," in *In the Valley of Vision* (Oxford, 1918), 53–54.

25. James E. Miller, Jr., *T. S. Eliot's Personal Waste Land: Exorcism of the Demons* (University Park, Pa., 1977).

26. George Watson, "Quest for a Frenchman," *Sewanee Review* 84 (Summer 1976): 466–75.

27. T. S. Eliot, "A Commentary," *Criterion* 13 (April 1934): 452.

28. Miller, *Eliot's Personal Waste Land*, 66.

29. Wyndham Lewis, *Tarr* (London, 1919), 220.

30. T. S. Eliot, "The Rock," in *CPP*, 97.

31. T. S. Eliot, *The Family Reunion*, 1.1, in *CPP*, 225–26.

32. A. C. Benson, *Edward Fitzgerald* (London, 1905), 181.

33. Ibid., 187.

34. Ibid., 190.

35. Job 8:11 and 16–17.

36. T. S. Eliot, *The Family Reunion*, 2.2, in *CPP*, 281.

37. John Webster, *The Duchess of Malfi*, 2.2, in *The Duchess of Malfi and the White Devil* (London and New York), 1930.

38. James Frazer, *The Golden Bough* (New York, 1911–15), 5:120.

39. Ibid., 121.

40. Dante, *Purgatory*, 3.16–18, in *La Divina Commedia*, ed. H. Oelsner (New York, 1933), pt. 2, p. 26. My translation.

41. Virgil, *Aeneid*, 3. 443–44, in *Works* (New York, 1952), 84. My translation.

42. Larisch, *My Past*, 175.

43. Herbert Knust, *Wagner, the King, and "The Waste Land"* (University Park, Pa., 1967), 14.

44. Eliot, *Facsimile*, 91, 95.

45. John Donne, *Devotions upon Emergent Occasions*, 4, in *Complete Poetry and Selected Prose of Jonh Donne and Complete Poetry of William Blake* (New York: 1946), 313.

46. Larisch, *My Past*, 152–53.

47. F. O. Matthiessen, *The Achievement of T. S. Eliot: An Essay on the Nature of Poetry*, rev. ed. (New York, 1959), 92.

48. Quoted in ibid, 92–93.

49. It is difficult not to detect in "La Figlia che Piange" the influence of D. G. Rossetti's "The Blessed Damozel."

50. Smith, *Eliot's Poems and Plays*, 27.

51. Leonard H. Unger, *T. S. Eliot: Moments and Patterns* (Minneapolis, 1956), 69–91.

52. Walter J. Ong, "'Burnt Norton' in St. Louis," *American Literature* 33 (January 1962): 522–26.

53. Dante, *Inferno*, 34.22–27, in *La Divina Commedia*, pt. 1, p. 384. Translation modified.

54. Larisch, *My Past*, 294.

55. Geoffrey Faber, "Nights in England at War, Winter and Summer," in *Valley of Vision*, 14–15.

56. Bradley, *Essays on Truth and Reality* (London, 1914), 116.

57. Ibid., 132.

58. Dante, *Paradise*, 12.28–30, in *La Divina Commedia*, pt. 3, p. 144. Translation modified.

59. Eliot, *Family Reunion*, 2.1, in *CPP*, 260.

60. Joseph Conrad, *Heart of Darkness*, 48.

61. Joseph Campbell, "Days," in *Earth of Cualann* (Dublin and London, 1917), 9–10.

62. Aldous Huxley, *Crome Yellow* (New York and Evanston, Ill., 1922), 260.

63. Ibid., 17.

64. Ibid., 18–19.

65. Ibid., 19.

66. Marion Montgomery, "Lord Russell and Madame Sosostris," *Georgia Review* 28 (Summer 1974): 281.

67. Larisch, *My Past*, 340.

68. Ibid., 98–99.

69. Ibid., 137.

70. Ibid., 137–38.

71. Ibid., 101.

72. Gertrude Moakley, "The Waite-Smith 'Tarot': A Footnote to *The Waste Land*," *Bulletin of the New York Public Library* 58 (October 1954): 471–75.

73. Arthur Edward Waite, *The Pictorial Key to the Tarot* (1910; reprint, New Hyde Park, N.Y., 1959), 192.

74. Ibid., 111.

75. Herbert Knust, "What's the Matter with One-eyed Riley?" *Comparative Literature* 17 (Fall 1965): 289–98.

76. T. S. Eliot, "*Ulysses*, Order, and Myth," in *Selected Prose*, ed. Frank Kermode (New York, 1975), 177. The article originally appeared in the *Dial* 75 (November 1923): 480–83.

77. James Joyce, *Ulysses* (1918; reprint, New York, 1934), 34–35.

78. Waite, *Pictorial Key*, 22–23.

79. Ibid., 116.

80. Ibid., 119.

81. Dante, *Inferno*, 3.52–57, in *La Divina Commedia*, pt. 1, pp. 28–30. Carlyle translation.

82. Virgil, *Aeneid*, 6.425–28, in *Works*, 170. My translation.

83. Conrad, *Heart of Darkness*, 40.

84. Baudelaire, "Les Sept Vieillards," in *Oeuvres Complètes*, ed. Y.-G. Le Dantec (Paris, 1954), 159–60.

85. Larisch, *My Past*, 209.

86. Dante, *Inferno*, 3.1–3, in *La Divina Commedia*, pt. 1, p. 26. Carlyle translation, but his "people lost" has been inverted to the order employed by Dante, "perduta gente."

87. Ibid., 3.55–57, 1.30, in *La Divina Commedia*, pt. 1, p. 30. Carlyle translation.

88. Igor Stravinsky, "Memoires of T. S. Eliot," *Esquire*, August 1965, 92–93.

89. Knust, *Wagner*, 22–24.

90. Ibid., 49.

91. Dante, *Inferno*, 4.25–30, in *La Divina Commedia*, pt. 1, p. 38. Translation modified from Carlyle.

92. Robert A. Day, "The 'City Man' in *The Waste Land*: The Geography of Reminiscence," *PMLA* 80 (June 1965); 290.

93. Frazer, *Golden Bough*, 6:88.

94. Dante, *Inferno*, 3.58–60, in *La Divina Commedia*, pt. 1, p. 30. Carlyle translation, except that "great" has been changed to "grand."

95. Dryden, *Annus Mirabilis*, 172, in *Poetical Works*, ed. W. D. Christie (London and New York, 1900), 67.

96. *London Times Literary Supplement*, 11 May 1972, 529. Mrs. Eliot made her remarks in a brief letter to the editor.

97. Joyce, *Ulysses*, 111.

98. Lewis, *Tarr*, 38.

99. John Webster, *The White Devil*, 5.4, in *The Duchess of Malfi and The White Devil* (London and New York, 1930).

100. John Webster, *The Duchess of Malfi*, 4.2.

101. Frazer, *Golden Bough*, 2:153.

102. Joyce, *Ulysses*, 47.

103. Ibid., 50.

104. Baudelaire, "Au Lecteur," *Les Fleurs du Mal*, in *Oeuvres Complètes*, ed. Y.-G. Le Dantec (Paris, 1954), 82. My translation.

105. Eliot, *Murder in the Cathedral*, 1, in *CPP*, 194.

Chapter 4. A Game of Chess

1. Webster, *Duchess of Malfi*, 3.2.

2. Ibid.

3. Miller, *Eliot's Personal Waste Land*.

4. Eliot, "Thomas Middleton," in *Selected Essays*, 141.

5. Arthur Symons, "Middleton and Rowley," in *The Cambridge History of English Literature*, ed. A. W. Ward and A. R. Waller (Cambridge, 1919), 6:79.

6. Eliot, "Middleton," 145.

7. William Shakespeare, *Anthony and Cleopatra*, 2.2, in *Works* (New York, 1938).

8. Quoted in Benson, *Fitzgerald*, 12.

9. Charles Baudelaire, "Une Martyre," *Les Fleurs du Mal*, in *Ouevres Complètes*, 181–82. My translation.

10. J. C. Maxwell, "Flaubert in *The Waste Land*," *English Studies* 44 (1963): 279, traces the word to *Madame Bovary*, 3:5 "Il y avait sur la pendule un petit Cupidon de bronze, qui minaudait, en arrondissant les bras sous une guirlande dorée." [There was on the clock a small bronze Cupidon, who struck an affected pose, his arms encircling a golden garland.] Emma sees this in the apartment of her lover, Leon Dupuis. Maxwell points out that, after leaving the apartment, riding about in her carriage, she encounters "un pauvre diable vagabondant avec son baton" [a poor devil of a vagabond with his stick] who follows after carriages singing that in the heat of day a young girl's fancies often turn to thoughts of love. Where his eyes would be there were only "deux orbites béantes tout ensanglantées" [two gaping sockets all bloodied], which could be linked with "Those were pearls that were his eyes."

11. Virgil, *Aeneid*, 1.726, in *Works*, 36. My translation.

12. Douglas Bush, *English Literature in the Earlier Seventeenth Century: 1600–1660* (New York, 1945), 130–31.

13. Jessie L. Weston, *From Ritual to Romance* (1919; reprint, Garden City, N.Y., 1957).

14. Frazer, *Golden Bough*, 5:122, 123.

15. John Lyly, "Song" from *Campaspe* in *Elizabethan Verse and Prose*, ed. George Reuben Potter (New York, 1928), 79, lines 1–4.

16. John Lyly, "Apelles' Song" from *Campaspe*, in ibid, 79, lines 1–2.

17. David Ward, *T. S. Eliot between Two Worlds* (London and Boston, 1973), 97.

18. Plato, *Phaedo*, 85A. Quoted in ibid., 97–98.

19. William Shakespeare, *Titus Andronicus*, 5.2.

20. Cf. William Cowper, "Conversation," 51: "So wither'd stumps disgrace the sylvan scene." Unconscious influence is possible but highly speculative.

21. Tennyson, "The Mermaid," in *Complete Poetical Works*, ed. W. J. Rolfe (Boston, 1898), 19.

22. D. G. Rossetti, "The Blessed Damozel," in *Poetry of the Victoprian Period*, ed. George Benjamin Woods (New York, 1930), 501, lines 1–6.

23. Eliot, *Facsimile*, 105.

24. Eliot, *Murder in the Cathedral*, 2, in *CPP*, 210.

25. Eliot, "Burnt Norton," pt. 1, lines 6–14, in *CPP*, 117.

26. Ford Madox Hueffer, *On Heaven and Poems Written on Active Duty* (New York, 1918), 33–34.

27. P. B. Shelley, "Ode to the West Wind," in *Oxford Book of Nineteenth Century English Verse*, ed. John Hayward (Oxford, 1964), 280, line 2.

28. William Shakespeare, *Hamlet*, 1.5.

29. Virgil, *Aeneid* 4.509, 6.47, in *Works*, 114, 156. My translation.

30. Vivien was no doubt keenly aware of the situation and felt sensitive about it, as witnessed by her insistence on Eliot's removing the line about there being only chessmen between them.

31. Hermann Hesse, "The Brothers Karamazov, or The Decline of Europe," in *My Belief: Essays on Life and Art*, ed. Theodore Ziolkowski, trans. Denver Lindley (New York, 1974), 76.

32. Ezekiel 36 and 37.

33. Joyce, *Ulysses*, 112–13.

34. Eliot, *Murder in the Cathedral*, 1, in *CPP*, 194.

35. Dante, *Inferno*, 5.73–75, in *La Divina Commedia*, pt. 1, p. 52. My translation.

36. 5.121–23, in ibid., 54. My translation.

37. Conrad, *Heart of Darkness*, 44.

38. Further details may be found in Bruce R. McElderry, Jr., "Eliot's 'Shake-speherian Rag,'" *American Quarterly* 9 (Spring 1957): 185–86. Reprinted in *A Collection of Critical Essays on "The Waste Land,"* ed. Jay Martin (Englewood Cliffs, N.J., 1968), 29–31, from which the present lyric is quoted.

39. Smith, *Eliot's Poetry and Plays*, 82.

40. Ibid., 327 n. 34.

41. Beaumont and Fletcher, *Philaster*, 2.3, in *Elizabethan and Stuart Plays*, ed. Charles Read Baskervill, Virgil B. Heltzel, and Arthur H. Nethercot (New York, 1934), 1213.

42. Webster, *Duchess of Malfi*, 4.2.

43. Robert Sencourt, *T. S. Eliot: A Memoir*, ed. Donald Adamson (New York, 1971), 54–55.

44. Shakespeare, *Hamlet*, 4.5.72–3.

Chapter 5. The Fire Sermon

1. Quoted in Margolis, *Eliot's Intellectual Development*, 142.

2. Eliot, *Facsimile*, 31.

3. Edmund Spenser, "Prothalamion," in *Complete Poetical Works*, ed. R.E. Neil Dodge (Boston and New York, 1908), 459–60, lines 1–18.

4. Ibid., 19–36, 760.

5. Jules Laforgue, "Dimanches," in *Poems*, trans. Patricia Terry (Berkeley and Los Angeles, 1958), 94. My translation.

6. Andrew Marvell, "To His Coy Mistress," in *New Oxford Book of English Verse*, ed. Sir Arthur Quiller-Couch (Oxford, 1939), 399–400.

7. Joyce, *Ulysses*, 95. Words, music, and commentary may be found in Helen Kendrick Johnson, *Our Familiar Songs and Those Who Made Them* (New York, 1881).The song was recorded by the New Hutchinson Family Singers in *Homespun America*, Vox SVBX 5309.

8. Ibid., 93.

9. Ibid., 112.

10. Ibid., 43.

11. Ibid., 89.

12. Ibid.

13. William Shakespeare, *The Tempest*, 1.2.387–402.

14. T. S. Eliot, "A Commentary," *Criterion* 13 (April 1934): 452.

15. Fyodor Dostoyevsky, *Crime and Punishment*, trans. Constance Garnett (New York, 1932), 474.

16. Ibid., 477–78.

17. John Day, *The Parliament of Bees*, character 3, 11–37, in *The Viking Book of Poetry*, ed. Richard Aldington (New York, 1941), 242.

18. Larisch, *My Past*, 179.

19. Quoted in Smith, *T. S. Eliot's Poetry and Plays* (Chicago, 1974), 86. In Smith, a dash is used to omit the four-letter word.

20. Paul Verlaine, "Parsifal," in *Oeuvres Poetiques Complètes*, ed. Y.-G. Le Dantec and Jacques Borel (Paris, 1962), 427. My translation.

21. Eliot, *Facsimile*, 43.

22. A. C. Swinburne, "Tiresias," 141–58, in Vol. 2 of *Complete Works*, ed. Sir Edmund Gosse and Thomas James Wise (New York and London, 1925), 236–37.

23. Quoted in *Reading Poems: An Introduction to Critical Study*, ed. Wright Thomas and Stuart Gerry Brown (New York, 1941), 726. No translator given.

24. Byron, *Don Juan*, 3.107, in *Complete Poetical Works* (Boston, 1905), 815.

25. Robert Louis Stevenson, "Requiem," in *Poetry of the Victorian Period*, ed. George Benjamin Woods (New York, 1930), 807.

26. Keats, "Ode to a Nightingale," in *New Oxford Book of English Verse*, 744, lines 61–70.

27. Eliot, *Facsimile*, 33.

28. Milton, *Paradise Lost*, 9.499–500, in *Poetical Works*, ed. H. C. Beeching (London, 1928), 363.

29. Ibid., 353.

30. Aldous Huxley, *Crome Yellow*, 220.

31. Larisch, *My Past*, 307.

32. Oliver Goldsmith, "Woman," in *New Oxford Book of English Verse*, 559.

33. Conrad, *Heart of Darkness*, 34–35.

34. Ibid., 27.

35. Quoted in Edward Walford, *Greater London: A Narrative of Its History, Its People, and Its Places* (London, n.d.), 1:573.

36. Knust, *Wagner*, 56–57.

37. Quoted in Eliot, *CPP*, 53.

38. Shakespeare, *Anthony and Cleopatra*, 2.2.195–98.

39. Dante, *Purgatorio*, 5.130–36, in *La Divina Commedia*, pt. 2, p. 56. My translation.

40. Eliot, *After Strange Gods* (London, 1934), 42.

41. T. S. Eliot, "Baudelaire," in *Selected Essays*, 380.

42. Eliot, *Murder in the Cathedral*, 2, in *CPP*, 210.

43. Smith, *Eliot's Poetry and Plays*, 90.

44. Webster, *Duchess of Malfi*, 3.5.81–82.

45. Ovid, *The Heroides*, 7.23–24, trans. Grant Showerman (London and New York, 1914), 84. My translation.

46. Larisch, *My Past*, 200–201.

47. St. Augustine, *Confessions*, trans. Edward B. Pusey (New York, 1909), 197.

48. Ibid., 196.

Chapter 6. Death by Water

1. Eliot, *Use of Poetry and Use of Criticism*, 60–61.

2. Tennyson, "Ulysses," in *Poetry of the Victorian Period*, ed. George Benjamin Woods (New York, 1930), 43, lines 6–16.

3. Knust, *Wagner*, 33–43.

4. Larisch, *My Past*, 178.

5. Ibid., 137.

6. Joyce, *Ulysses*, 113.

7. Ibid., 109.

8. Ibid., 34.

9. Dante, Inferno, 26.112–30, in La Divina Commedia, pt. 1, pp. 292–94. Translation adopted from that of Carlyle.

Chapter 7. What the Thunder Said

1. From a letter to Bertrand Russell, 15 October, 1923, quoted in Eliot, Facsimile, 129.

2. The Upanishads: Breath of the Eternal, trans. Swami Prabhavananda and Frederick Manchester (Hollywood, Calif., 1948; reprint, New York, 1957), 112.

3. John D. Vickery, The Literary Impact of The Golden Bough (Princeton, 1973), 264.

4. Eliot, Facsimile, 109.

5. Alan Seeger, Poems (New York, 1916), 16.

6. Ibid., 12.

7. Rudyard Kipling, Kim (New York, 1962), 198.

8. Ibid.

9. Larisch, My Past, 179.

10. Ibid., 199–200.

11. Ibid., 202.

12. Smith, Eliot's Poetry and Plays, 94.

13. Eliot, "The Rock," in CPP, 103–4, line 3.

14. Hermann Hesse, "The Brothers Karamazov," in My Belief, 85.

15. Theodore Ziolkowski, introduction to ibid., ix.

16. Hesse, My Belief, 70, 72.

17. Eliot, Use of Poetry and Use of Criticism, 106.

18. Hesse, My Belief, 71, 72, 76.

19. Eliot, "Baudelaire," in Selected Essays, 379.

20. Dryden, "Annus Mirabilis," in Poetical Works, ed. W. D. Christie (New York, 1900), 79, line 227.

21. Shakespeare, Macbeth, 2.3.55–62.

22. Dante, Inferno, 3.22–23, in La Divina Commedia, pt. 3, p. 28.

23. Frazer, Golden Bough, 6:31.

24. Ernest Shackleton, South: The Story of Shackleton's Last Expedition 1914–1917 (London, 1919), 60.

25. Ibid., 43, 33.

26. Eliot, Facsimile, 113.

27. Lee J. Richmond, "Eliot's The Waste Land, 380–395," The Explicator 30 (November 1971): item 23.

28. Quoted in ibid., with original italics.

29. Ibid.

30. Weston, Ritual to Romance, 175.

31. Eliot, "The Rock," in CPP, 108, line 7.

32. Waite, Pictorial Key, 132.

33. Virgil, Aeneid, 6.553, in Works, 175. My translation.

34. Martin Puhvel, "Reminiscent Bells in 'The Waste Land,'" English Language Notes 2 (June 1965): 286–87, suggests Browning's "Childe Roland to the Dark Tower Came," 193–98, as a source for the tower and bells motif, but the parallel is strictly peripheral.

J. C. Maxwell, "'Gareth and Lynette' and 'The Waste Land,'" *Notes and Queries* 17 (December 1970): 458, offers as a source for "And upside down in air were towers" the line, "And solid turrets topsy-turvy in air" from Tennyson's "Gareth and Lynette," 251. This is certainly a possible source.

35. Shackleton, *South*, 33.

36. Larisch, *My Past*, 335.

37. Matthew Arnold, "Philomela," in *Poetry of the Victorian Period*, ed. George Benjamin Woods (New York, 1930), 470.

38. Smith, *Eliot's Poetry and Plays*, 95.

39. Knust, *Wagner*, 27.

40. Frazer, *Golden Bough*, 6:107.

41. Miller, *Eliot's Personal Waste Land*, 126–28.

42. Webster, *White Devil*, 5.6.

43. Dante, *Inferno*, 33.46–47. My translation.

44. Charles Baudelaire, "À Une Heure du Matin," in *Oeuvres Complètes*, 292.

45. James Joyce, *Portrait of the Artist as a Young Man* (1916; reprint, New York, 1956), 135–36.

46. When Marie Larisch delivered Marie Vetsera to Rudolph ostensibly for a short meeting, he requested ten minutes alone with the girl. The latter slipped into the smoking-room: "The Crown Prince followed her. 'Only ten minutes,' he repeated, as he closed the door, and I heard him turn the key in the lock." Larisch, *My Past*, 307.

47. Isaiah 38:1.

48. Milton Miller, "What the Thunder Meant," *Journal of English Literary History* 36 (June 1969): 449.

49. Thomas Kyd, *The Spanish Tragedy*, 4.1, in *Elizabethan and Stuart Plays*, 465.

50. Ibid., 467.

51. J. W. Mackail, *Latin Literature* (New York, 1895), 243–44.

52. *Vigil of Venus*, trans. Elizabeth Hickman Du Bois (Woodstock, Vt., 1911), passim. My translation.

53. Ibid., 21. My translation.

54. Tennyson, "O Swallow, Swallow," from *The Princess*, in *Poetry of the Victorian Period*, 55, lines 1–3.

55. A. C. Swinburne, "Itylus," in ibid., 675, lines 1–6.

56. My translation. Though it probably did not influence Eliot to choose this poem as a source, it is nevertheless interesting to note that Nerval committed suicide by hanging himself, on a day apparently calculated in advance on astrological and numerological considerations. It is tempting to relate him to the Hanged God. [*Amour* is the French name for Eros as well as the word for love.]

57. Consult especially Jean Richer, *Nerval: Expérience et Création* (Paris, 1963), 555–81; and Andre Lebois, *Fabuleux Nerval* (Paris, 1972), 201–13.

Bibliography

Aldington, Richard, ed. *The Viking Book of Poetry of the English-Speaking World*. New York: Viking Press, 1941.

Augustine, Saint. *Confessions*. Translated by Edward B. Pusey. New York: P. F. Collier, Harvard Classics, 1909.

Baskervill, Charles Read, Virgil B. Heltzel, and Arthur H. Nethercot, eds. *Elizabethan and Stuart Plays*. New York: Henry Holt, 1934.

Baudelaire, Charles. *Oeuvres Complètes*. Edited by Y.-G. Le Dantec. Paris: Gallimard, 1954.

Benson, Arthur Christopher. *Edward Fitzgerald*. London: Macmillan, 1905.

Bergin, Thomas G. *Dante*. New York: Orion Press, 1965.

Bertocci, Angelo. *From Symbolism to Baudelaire*. Carbondale: Southern Illinois University Press, 1964.

Bradley, F. H. *Appearance and Reality: A Metaphysical Essay*. Oxford: Clarendon Press, 1897.

——. *Essays on Truth and Reality*. Oxford: Clarendon Press, 1914.

Brooks, Cleanth. *The Well Wrought Urn*. New York: Harcourt, Brace, Harvest Books, 1947.

Bush, Douglas. *English Literature in the Earlier Seventeenth Century: 1600–1660*. New York: Oxford University Press, 1945.

Byron, Lord. *Complete Poetical Works*. Boston: Houghton Mifflin, 1905.

Campbell, Joseph. *Earth of Cualann*. Dublin and London: Maunsel, 1917.

Chaucer, Geoffrey. *Works*. 2d ed. Edited by F. N. Robinson. Boston: Houghton Mifflin, 1957.

Conrad, Joseph. *A Conrad Argosy*. With an introduction by William McFee. Garden City, N. Y.: Doubleday, Doran, 1942.

Dante Alighieri. *La Divina Commedia*. Italian text edited by H. Oelsner. Translated by J. A. Carlyle, Thomas Okey, and P. H. Wicksteed. Temple Classics, 1899–1901. Reprint. London and Toronto: J. M. Dent; New York: E. P. Dutton, 1933.

Day, Robert A. "The 'City Man' in *The Waste Land*: The Geography of Reminiscence." *PMLA* 80, no. 3 (June 1965): 285–91.

Dickens, Charles. *Our Mutual Friend*. 1865. Reprint. New York: Heritage Press, 1957.

Donne, John. *The Complete Poetry and Selected Prose of John Donne and the Complete Poetry of William Blake*. With an introduction by Robert Silliman Hillyer. New York: Random House, Modern Library, 1946.

Dostoyevsky, Fyodor. *Crime and Punishment*. Translated by Constance Garnett. New York: Modern Library, 1932.

Dryden, John. *Poetical Works*. Edited by W. D. Christie. New York: Macmillan, 1900.

Eliot, T. S. "A Commentary." *Criterion* 2, no. 7 (April 1924): 231–35.

————. "A Commentary." *Criterion* 13, no. 52 (April 1934): 451–54.

————. *After Strange Gods*. London: Faber and Faber, 1934.

————. "The Art of Poetry, I: T. S. Eliot." *Paris Review* 21 (Spring–Summer 1959): [47]–70.

————. *The Complete Poems and Plays: 1909–1950*. New York: Harcourt, Brace, 1952.

————. "The Idea of a Literary Review." *Criterion* 4, no. 1 (January 1926): 1–6.

————. *Knowledge and Experience in the Philosophy of F. H. Bradley*. New York: Farrar, Straus & Giroux. 1964.

————. *On Poetry and Poets*. New York: Farrar, Straus & Cudahy, 1957.

————. Preface to Saint-John Perse. *Anabasis: A Poem*. Translated by T. S. Eliot, 3d ed. New York: Harcourt, Brace, 1949.

————. *Selected Essays*. 2d ed. New York: Harcourt, Brace, 1950.

————. *Selected Prose*. Edited by Frank Kermode. New York: Harcourt Brace Jovanovich / Farrar, Straus & Giroux, 1975.

————. *The Use of Poetry and the Use of Criticism*. Cambridge: Harvard University Press, 1933.

————. *The Waste Land: A Facsimile and Transcript of the Original Drafts Including the Annotations of Ezra Pound*. Edited by Valerie Eliot. New York: Harcourt Brace Jovanovich, 1971.

Faber, Geoffrey. *In the Valley of Vision: Poems Written in Times of War*. Oxford: B. H. Blackwell; New York: Longmans, Green, 1918.

Foulkes, David. *The Psychology of Sleep*. New York: Scribners, 1966.

Frazer, James. *The Golden Bough*. 12 vols. New York: Macmillan, 1911–1915.

Gregory, Horace, and Marya Zaturenska. *A History of American Poetry 1900–1940*. New York: Harcourt, Brace, 1946.

Hayward, John, ed. *The Oxford Book of Nineteenth Century Verse*. Oxford: Clarendon Press, 1964.

Hesse, Hermann. *My Belief: Essays on Life and Art*. Edited by Theodore Ziolkowski. Translated by Denver Lindley. New York: Farrar, Straus & Giroux, 1974.

Horowitz, Mardi J. *Image Formation and Cognition*. New York: Appleton, Century, Crofts, 1970.

Hueffer, Ford Madox. *On Heaven and Poems Written on Active Service*. London and New York: John Lane, 1918.

Huxley, Aldous. *Crome Yellow*. New York and Evanston, Ill.: George H. Doran, 1922.

Johnson, Helen Kendrick. *Our Familiar Songs and Those Who Made Them Famous*. New York: Holt, 1881.

Jones, Genesius. *Approach to the Purpose: A Study of the Poetry of T. S. Eliot*. New York: Barnes and Noble, 1964.

Joyce, James. *Portrait of the Artist as a Young Man*. 1916. Reprint. New York: Viking Press, Compass Books, 1956.

──. *Ulysses*. 1918. Reprint. New York: Random House, Modern Library, 1934.

Kenner, Hugh, ed. *T. S. Eliot: A Collection of Critical Essays*. Englewood Cliffs, N.J.: Prentice-Hall, 1962.

Kipling, Rudyard. *Kim*. 1901. Reprint. New York: Dodd, Mead, 1962.

Knust, Herbert. "What's the Matter with One-eyed Riley?" *Comparative Literature* 17 (Fall 1965): 289–98.

──. *Wagner, the King, and "The Waste Land."* University Park: Pennsylvania State University Press, 1967.

Kojecky, Roger. *T. S. Eliot's Social Criticism*. New York: Farrar, Straus & Giroux, 1972.

Laffal, Julius. *Pathological and Normal Language*. New York: Atherton Press, 1965.

Laforgue, Jules. *Poems*. Translated by Patricia Terry. Berkeley and Los Angeles: University of California Press, 1958.

Larisch, Countess Marie. *My Past*. New York: E. Nash, 1913.

Lebois, André. *Fabuleux Nerval*. Paris: Denoel, 1972.

Lewis, Wyndham. *Tarr*. London: Methuen, 1918.

Litz, A. Walton, ed. *Eliot in his Time: Essays on the Occasion of the Fiftieth Anniversary of The Waste Land*. Princeton: Princeton University Press; London, Oxford University Press, 1973.

de Lorris, Guillaume, and Jean de Meun. *The Romance of the Rose*. Translated by Charles Dahlberg. Princeton: Princeton University Press, 1971.

Mackail, J. W. *Latin Literature*. New York: Scribners, 1895.

Mallarmé, Stephane. *Oeuvres Complètes*. Edited by H. Mondor and G. Jean-Aubry. Paris: Gallimard, 1945.

Margolis, John G. *T. S. Eliot's Intellectual Development: 1922–1939*. Chicago: University of Chicago Press, 1972.

Martin, Jay, ed. *A Collection of Critical Essays on "The Waste Land."* Englewood Cliffs, N.J.: Prentice-Hall, 1968.

Matthews, T. S. *Great Tom: Notes toward the Definition of T. S. Eliot*. London and New York: Harper & Row, 1973.

Matthiessen, F. O. *The Achievement of T. S. Eliot: An Essay on the Nature of Poetry*. New York: Oxford University Press, 1935. Rev. ed. 1959.

Maxwell, J. C. "'Gareth and Lynette' and 'The Waste Land.'" *Notes and Queries* 17 (December 1970): 458.

──. "Flaubert in The Waste Land." *English Studies* 44 (August 1963): 279.

McElderly, Bruce R. "Eliot's 'Shakespeherian Rag.'" *American Quarterly* 9 (Spring 1957): 185–86.

Miller, James E., Jr. *T. S. Eliot's Personal Waste Land: Exorcism of the Demons*. London and University Park: Pennsylvania State University Press, 1977.

Miller, Milton. "What the Thunder Meant." *Journal of English Literary History* 36 (June 1969): 440–54.

Milton, John. *Poetical Works*. Edited by H. C. Beeching. London: Oxford University Press, 1928.

Moakley, Gertrude. "The Waite-Smith 'Tarot': A Footnote to The Waste Land." Bulletin of the New York Public Library 58 (October 1954): 471–75.

Montgomery, Marion. "Lord Russell and Madame Sosostris." Georgia Review 28 (Summer 1974): 269–82.

Morgan, Kenneth, ed. The Religion of the Hindus. New York: Ronald Press, 1953.

Morris, George L. K. "Marie, Marie, Hold on Tight." Partisan Review 21 (March–April 1954): 231–33.

Ong, Walter J. " 'Burnt Norton' in St. Louis." American Literature 33 (January 1962): 522–26.

Ovid. Heroides and Amores. Translated by Grant Showerman. Loeb Classical Library. London and New York: William Heinemann / Macmillan, 1914.

Patterson, Gertrude. T. S. Eliot: Poems in the Making. New York: Barnes & Noble, 1971.

Philippe, Charles Louis. Bubu of Montparnasse. With an introduction by T. S. Eliot. New York: Shakespeare House, 1951.

Potter, George Reuben, ed. Elizabethan Verse and Prose. New York: Henry Holt, 1928.

Pound, Ezra. The Spirit of Romance. New York: New Directions, n.d.

Puhvel, Martin. "Reminiscent Bells in 'The Waste Land.' " English Language Notes 2 (June 1965); 286–87.

Quiller-Couch, Arthur, ed. The New Oxford Book of English Verse. 2d ed. Oxford: Clarendon Press, 1939.

Rexroth, Kenneth. American Poetry in the Twentieth Century. New York: Herder & Herder, 1971.

Richards, I. A. Principles of Literary Criticism. New York: Harcourt, Brace, n.d.

Richer, Jean. Nerval: Expérience et Création. Paris: Hachette, 1963.

Richmond, Lee J. "Eliot's The Waste Land: 380–395." The Explicator 30 (November 1971): item 23.

Seeger, Alan. Poems. New York: Scribners, 1916.

Sencourt, Robert. T. S. Eliot: A Memoir. Edited by Donald Adamson. New York: Dodd, Mead, 1971.

Shackleton, Ernest. South: The Story of Shackleton's Last Expedition 1914–1917. London: Heinemann, 1919.

Shakespeare, William. Works. New York: Oxford University Press / Shakespearehead Press, 1938.

Smith, Grover. T. S. Eliot's Poetry and Plays: A Study in Sources and Meaning. 2d ed. Chicago: University of Chicago Press, 1974.

Spenser, Edmund. Complete Poetical Works. Edited by R. E. Neil Dodge. Boston and New York: Houghton Mifflin, 1908.

Stearns, Monroe. Dante: Poet of Love. New York: Franklin Watts, 1965.

Stravinsky, Igor. "Memories of T. S. Eliot." Esquire 64, no. 2 (August 1965): 92–93.

Streng, Frederick J. Emptiness: A Study in Religious Meaning. Nashville and New York: Abingdon Press, 1967.

Suzuki, D. T. Zen Buddhism. Edited by William Barrett. New York: Doubleday, Anchor Books, 1956.

Swinburne, Algernon Charles. *Complete Works*. Edited by Edmund Gosse and Thomas James Wise. 20 vols. London: William Heinemann; New York: Gabriel Wells, Bonchurch edition, 1925.

Symons, Arthur. *The Symbolist Movement in Literature*. New York: E. P. Dutton, 1919.

Tauber, Edward S., and Maurice R. Green. *Prelogical Experience: An Inquiry into Dreams and Other Creative Processes*. New York: Basic Books, 1959.

Tennyson, Alford Lord. *Complete Poetical Works*. Edited by W. J. Rolfe. Boston: Houghton Mifflin, 1898.

Thomas, Wright, and Stuart Gerry Brown, eds. *Reading Poems: An Introduction to Critical Study*. New York: Oxford University Press, 1941.

Tindall, William York. *Forces in Modern British Literature: 1885–1956*. 1947. Reprint. New York: Vintage Books, 1956.

Unger, Leonard H. *T. S. Eliot: Moments and Patterns*. Minneapolis: Minnesota University Press, 1956.

Unterecker, John. *Voyager: A Life of Hart Crane*. New York: Farrar, Straus & Giroux, 1969.

The Unapishads: Breath of the Eternal. Translated by Swami Prabhavananda and Frederick Manchester. Hollywood, Calif.: The Vedanta Society of Southern California. Reprint. New York: New American Library, Mentor Books, 1957.

Valery, Paul. *The Art of Poetry*. Translated by Denise Folliot. Introduction by T. S. Eliot. Bollingen Foundation, 1958. Reprint. New York: Vintage Books, 1961.

Verlaine, Paul. *Oeuvres Poetiques Complètes*. Edited by V.-G. Le Dantec and Jacques Borel. Paris: Gallimard, 1962.

Vickery, John D. *The Literary Impact of The Golden Bough*. Princeton: Princeton University Press, 1973.

Vigil of Venus (Perviqilium Veneris). Translated by Elizabeth Hickman du Bois. Woodstock, Vt.: Elm Tree Press, 1911.

Virgil (P. Virgilius Maro). *Works*. Interlinear translation by Levi Hart and V. R. Osborn. 1882. Reprint. New York: David McKay, 1952.

Waite, Arthur Edward. *The Pictorial Key to the Tarot*. 1910. Reprint. New Hyde Park, N.Y.: University Books, 1959.

Walford, Edward. *Greater London: A Narrative of Its History, Its People, and Its Places*. 2 vols. London, New York, Paris, and Melbourne: Cassell, n.d.

Ward, David. *T. S. Eliot Between Two Worlds: A Reading of T. S. Eliot's Poetry and Plays*. London and Boston: Routledge & Kegan Paul, 1973.

Watson, George. "Quest for a Frenchman." *Sewanee Review* 84 (Summer 1976): 466–75.

Webster, John. *The Duchess of Malfi and The White Devil*. Illustrated by Henry Keen. London: John Lane, The Bodley Head; New York: Dodd, Mead, 1930.

Wells, Henry W. *Poetic Imagery: Illustrated from Elizabethan Literature*. New York: Columbia University Press, 1924.

Weston, Jessie L. *From Ritual to Romance*. 1919. Reprint. Garden City, N. Y.: Doubleday, Anchor Books, 1957.

Wilkins, Ernest Hatch. *A History of Italian Literature*. Cambridge: Harvard University Press, 1954.

Wolberg, Lewis R. *The Technique of Psychotherapy*. 2 vols. 2d ed. New York: Grune & Stratton, 1967.

Woods, George Benjamin, ed. *Poetry of the Victorian Period*. New York: Scott, Foresman, 1930.

Wundt, Wilhelm. *Elements of Folk Psychology: Outlines of a Psychological History of the Development of Mankind*. Translated by Edward Leroy Schaub. London: Allen & Unwin; New York: Macmillan, 1916.

Yeats, John Butler. *Passages from the Letters*. Edited by Ezra Pound. Churchtown, Dundrum: Cuala Press, 1918.

Index

About the Author

Due to a physical handicap, Robert L. Schwarz did not attend public schools but was self-educated until he entered college. He graduated *summa cum laude* from Garfield Senior College, where he also subsequently became an instructor. He has worked as an editorial contributor for World Publishing Company and has taught in special programs in the school system of Cleveland Heights, Ohio. As a free-lance writer and editor, he has done major projects for Merrill Lynch, and he does ongoing departmental work for technical trade publications. In 1972, he was the recipient of a research grant from the Martha Holden Jennings Foundation. Mr. Schwarz is a long-time collector of books and phonograph records and entertains a wide range of interests.